TAKENOTE!

DARREN ANDERTON

Dedication

To Dad

(Norman Alexander McKenzie Anderton,
19 September 1942 to 25 February 2009)

My best friend, an incredible character, who helped me every step
along the way. None of what I achieved would have been possible
without him.

He will never be forgotten.

TAKENOTE!

DARREN ANDERTON

The Autobiography with Mike Donovan

Foreword by Terry Venables

First published in Great Britain in 2010 by The Derby Books Publishing Company Limited, 3 The Parker Centre, Derby, DE21 4SZ

ISBN 978-1-85983-870-9

Printed and bound in Rzeszowskie Zakłady Graficzne S.A., Poland.

Contents

Acknowledgements

DARREN ANDERTON

There are so many people I'm grateful to for helping me through my life and career, starting with my Dad, to whom I've dedicated the book.

My thanks to Mum, Scott, Ben and Kelly for all her love, help and support and keeping my feet on the ground, and to Katie for all her love, support and patience throughout the ups and downs of the latter years of my career.

My appreciation to Gran and Grandad for always showing their support and always saying it how it was and not beating around the bush, Ian Parker for being a great friend and always being there to help with anything, Dave Fudge for looking after me on the many great nights out and dropping everything at the drop of a hat to be there as a friend if needed, the American Clan for being such good friends and allowing me to visit and have so many holidays of a lifetime, and all my other friends – you know who you are.

Also, thanks to Terry Venables for being the most important and biggest influence on my professional career and doing the foreword, Dave Hurst for finding me and spotting that little bit of potential, Graham Paddon for being a huge influence on my improvement as a young player, giving me a great upbringing in the game and showing great belief in my ability, Alan Ball for showing me the right way to play and giving me an apprenticeship, Jim Smith for giving me the chance and turning me into the player I became, Gerry Francis for taking me to the next level as a player, and wanting to build his team around me as a central-midfielder, Glenn Hoddle for giving me my World Cup dream which I'll never forget, George Graham for being a great guy and pleasure to work with, Dr Mueller-Wohlfahrt for all his help in getting me back to fitness, Dr McShane for all of his help when no one could diagnose my Achilles injuries in England, Leon Angel for being an honest agent/accountant and not pushing for me to move clubs for a quick buck and in my opinion getting the better of Alan Sugar a couple of times.

Also, thanks to John Gregory, Frank Burrows, Ray Clemence, Dougie Livermore, Dave Butler, Terry Byrne, Ossie Ardiles, Peter Osgood, Chris Hughton, Steve Perryman, Roger Cross, John Gorman, Steve Bruce, Eric Black, Gary Lewin, Stuart Gray, Neil McDiarmid, Kevin Bond, Rob Newman, Stuart Murdoch, Kevin Keegan, Joe Roach, Eileen Drewery, Tony Barton and Steve Wicks. My thanks to all at DB Publishing including Steve, Alex, Jo and Matt for your faith and support. Also thanks to Mike Donovan, who approached me with the belief my story was worth telling.

MIKE DONOVAN

My thanks for the support, encouragement and/or invaluable assistance to: John Fennelly and Andy Porter at Tottenham Hotspur FC, David Barber at the FA, Nick Noble at the FA Premier League, the Football League, Mark Storey at Portsmouth FC, Peter Lewis at Birmingham City FC, John Hendley at Wolverhampton Wanderers FC, Neil Vacher at AFC Bournemouth, Jane Devitt (Darren's Mum), Scott and Ben Anderton (and the rest of the brood), Ian Parker, David and Joe Roy, Katie Rata-McMahon and family, Leon Angel, Terry Venables, David Luxton, Mike McNamara (have camera, will travel) David Juson, Tim McNamara (for the loan of the hotel!), Nick, Jan and Debbie Saloman, Mark Friedlander, Kevin Rogers, Dave Harley, Tony Harris, Bill Pierce, Glenda and Jack Rollin's *Sky Sports Football Yearbook*, Graham Cumming, Sean Donovan and Christine Tobin (I pray you can work it out!), Steve Hollis, Bruce Talbot, Chris Giles, Mike Legg, all on the *Sun*, *News of the World*, *The Argus*, *Backpass* sports desks and others who've helped put bread on my family's table, the Loughton five-a-siders (I'll be back), Mims, Mum, my late Dad's memory, my fantastic son Matthew and Rosie (the love of my life).

I owe a special debt of gratitude to my 'mentor' Kevin Brennan.

My biggest thanks go to Darren himself for his time, cooperation, companionship, professionalism and consideration – and a laptop charger! – which ensured the completion of my most life-affirming project in more than 35 years of sports writing. He is much more than one of Tottenham Hotspur's greatest footballers of the modern era.

Finally, I'd like to declare my appreciation of the role played by BBC Radio 6 Music, Debbie Duveen and the Millbanks, the Beatles, jammy Wagon Wheels and countless cups of tea in sustaining me through so many days of solitary confinement at home getting the job done.

Foreword

I remember when I first decided I wanted to sign Darren. I was in the crowd at Highbury when he played for Portsmouth in the FA Cup semi-final against Liverpool in 1992.

He was outstanding, not flashy. He had two good feet and, although he played wide, was also like a central-midfield player. Central-midfield players are more careful with their passing. I liked those things about him.

In Euro '96, those qualities enabled me to play Darren on the left – as well as the right – and he could get crosses in with his left foot. It seems practising to be two-footed is pretty much unheard of these days. I also noticed he could run all day. He had that marathon runner's build, tall and slim like Steve McManaman. I knew he was my sort of player.

I thought I was going to have to battle all the other clubs when I was at Tottenham. Not really. I was delighted and fortunate to get him.

Darren is one of the best players I've worked with. Not just a good player, but right up there with the very best. I rate David Beckham highly, but Darren was every bit as good. In fact, he might have the edge because he could also play on the left.

To me, he was a champion. People talk about stars, but stars only come out at night. There are few champions about. People who never cause a problem to you as a coach. He was the perfect person to work with at Tottenham Hotspur and England; a joy. He was a great lad and could do everything you asked of him. He'd pick things up so quickly. He had a football brain as good as ANYONE else I've known.

People think he was quiet and gentle, but he was strong. You can't get to the level he got to without being strong-minded, mentally tough.

He could do everything.

When I gave him his full England debut against Denmark I knew it didn't matter if I played Darren right, left or through the middle. He could do all of that. And he could make and score goals and always took responsibility for whatever was needed. He was also courageous.

I knew from when I took over he was going to be in my thoughts for as long as I was in the post. He played in every game in a fantastic England team at Euro '96.

People kept saying when I took over that we didn't have any left-sided players. But that changed with Darren. He started on the right with Steve McManaman on the left for the first game against Switzerland. Steve said he liked it on the left, so we did that. They equalised with a penalty and it ended in a draw, which was frustrating, so from then on we switched it with Darren and Steve.

It was from the left that Darren made that goal for Paul Gascoigne against Scotland. There were seven or eight passes and the ball came right across to Darren. Instinctively he took up the right position, with his back to the left-hand touchline so he could see where the ball was coming from and a run Gazza was making. We were all screaming for him to hit it first time because we'd seen Gazza running. Darren couldn't hear us, but he'd seen it before any of us on the bench did. He knocked it on first time with his right foot to Gazza and the rest, as they say, is history. An amazing goal, an amazing moment.

Darren was also one of the great Tottenham players of the modern era.

I felt devastated not to be able to carry on working with him and players like him with Tottenham – where he was part of a team I believed was developing into League winners – and England for longer. And I wonder what would have happened if I had been?

I was proud of him and all the players I worked with who went on to the 1998 World Cup. It gave me a sense of satisfaction, although also one of frustration as I wasn't involved.

Some didn't appreciate just how good Darren was. That is their ignorance. I don't give a damn what anyone else thinks, to me he was top, top class.

Players will tell you the same. I know Teddy Sheringham thinks he is the best or at least one of the best players he ever played with. And, from what Darren says in the book, Alex Ferguson was keen to have him for Manchester United.

I CAN'T SAY ENOUGH ABOUT THIS BOY. HE IS AN ABSOLUTE GEM. I HAVE THE UTMOST RESPECT FOR HIM AS A MAN AND A FOOTBALLER.

Because of his bravery as a player, it hurts me to hear this 'Sicknote' stuff about him.

It is clear from this book how it gnaws at him, and it would do me as well. It is hard to deal with this foolishness. People saying things that are just so wrong. They couldn't be further from the truth. Those people must know themselves that if they break a leg they can't walk across the road no matter how much they want to.

Darren played with injuries other players would not have played with. If all the players were as cooperative in playing with injuries, I'd like to find them! It is not possible for anyone to play with a pulled muscle, groin trouble, an Achilles injury or other problems like that. You can't play with an Achilles until it is more than right, 100 per cent right. Darren refers to Christian Gross telling him his injury was all in the mind. Absolute madness! Although it is rare that something so stupid is said in football.

Why would you want criticise and make jokes against someone for not doing what he wants to do more than anything else – play football? It was killing Darren when he couldn't play. To think he didn't want to play was so unkind. It was what Darren and players like him had wanted to do from as far back as they remember. So why would they want to stop when they got to the top?

It doesn't make sense. It should just be put down to absolute rubbish. Darren should treat it with the contempt it deserves. You can't blame someone for not doing something that was impossible.

When Darren came to Tottenham, you could see early on he was a bit nervous, and I tried to be encouraging and available to him. I remember coming into the dressing room when we were playing Everton early on. I told him not to worry, that it would be all right. It was a big move for him. Massive really, because he hadn't played in that top division.

People expect footballers getting to the top of their trade aged 20 or 21 to have developed life skills. But who else is at the top of their trade at that age? No one.

It was only a matter of time before he would pick everything up by learning quickly. He had to fast track by listening to people who have been through it. There was no time to experience things first.

I told him: 'Just keep doing what you was doing. I can see what you are doing and that's all that matters, so if you stick with that you are going to go right to the top.'

When he settled I wanted to challenge him to be even better because I knew he was good enough to play for England.

As a manager, you want to be friendly. You are nearly 'one of the boys', but not quite, but you understand the problems players have got. Sometimes you give them what they want, but at the same time they have to earn what they get because it is a hard business at the top.

I was fortunate to have players like Darren who responded positively, for instance, to the training I put on to suit them at Tottenham, QPR and Barcelona.

I noticed how Darren grew up as he got older. He would never say anything nasty at first. But then, after a while, if he had something to say he would say it. I thought: 'Good for you.'

And his more spiky attitude now stands him in good stead.

He certainly speaks up in this book. Very forthright. He had to show himself to be a really plucky guy to get his point across. And he does when he says that, although he kept quiet at the time because he didn't want to give Tottenham adverse publicity, he still hasn't forgotten about the bad things that happened to him as well as the good. It makes for an excellent story, something people will want to read. It is what helps make it different.

I was sad to read about his Dad dying. I remember he came into the Spurs boardroom with Darren, and I told him: 'Make sure Darren keeps doing what he's doing. There's not a doubt in my mind about what he can achieve, so don't let me be wrong.' Darren's Dad was a good bloke. I liked him.

I can understand how Darren has been hit for six with his passing. It's a big blow in your life.

But, with the way he has matured, Darren has become a man who knows what he is about. He's had a tough knockback with losing his Dad, but such things, they say, make you stronger. He's finding it hard. I did when my Dad died. You only ever have one of them. But what his Dad would want him to do now is fight back. To choose the right things to do and say and stand up for himself. That is what he is doing with this book.

Terry Venables
London, 23 July 2010

Prologue

I've had such an incredible life so far thanks to realising the dream of being a professional footballer. Myself, my family and friends have enjoyed the rewards, but the journey has been full of ups and downs.

There are so many good memories I wanted to share, from growing up to playing at the top flight for a great club like Tottenham Hotspur for 12 years to performing for my country at Euro '96 and in the World Cup finals in 1998 when I scored a goal which means so much to me.

I wanted to be able to thank all the wonderful people who have helped me along the way. And I wanted to keep a promise to my Dad, my best friend.

There are people who remember me as a good footballer but, unfortunately, many people think of Sicknote when my name is mentioned, and I think they will be horrified to read how my injuries were handled and treated.

I told my Dad I would one day let the public know the truth. I'd always felt I shouldn't speak about it while I was employed by Spurs. But the end of my career coinciding with the passing of my Dad has given me the motivation to honour that promise.

This book is to put the record straight. Now TAKENOTE! and enjoy my true story.

1
My Rock

My Dad's passing on 25 February 2009 has hit me hard. I will always recall when I looked into his eyes as we sat in the lounge of the family home and asked him: 'Have you had enough?' A few months earlier he had made the same inquiry of me. We each answered 'yes'.

My reply was to confirm I wanted to retire as a professional footballer. All it meant was, of course, that I had chosen to give up on living the dream. My Dad's reply revealed he wanted to give up on living. The pain from his fast-deteriorating emphysema was too much for him to bear.

I fought back the tears and told him: 'You're the best Dad in the world'. He smiled: 'Not bad.' Typical self-effacing understatement. It was our last conversation. He died in his sleep during the early hours of the following morning, aged 66.

He had always been my best friend and biggest fan, forever boosting my confidence. Without his support, there would have been no European Championships or World Cup Finals for me. No 12 years in the Premier League with one of football's greatest clubs. No career in the paid ranks of a sport I'd have played for nothing. Like most football-mad kids, my aspirations would have remained unrealised.

Yes, he was useless at football, and I remember him breaking his toe once proving the point, displaying a total lack of technique. And he struggled to even boil an egg when he brought up me and my brothers, Scott and Ben, and my sister Kelly. But Dad was my rock every step of the way and ensured I climbed my mountain. It was quite a feat considering my lack of self-confidence.

All us children ended up living with Dad after my parents divorced. I'm sure it was a struggle for him, although my Mum helped him no end. As 'thanks' us kids used to terrorise him. We would ring the house number and when he picked up the receiver the phone kept ringing as we'd taped the dial-tone button down. He wondered what the hell was going on.

Dad loved his steak and kidney pies – he was a simple man of simple tastes. We used to take his pie out of its wrapper while he wasn't looking, remove the filling and place the crust back on top before he microwaved it. When he sat down to eat it he would catch on after the first cut there was no filling – just the crust. He exclaimed: 'You idiots, go down the shop and get me another one!'

He'd spend most of the day drinking tea – and, unfortunately, smoking. A few times, Ben drilled a tiny hole in the bottom of his mug and when he poured the milk in it seeped through all over the kitchen work top and he wondered what on earth had caused it – until he turned round to see us all giggling.

I told him once Ben had nicked a load of car radios and hidden them in his wardrobe. His jaw dropped and he said 'you're joking' and rushed up the stairs to fling open the doors of it to discover he'd been the victim of a wind-up.

His children could have turned out to be brats. But we haven't. We are all grounded and appreciative of what he did for us.

Our home at Oak Tree Road, Bitterne, a district of Southampton, became a mini sports centre, with our mates being around all the time. I am sure he hated it at times, with screaming kids everywhere. But he never stopped them visiting because he could see we were so happy. Our friends loved him so much they became mates with him as well. His humour would have everyone in stitches. Dad was, without doubt, our best friend. You always knew what he was thinking – angry or happy – through the colourful language he often used.

There was a snooker table in mine and Scott's bedroom. We all used it every day. I remember one night playing against my Dad. We started at 25p a frame. After a few hours, I had won every game and wanted to go to bed. He wouldn't let me until he'd won. We were playing double or nothing on every frame. By the time he'd won I was up over £250,000! He could see I was gutted so he gave me £20 anyway. That summed him up for me – crap at sport but with a heart of gold.

I played football in the garden with my brothers and friends. It could get like a quagmire at times. And my sister Kelly often suffered when she and her friends got in the way trying to practice their gymnastics. We even tried football indoors.

Dad always encouraged us with our sports. He was a cross-country runner as a school kid. He won his school runs every day. I inherited the ability but hated it. One Friday, when I was about 10 or 11, I got a note in school from a teacher which said 'you are running this evening'. It was the first race of the season. I went to see him and mentioned I hadn't trained once and didn't want to do it as I hadn't enjoyed it the year before. He told me I should give it a go as he thought I'd do well.

I was still looking for a way out and said I hadn't got any spikes. 'Wear your trainers', he suggested. I gave in. That night I finished fifth in the

Southampton and District Schools Cross Country Championships against kids two years older than me. And my dad piped up: 'See how good you are at it? You should do it regularly. It'll help you with your football because it'll give you more stamina.'

He knew football was what I wanted to do and clearly aware that running would do me a world of good as far as my number one sporting priority was concerned. I carried on and two years later – in my final year at middle school – became Hampshire county champion. I liked winning the medals and the feeling that came with it, but not the actual running itself.

My running ability did stand me in good stead throughout my playing career, although I STILL couldn't stand cross country. I don't miss those pre-season training runs, I can tell you.

Dad and Mum gladly acted as my chauffeurs when I began playing organised football for youth and district sides. I started with Itchen Saints Under-10s even though I was only seven. I remember losing my first game 15–0! When Dad was in hospital near the end I used to drive past the pitch from that unforgettable day on the way to visit him, and it always brought a wry smile to my face.

Next season, Bitterne Park Rangers were formed, a team made up of all my school friends. There was no Under-9s football back then, so some of us, including me, had to play above our age group. The following year, the squad was broken up into Under-10s and Under-11s teams. I was put in the older group, although still eligible to play in the younger one. My side won division two in the Southampton Tyro League. My first success in football. My future Portsmouth captain Kevin Ball presented me with my medal, although I didn't know who he was at the time! Ironically, six years later I ended up cleaning his boots at Pompey.

I dropped back into my own age group when asked to join Winsor United at Under-13s. My Dad's friend Henry had a son in the team and suggested I played for them as they were one of the better teams in the area. It was a great first year as we went on to win the top division in the Tyro League, along with the district and Hampshire Cups.

When I finished my last year of junior football at Under-15s, I then moved on with a few of my Winsor and Southampton and District teammates to play for Totton Youth Under-18s, which was very enjoyable. I was their player of the year – nice.

Dad ran a removal firm before becoming a taxi driver after the 1986 property crash, so I guess it was a bit of a busman's holiday for him to make sure I got to games. He also took me on some work trips and roped me in to doing some removals. Dad always said I didn't help much. He was right. I used to take one chair off the lorry and plonk it outside the front door of the house we were moving things to. That was all I did! I drove him mad. But I enjoyed the long journeys back to his homeland in Scotland. His work colleague Johnny Harrop used to tell us stories of how Dad played for Rangers when we went to Glasgow. I totally believed them – until I saw him kick a ball.

It was through my Dad I got hooked up with my first professional club. Off his own back, and without telling me, he phoned up Southampton's south-coast rivals Portsmouth and spoke to Dave Hurst, the club's youth development officer. That got the ball rolling professionally for me.

Dad was also my agent, albeit loosely, when things started to go well at Portsmouth. He always came along to watch me when I was in the Reserves and was there when I signed my first pro deal.

A lot of people began talking about me when I helped Pompey get to the FA Cup semi-finals. Top agents wanted to act for me. I remember Eric Hall, with his 'Monster, Monster' catchphrase, was one who was keen. Eric was constantly on the phone to my Dad saying he could get me this and that. I wasn't ready for all that and wanted Dad to help me on that side of things. I remember watching Dad trying to get off the phone to Eric as he was making all these promises.

Jim Smith had by this time taken over as Portsmouth manager and wanted me to sign another deal. One day, Jim phoned Dad while he was driving me to training. Dad told him 'I know what you are offering is good, but this is what he wants'. Jim was fuming and shouted 'I'll f***ing sell him'. My Dad replied 'Yeah, I don't blame you'.

Jim phoned my Dad back later and told him the club would give me what I wanted. My Dad had done a good job. I would have signed anyway. I never wanted to go. I was happy. Jim loved my Dad, always asked after him.

I consulted Dad on everything, so when the chance to join Tottenham Hotspur came up we talked it through. I had got my accountant Leon Angel to act as my agent by then, but it was my Dad – and Mum's – opinions which mattered most to me.

I had met up with chairman Alan Sugar and manager Terry Venables, who had bossed Barcelona, at a Spurs game a few months earlier. I'd been quite shy and a bit daunted at meeting these household names. My Dad wasn't overawed in the slightest. He spoke to Sugar and Venables the same way he'd speak to anyone. He was just himself.

Now, although I was excited to be linking up with Spurs, it had only been two years since I'd made my Portsmouth debut. It was quite a leap for me. Dad made me feel comfortable about the situation. He always had a sense of whether something was right for his eldest and told me the move was a good one. To not worry. Be proud of how far I'd come. That it was something I deserved. And I'd be absolutely fine.

When I actually signed, Dad was positive. He always was. He said to me when I was 16 that I'd become a top player by the time I was 23 or 24, and I'd like to think he was spot on. He helped keep me going through long-term injuries with his upbeat philosophy.

Dad was vital in me having a decent World Cup in 1998. I was getting grief from supporters because they thought I was keeping David Beckham out of the side. He knew what I had accomplished merely to be fit and was angry about the reaction, but he kept it to himself as he sat in the stands. Then he told me afterwards: 'Screw them, they are clowns. Just go out and enjoy the matches with a smile on your face. You are in the World Cup.' I didn't have a care in the world after that. His quiet word helped make my World Cup.

He wasn't so quiet though, when England supporters gave Teddy Sheringham some stick, calling for Michael Owen to replace him. Teddy's son Charlie was sitting alongside him. He spun round and gave those fans what for!

Nearing The End

Dad went to most of my matches. There were times when I got frustrated and he would be reassuring, telling me that if I had enough of the ball I would play well in my next match. Even in the players' lounge he never got over-excited. A quick 'you played well today' or, if I didn't, it was 'don't worry, it doesn't happen too often'.

When I left Spurs for Birmingham, Wolves and Bournemouth he didn't go to the games so much. His attendances were fewer in the last 10 years of his life because he knew I could stand on my own two feet and because he wasn't always feeling that great. The emphysema had taken hold. I spoke to him after every match. I often still think 'I'll give Dad a call'. That's one of the hardest things for me now.

During my last three or four years at Tottenham, I bought a hospitality box for family and friends, but especially Dad because he was starting to feel the cold. He quite enjoyed that and made a day of it. But the illness got worse because he kept smoking.

When he was first diagnosed I asked the Tottenham doctor whether there was an emphysema specialist he could see. He said there was, and the expert told Dad there were things he could do for him but the only doctor he needed was himself. He needed to stop smoking. Simple! I'm sure that disappointed Dad. There were times he was down to a few cigarettes a day. But he never wanted to give up on a habit he had picked up as an 11-year-old at boarding school.

I was angry with him. I thought he was selfish, not seeming to be concerned about how it was affecting everyone else. I told him he would have gone spare at me if I had started to kick a ball around the garden at home when I had a serious injury. And that that was only my football career. This is your life. What are you doing? He agreed I was right, that it was stupid and that he'd try to stop. But it was an addiction.

It meant he was unable to attend my final match as a professional footballer, for Bournemouth against Chester at Dean Court on Saturday 6 December 2008.

I spoke to him on the Wednesday and told him I would be playing my last game at the weekend. We'd chatted a few times about my retirement. He had said you are a long time retired and football had always been what I wanted to do. I explained I wasn't enjoying it like I had done. That's when he told me stopping was the right decision and he'd be along for the game.

But on the morning of the match he was too ill to come, which upset me. After all he'd done for me, of course, I wanted him to be there.

The Final Weeks
During Dad's final few years, there were times he was so bad he had to go into hospital where he would be treated for a week or two. He'd come out feeling a thousand times better. This gave him a false sense of security, that he could keep smoking and when he felt bad again he could just go into hospital for at least a week and he'd be fine.

The final sequence of events in my Dad's life happened so quickly. He wasn't feeling well and went into hospital. We all thought he was relatively fine, and I was due to go to my first Super Bowl. While I was out in America, enjoying a game of golf with friends before the game between the Pittsburgh Steelers and the Arizona Cardinals in Tampa, Florida, I had calls from Scott and my now fiancée Katie Rata-McMahon to say he had checked himself out. Katie told me that when she spoke to him he was so out of breath he could hardly speak.

I phoned Dad and he sounded awful. I told my brothers and sister to try and make sure he went back to hospital. Thankfully, he did. But all through the 2009 Super Bowl the next day I kept thinking about him and phoned Kelly to say I would fly home the next day. London was snowbound, and I eventually got back 24 hours later and went straight to Southampton General Hospital. Dad was asleep.

He woke up when I returned the following day but was not with it at all. I spoke to the doctor in charge. He said: 'We nearly lost your Dad last night'. I replied: 'Why weren't the family told this?' Then he informed me that Dad had almost died on the day my brothers and sister had checked him back in. They weren't told, either. Nor was Dad. Why did they not think to tell us all? It was mind-boggling.

The doctor's assistant asked me whether I wanted to let my Dad go and just keep him comfortable because the hospital had done all they could for him. I broke down in tears, and he said to 'have a walk and come back and let me know what you think.' When I returned, he wasn't around to speak to.

I phoned my brothers and sister to say Dad was in a really bad way and then they came up to the hospital. We noticed a few hours later there was nothing monitoring how he was. I asked a female nurse who told me the assistant doctor had said I had made the decision to allow him to die in peace earlier. I told her I hadn't made any such decision. I went berserk, and then called the main doctor, Dr Marshall, who explained Dad was coming to the end of his life. I mentioned what had happened earlier with his assistant, and he agreed to put all the monitoring equipment back on and resume his treatments because of the misunderstanding.

Dr Marshall's treatment of Dad had been fantastic, especially with Dad's stubborn ways, although the situation before I'd spoken to the doctor that day had been handled extremely badly at the hospital. Dad recovered a bit and was able to go home a week later.

He could not sleep a lot or walk, but was in good spirits and eating well. At times, he was like his old self. But I discovered he didn't really know how bad he was. While having dinner one night, he spoke to one of his taxi buddies on the phone and told him: 'I'll be down on the rank later tonight.' We looked at him and said: 'Don't be so ridiculous.'

I told him how he'd nearly died a couple of times in hospital, and it nearly shocked him to death. Perhaps if he'd been told about the severity of his condition a lot earlier it might have made a difference, although I doubt it.

Dad stopped eating and sleeping the next weekend and complained he was in a lot of pain on the Monday. He lay there shouting and swearing because he was so short of breath. We phoned the family doctor asking for something that would settle him. We were told he was dying and probably only had about 72 hours left to live, whether he had morphine to ease the discomfort or not.

We got the morphine and the doctor advised us to speak to Dad before they gave him the drug as it was likely to be our last opportunity to do so. That's when he said he'd had enough of living and pleaded with me to stop the pain.

Myself, Scott, Ben and Kelly were all in the living room with him for his final hours. He looked relaxed and tired and we didn't get a lot out of him. We watched Manchester United against Inter Milan in the Champions League on television and then put on a DVD of a comedy film called *Role Models*. My brother Scott went to check on him and told us 'I think he's gone'. He looked peaceful. We were all heart-broken. It was a night we'll never forget.

Dad always hated funerals. He hated anything sad. He just wanted to remember the good times, the good memories. So we made his more of a celebration.

I did a eulogy. It was difficult but nice to be able to do it. And I tried to speak about him in a light-hearted way. The stories made people smile. He'd have revelled in seeing everyone laughing. There were a lot of young as well as old there. Our friends had remained his friends. They were very fond of him. There was no generation gap.

I reminded the congregation of when his kids grew older and started going out, I would drive down after matches on Saturday nights and hit the town with Scott, Ben, Kelly and friends in Southampton. It was real fun, but the highlight of the evening was always heading back to our family home.

All our friends would want to come back and have a drink with Dad when he finished his evening shift as a taxi driver. We would all sit around the living room, laughing and joking for hours, listening to Dad telling us stories about his glory days growing up. He'd make fun of all our friends as he sat there smoking 'the funny stuff' – cannabis – in one hand and holding a glass of whisky and lemonade in the other.

After a few hours, when he was starting to feel the worse for wear, we would often bet him he couldn't hit the garage window with an egg. He would always take up the challenge. Unfortunately for him he would always miss – and then ask for another chance. Before you knew it, there would be egg yolks running down the garage wall, much to our amusement.

I looked out of my bedroom window after waking up one morning to see Dad scrubbing the garage wall. So I opened it and shouted: 'What are you doing?' He turned round and shouted back: 'Stop betting me to throw eggs when I'm pissed you idiot! Now go down to the shop and buy some eggs for breakfast as there's none left.' I rolled around with laughter.

A few years later, we started going to Puerto Banus in Spain on golf holidays. Dad absolutely loved them. Playing golf. Nights out. He was in his element. On one trip, a group of us were shattered after finishing golf at about eight o'clock at night. We had dinner and decided on a night in, watching TV at our apartment. Someone said 'Where's Dad?' I went to have a look in his bedroom. There he was, ready to go out. I said: 'What are you doing?' He replied 'I'm going down to the port, I'm not staying in with you muppets.' I said: 'OK, wait five minutes and I'll come with you.'

I went back to the lounge and said: 'You'll never guess what. Captain Busy has got his gear on and is going out.'

Everyone laughed and said 'Oh, well, I guess we're going out then.' No one wanted to miss a night out with Dad. He loved it in the port. He always seemed to have a gaggle of girls around him giggling at whatever he was saying. He always wanted to end up in a certain piano bar, sitting up by the guy tinkling the ivories who would always play a Neil Diamond song for him. Dad became a legend in there. Whenever we go back there now they always ask: 'Where's Normy Wormy?'

He had an effect on everyone he met.

I'll never forget one late-night disco. It was about five in the morning and the bouncer came over and said: 'Could you get him down, please? There is no dancing allowed on bar stools in here.' It was Dad, of course. Priceless. He really did love those trips.

The last few months became a real struggle for Dad, but he retained his humour, leaving various phone messages making fun of everyone. Even on coach trips back from away games for Bournemouth, my teammates would ask me to call Dad and put him on loudspeaker so they could listen to him taking the mickey out of one of them, Warren Cummings, who got on really well with him. They loved his humour and would often keep him on the phone for ages. He certainly made the journey home more enjoyable.

Dad lived life. He loved his kids, his friends, his dogs, his cigarettes and whisky and, of course, his endless mugs of tea. He was a man of habit who loved the simple things. He would walk the dogs, Boss and Sky, every day. Even if he didn't feel great, he didn't want them to miss out on their exercise.

He'd eat the same things. It was soup followed by steak and chips in every restaurant we ate in. He refused to eat either Chinese or Indian food. He never ever ate either pasta or a pizza.

People told me what a great bloke he was, describing him in a variety of ways: caring, stubborn, generous, a joker, crazy, full of life, a legend. He would do anything for his family and friends.

Passing away at home with his four kids there would have been exactly what he would have wanted. Unfortunately, for us, he went far too soon. We feel like we've lost years of fun and good times with Dad, but so privileged and fortunate for the past 30-odd years of life we shared with him. Everything we have is because of him.

I have so many personal tales to tell. One I've often thought about since he passed away was when I bought him a Mercedes. He would joke with me that he would only believe I'd 'made it' if he woke up one morning to discover a brand new Merc on the lawn outside. I was 23 and had just signed a lucrative contract with Spurs and decided to get myself one and another for Dad as a gesture for everything he'd done for me.

It was all cloak and dagger as I arranged to surprise him. I drove his car down to Southampton, put it in a garage at my Mum's place and went to collect it early in the morning to bring it across the city and put on Dad's lawn.

I got some of my friends to go into the house to check the path was clear. Dad had got up a lot earlier than normal so the curtains had to be kept closed so he wouldn't see the car being put into position. He screamed at one of my mates, Ian Parker, to open them as it was pitch black in the house. Parker told him 'Norm, it's boiling out and I've got a hangover'.

I got the car on the lawn and came in with some more friends. He said: 'Why are all you idiots here?' Mum was there too. Then I gave him a card which said: 'Thanks for everything. If it hadn't been for you I wouldn't be where I am now.' The car's key was taped inside the card with another message attached: 'Do you think I've made it, now?!'

Parker – that's what we call him – then opened the curtains to reveal my gift to him – a brand new blue Mercedes 300.

Dad spluttered: 'Is this a f***ing wind up?' Then he choked up.

There are a million things that make his death difficult. We – as a family – want to keep the house because of all the good memories, but then you walk in and there's the chair he used to sit on. There's his phone number in your mobile that you don't want to take out.

As the oldest, I make sure my siblings are all right and speak to Mum all the time. Katie helps me cope.

But I'm still grieving for Dad. Always will.

2
Beginnings

I was born in the same hospital that my Dad spent an increasing amount of time in towards the end of his life. After an 18-hour labour (sorry Mum), I made my first appearance of any sort at 11.50am on Friday 3 March 1972 in the Victoria House wing of Southampton General, tipping the scales at 7lb 6oz. Dad was there, although he was sent out of the room when forceps came into play and left to read a magazine article on Peter Osgood, the Chelsea legend, in the corridor. Ironically, *Son of My Father* by Chicory Tip was No.1 in the UK pop charts.

I was the first of four children born to Norman and Jane Anderton. We were a working-class family in the city famous for its association with ocean liners like the ill-fated *Titanic* and the *Queen Elizabeth II*. Mum was a waitress at the local Beefeater restaurant before she had us, and Dad was the owner of a removal firm he ran from the family home.

My parents met during the Swinging Sixties. Dad had been a biker and Mum a bit of a mod. It seemed a case of opposites attracting. Mum tells me, with a bit of irony, that there is a thin line between love and hate and that she and my Dad walked it at the start of their relationship. She laughs about how they used to throw plenty of verbal abuse at each other after becoming acquainted in the basement of the Checkpoint Café in Southampton over a frothy coffee. They were just friends at first and hung around in a group. She would turn him down on the regular occasions he suggested a date. But she finally said 'yes' after returning from a holiday bored and thought a night out with Dad would liven up her dull existence.

Their romance blossomed and they enjoyed a lot of good times. They had a shared interest in music; attending early concerts by the Small Faces, a pop rock band, at the Concorde Club in Southampton. Those gigs must have been nights of compromise for Dad as singer Steve Marriott and his Faces were mods! Mum and Dad also saw Manfred Mann, another chart group, down there. The courting couple also used to go to a dance hall at the end of the pier every Sunday to see bands and enjoyed attending a club in Bognor.

They became engaged, but my Mum decided to take a break from her life on the south coast of England. Taking £50 – the most you could take out of the country at the time – she went hitch-hiking round Europe with a friend of hers. She returned when the money ran out after six weeks. But in that time she discovered absence had made her heart grow fonder of Dad. They married at St Mark's Church – which is no longer there – in Southampton on 24 February 1968. And they lived happily ever after in the city…for 14 years.

A year was spent in a one-bedroom flat above a greengrocer that my grandad – Mum's dad Jack Smith – ran. Then they moved to a three-bedroom semi at Burnett Close, Bitterne Park, a suburban area of Southampton. That was my first home along with middle brother Scott, two years my junior.

Mum and Dad exchanged contracts on the house that was to become the main family home as she went into labour with my twin brother and sister, Ben and Kelly, when I was three-and-a-half. Oak Tree Road was another three-bedroom semi, but provided the increased living space needed.

Football in the Family
There was only a little in the family tree to suggest Mum and Dad would produce a footballer.

My Mum's Dad was a soldier who saw action in France and Burma during World War Two and, later, in Korea. He never spoke about his experiences, along with many who were traumatised by the horrific reality of war. Once out of the Army, he established himself as a cobbler to the well-heeled in Bournemouth and Poole, where my Mum grew up. He uprooted the family to Southampton when Mum was eight to set himself up in the fruit and veg retail business.

Mum tells me he was laid back in his younger days. It seemed he would have sat quietly in his favourite chair watching the telly even if the roof had caved in. It was Gran Jean who wore the trousers in the house. But he changed in character, understandably becoming less easy-going after he had a stroke. He had a tough time in the end, contracting diabetes and blindness.

Grandad was, I'm told, a useful footballer. I heard he might have joined Charlton but the war, like it did for so many budding footballers, got in the way. He turned out for non-League Poole Town. My Gran used to go along with my Mum to watch him.

Mum was the son he didn't have for 10 years until her brother Kent was born. She watched the 1958 World Cup Finals in Sweden, from which Pelé emerged, on television with him and developed into a big

Southampton fan, following the Saints all round the country when the likes of Ron Davies, Terry Paine, Micky Channon and Martin Chivers donned the red-and-white-stripes.

My uncle Kent played non-League and his son Michael got as far as being an associated schoolboy with Portsmouth before suffering an accident which affected his sight. There was also a distant cousin of mine called Peter who had a trial with Saints.

My Parents

Mum picked up on my abilities early on. She says I was more interested in kicking a ball than learning to walk during my crawling days. I used to haul myself upright either via a chair or table leg in the house to swing at one whenever I had the chance. It certainly delayed my ability to put one foot in front of the other. I didn't take my first steps until I was 14 months. At the age of two, I was apparently able to volley a leather ball in the garden.

I wasn't interested in *any* toys. It was all about football. The only time I might do something else was when it was pouring with rain outside and the Lego came out.

Apparently, I had a short temper but was generally a 'good boy'. The only time Mum remembers me really stepping out of line was through my obsession with football. It resulted in me being briefly shown the inside of a police cell. I was about seven or eight and stole some money from coins my Dad left out on the sideboard so I could go to the local newsagent and buy some football cards of my favourite players. When my parents found out they decided to take firm action. Dad took me down the station, after arranging things with the police, to give me a fright. I was made to pack a bag and say goodbye to my brothers and sister. I was scared out of my wits and it taught me a life lesson.

Dad's background in football was minimal. He was bought up in Motherwell, 13.5 miles south-east of Glasgow. His family supported the home-town team, which included the likes of Ian St John, en route to becoming a legendary striker for Bill Shankly's all-conquering Liverpool team of the 1960s and one half of the TV team of Saint and Greavsie. But the sport didn't really figure much in his life in those days.

His childhood, generally, was a miserable one. His Dad (Alexander McKenzie), who was a doctor, died when he was two so he didn't have any memories of him. His Mum remarried, to Harry Anderton, who, I'm told, liked his drink, and was not the nicest guy in the world. Dad got packed off to a Scottish boarding school, which he didn't overly like, and discovered athletics – as well as his smoking habit – at the age of 11.

He found he was a natural cross country runner, the main sporting attribute he passed down to me. Come to think of it, it's the only one! Dad also spoke about how he played a bit of cricket and was a decent spin bowler, although I didn't see any proof of it.

One sporting highlight we did see was when he won a 10-pin bowling competition against other parents from one of my youth teams. First thing I knew of it was the next morning when I came down for breakfast and noticed my sports awards had disappeared from the display shelf and been replaced by the tiniest bowling medal you could wish to see. That summed up his humour.

Dad ended up leaving school at 13 and went to live with his Mum and step-dad in Jersey. He made us watch the detective programme *Bergerac*, with the actor John Nettles, because it was based there. As we sat in front of the box, it provoked memories of his time on the island and he shared them with us. He loved his time there, often going round the island on bikes with his mates, although he was in and out of jobs before settling in Southampton with his family in his late teens. Football remained off his radar until I started taking a big interest in it.

Mum and Dad decided to take me to my first professional game, which was Southampton versus Manchester City, when I was about eight. I remember Dave Watson, who was playing for Saints and had played for City, getting knocked out. The excitement and the atmosphere were incredible. I was buzzing. Mum and Dad said I had the biggest smile – from ear to ear. I was hooked. My imagination ran away with me. I wanted to be a Saint.

The Dell was a ground typical of the time, characterised by Victorian structures of metal and wood, pongy loos and dodgy burgers before the Taylor Report brought about all-seater stadia following the Hillsborough disaster in 1989 and eventually saw Saints switch to the club's current state-of-the-art home at the St Mary's Stadium.

I might have been uncomfortable surrounded by health and safety issues, but I loved every visit. It excited my senses. The sight, sounds and smells of 15,000 squeezed together to watch 22 footballers perform are still with me. Dad and I got crushed against the bars that used to be on the terraces, which was really quite frightening.

When I was about 10, he got us season tickets in the Family Centre section and we were able to watch every home game. I saw some wonderful players like Kevin Keegan, Peter Shilton, Alan Ball, Mark Dennis, the Wallace brothers, Frank Worthington, Mick Mills and Steve Williams.

My parents, as I've indicated, were both determined their kids wouldn't suffer following their divorce in 1982. It seemed like they'd been arguing for years. They always tried to stay together for the sake of us children, but in the end they had to go their separate ways. I'm sure Dad's depressing experiences growing up were a big motivation for him to ensure we had a happy and settled upbringing despite the differences between him and my Mum. That was reflected in the fact that we all remained under the same roof after the marriage ended.

Eventually, though, Mum met another chap called Mike Devitt. Mike and Dad almost came to blows once outside the front door. She moved in with Mike, taking us kids with her; a night I'll never forget as I looked back into the kitchen to see Dad in tears as we were leaving.

Although Mike wasn't the reason our parents broke up, we saw him as the enemy. It wasn't that we hated him, it was just we thought he was obviously trying to take over from Dad. We were a pain in the backside and caused an absolute riot. We did not enjoy living in his house on the other side of the city. We were obviously missing our friends and Dad. We would deliberately eat food off the plates with our bare hands and spill gravy everywhere. Scott wound Mike up so much once that Mike stuffed his head in the food! I reacted by throwing roast potatoes at Mike's head and running out of the room to lock myself in the toilet.

We also didn't like the area we lived in. It was called Bevois Valley. An awful part of Southampton. There were hookers on the street nearby. Nasty. The house itself was an old building we thought haunted. We all moved to another place near Southampton's old Dell ground, but all the problems remained. We missed our home.

All four of us get on great with Mike now. He came to my Dad's funeral and was in tears. He grew to really care for him. But back then Norman's kids made it clear we wanted to be with our Dad at our true home.

So my parents came to an arrangement for us to move back to Oak Tree Road. It must have been hard for Mum to do that, but she understood the situation and put the children first. Dad could have gone off and lived in Spain or done whatever, but he too wanted to do what was best for his children. And so he put his own life on hold. No girlfriends, no social life. Just four monsters to look after, even though he struggled with the housework besides the cooking. Luckily, my Mum was a star. She would come to us after work to rustle up meals, tidy up and try to educate my Dad in the ways of domesticity. He'd obviously left all that to her while they were married. Shock, horror!

Everything worked out for all four of us. We didn't miss out on anything. Us Anderton kids still saw our Mum and Dad every day and lived in the family home. Eventually Dad got to grips with preparing meals, although what he produced made school dinners seem like something they'd serve up at the Ritz. But he got better.

Life was great. He spoilt us rotten. We got the best trainers, football boots, tennis racquets, snooker tables, clothes and holidays. Everything we wanted we could have. Even when it was 'can I have a couple of quid, Dad?' we got it. He just couldn't say no.

Football was, as I have revealed, my sole interest. Any toys I got for Christmas from well-meaning members of the family were either left in their wrapping or gathered dust in some dark, forgotten corner of the house.

As I developed, Mum and Dad were, thankfully, able to share in any success I had. Mum admits to being a 'proud mum'. As soon as I came out to see my parents after a game, she would want to know what the manager said to me, while all I wanted to do was chill out. Dad and I dubbed her Ceefax – after the teletext service – because she was so keen to get a full report. Dad would love it when she did it and joke with her, saying: 'Come on, Ceefax, give him five minutes.'

Brothers and sister

Scott and Ben shared my passion for football. We played a lot together growing up. Scott was usually in goal. Even when he was reluctant, I pulled rank on him as the oldest brother and forced him to stand in front of the garage door we used as a goal. Or between the jumpers either over the park or in the school playing fields at the back of Oak Tree Road. Ben joined in when he was old enough.

It wasn't the only sport we played. I remember ending up rolling around in the mud on a golf course fighting with Scott because we were both so competitive. Again, because I was the oldest, I felt I was the best – and it needed to stay that way! Dad picked us up and we weren't talking to each other.

We are all still the same. Not that long ago, before Dad died, Scott and Ben gave him a good laugh. They had a row on a tennis court. Ben shouted: 'I can't be dealing with this rubbish' – and stormed away from the court and drove off. That left Scott stranded, a mile and a half from the Oak Tree Road house they shared and still do.

Scott ran home, and when he got there decided to let down the tyres on Ben's car parked outside as revenge for leaving him high and dry. When Dad told me the story he was in fits of giggles. It was so childish, but the pair of them have the competitive gene most of us have inherited from Dad. Mum's the only placid one!

The banter when I get together with my brothers can be non-stop. It can make the impartial observer wonder whether we are fond of each other. The stick we dish out and receive over the clothes we wear can be merciless. Comments on each other's performances on either the golf course or tennis court, unsurprisingly, are nearly always far from complimentary. There are verbals aplenty at the snooker table, where cues have been known to be snapped in half, usually by me. But, in truth, we are all best friends. Even though we are the worst losers in the world.

We have spent a lot of time with each other, partly through our common interest in sport, and have all tried to develop any talent we had at whatever game we played. My sister tried to do her own thing with her gymnastic friends but she was constantly interrupted when practising in the garden as we kicked a football around. Kelly was a good gymnast, though, and a decent athlete – particularly at cross-country running – but she injured her ankles which prevented her from fully realising her potential in either sport.

It must have been hard for my sister on occasions to have three brothers sharing the family home with her. Especially when it came to boyfriends. We had to approve of whoever it was. If we didn't give him the thumbs up then she couldn't go out with him. I believe she feels a little sensitive to what we think even now! Poor Kelly. But she has done well for herself. She has got her own house in Southampton and works hard for an insurance firm.

Scott lived with me in Hemel Hempstead after I joined Spurs and got a job as a ski instructor at the town's dry slope facility. He then went on to do the same job in America and Australia. Scott has always been good at golf, getting down to a scratch handicap. He tried hard to get a card to play on a pro tour in Europe. He has now started a gardening business and might go off and work in either America or Australia in the future. Or do something totally different. We will see.

Ben could have joined me as a professional footballer. Unfortunately, he didn't have the same passion as I did for the game. He was very talented but stopped playing when he was only 11 or 12 because he didn't enjoy it. He restarted when he was 15 and, within six months, earned an apprenticeship with Portsmouth – as I was leaving for Tottenham.

The local media made a big deal of this, which I thought was unfair because it added extra pressure on him. His youth coach didn't have a professional career that matched those who helped me carve out my career there. And Ben might have come across as not showing him too much respect: Ben's his own person who does what he wants and says what he thinks, like Dad used to do. That might have come across as arrogance, especially after what I achieved at Pompey.

Sadly, Portsmouth did not offer him a professional contract, but Spurs gave him a trial after Steve Perryman, then assistant manager at

Tottenham, had a word with me because he had remembered seeing him in a Pompey youth game. Ben came and had a good week's training and had already been invited back for another week when disaster struck as he broke his leg playing for the youth team against Bristol City alongside Sol Campbell (more about this later). He tried to come back a couple of years later, but nothing materialised and he has followed Dad and become a taxi driver. That suits him down to the ground because he can work whenever he wants to.

Together, Ben and Kelly worked in the bars in Malia on Crete among the Greek Islands one summer, which they thoroughly enjoyed.

My relationships with both my brothers and sister have not changed because I went on and had a decent football career. We still always see a lot of each other and share the same group of friends. Whenever we go out I look after them, sort everything. As their big brother, it is my way of making sure they are OK. Yes, I do like spoiling them, just like Dad did with us.

They all came to watch me regularly early on. But when I started getting long-term injuries they got out of the habit, although Scott turned up at my last club, Bournemouth, more than the others. Yet they all still took an interest in my football career and were forever on the phone after games taking the piss out of me.

There is not an ounce of jealousy in any of them, and I am not the sort to become a Big-Time Charlie with anyone, let alone my brothers and sister, not that they'd ever let me get away with anything. They are proud of me as much as I am of them.

In my last ever game, against Chester just before Christmas in 2008, they all came and were pretty choked up.

School

I hated it at Bitterne Park School, apart from when we played football. They say your school years are the best of your life, but I don't think so. I couldn't be bothered to study. Dad, though, made me promise I would at least try and get my Maths and English GCSEs – which I did – so I would have something to fall back on if my hope of becoming a footballer didn't work out. It was quite funny considering he'd left school with no qualifications. But he had learned by his own mistakes.

There are two teachers I remember. Mr Swift was the sports teacher in charge of my football and cross-country teams at middle school. My form teacher Mrs Starks had me off to a T. If I played up in class she told me 'no work, no football'. She knew I'd have a terrible temper if I came into class after I'd lost a game in the playground and would calm me down. She was my favourite teacher.

I went back to see them when I was at Portsmouth and Tottenham. I also got them tickets for my first full England game as thanks for what they did for me and loved the fact they were able to see me fulfil my aspirations.

I played in school games alongside the youth matches with Bitterne Park Rangers, Winsor and Southampton and District. I was always serious about my football. It hit home how serious when I made a conscious decision to stop hanging around with a group of boys I had spent my childhood with. A couple were sons of neighbours. One was my best friend throughout school. There were others who were in my school team. They were good fun and loved football. We'd either play in the garden with my brothers or hop over the back fence into that school field. The school caretaker tried to keep us off it occasionally. Mum remembers him coming round to the house and accusing us of trespass.

When I was in my last year at school, a lot of these mates went to pubs, started smoking, hanging around with people I didn't like and walking the streets looking for fights. Two of them ended up in jail. They have straightened themselves out now. But at the time, I thought, 'enough of this'. It wasn't for me. I knew what I wanted to be – a professional footballer. It proved a good decision to stop seeing them. I didn't want to destroy my dream.

I have always had a radar which has enabled me to pick up on potential trouble. When I became known at Portsmouth I avoided going into the Southampton clubs my friends went in because the two clubs were such rivals. Footballers have to be so careful where they go and who they mix with.

My focus on football always remained total and paid off once the opportunity to link up with Pompey happened, although my life has not been without off-the-field incident since.

3
The Ball's Rolling

In a letter dated 23 February 1988, Portsmouth manager Alan Ball wrote to my parents to confirm that I would be offered an apprenticeship with Portsmouth on leaving school. A Southampton lad risks the wrath of his home city if he has anything to do with Portsmouth Football Club. However, it was a risk I took to launch my professional career, despite a rivalry between Pompey and Soton which dates back more than 900 years.

King John, according to Southampton FC historian Dave Juson, niggled Portsmouth traders by forcing them to pay their taxes and port and customs duties through Southampton. There were other political squabbles down the centuries, such as when it was revealed that Pompey would be a on a branch of a new railway mainline between London and Southampton. If Portsmouth weren't on a mainline to the capital the planners could forget it, according to some angry councillors.

The supporters of the respective football clubs coexisted without neighbourly spats until the 1960s. But that all changed, so the experts tell me, when both sets of fans clashed on the pitch after Saints beat Pompey at Fratton Park in 1966. The Blue and Red Noses became bitter enemies, with the 1970s hooligans stirring the pot. As Kevin Mitchell said in the *Observer* on 23 January 2005: 'This is very much a modern war, one built on sand but sustained in ignorance. It is about the idiocy and manufactured romance of football, which too often becomes a vehicle for deeper prejudice.'

As a local lad, I was only too aware of the animosity between my home club's supporters and Portsmouth's. It has become as intense as most in football when the two play each other, and it is potentially a rocky road for anyone who dares leave one for the other. As uneven as any trodden by players moving across town to 'rivals' in Glasgow, London, Manchester and Liverpool.

Sol Campbell, my teammate at Tottenham and in the 1998 World Cup, received a slating from the White Hart Lane faithful after he moved the handful of miles across north London to Arsenal in 2001. He might have developed into one of the world's greatest defenders, but that cut no ice with supporters who hero-worshipped him and felt betrayed at him joining the 'enemy'.

And those fans proved to have long memories when Campbell returned to White Hart Lane in April 2010. He had unexpectedly rejoined the Gunners after serving Portsmouth and got a verbal blasting throughout the game from home supporters anxious to rub his nose in the dirt as Spurs won 2–1.

Harry Redknapp also got tongue-lashed when he quit as Portsmouth manager to take up the hot seat at Southampton. The Blue Noses labelled him 'Judas' for what they believed was treacherous behaviour, even though he'd got Pompey into the Premier League for the first time. And when he went back as boss at Fratton Park, there were still many among his detractors who refused to forgive, even though Harry maintained their top-flight status and won the FA Cup before moving on to Tottenham.

When I threw my lot in with Pompey, however, there was no danger of enduring the sort of treatment meted out to Harry and Sol. I was just 'Darren who?', a skinny kid who wanted to be a professional footballer, like millions of others.

I had loved going down the Dell to cheer on the Saints. But, as I said earlier, there were no scouts tapping on Mum or Dad's shoulders to ask them if I wanted to come down to the club for a trial.

I was playing with some good players for Southampton and District Schools and Winsor. A couple of lads were training at Saints on schoolboy forms and there were one or two more at Swindon under a similar arrangement. But yours truly didn't seem to be impressing anyone beyond his parents, although I would hope my managers and teammates didn't think I was too bad. Bob Higgins from Saints used to watch my Southampton Schoolboys team play every Saturday morning, but obviously he didn't really notice me.

He was in charge of the club's youth set-up then. He had a good reputation and had helped to produce Alan Shearer and the Wallace brothers, Danny, Rod and Ray. I'd have loved to have gone down to the Dell. What could be better than playing for your home club? But I was clearly not in his thoughts.

That was when my Dad took it upon himself to make that call to Pompey. He knew how much a career in the game meant to me, and if Saints didn't want me maybe Portsmouth would. After all, I was 14 and in danger of missing the boat if there was one for me to board to the Land of the Professional Footballer.

One day at Eastleigh I turned out for Southampton Schools Under-14s. Dad wasn't there because he had taken Ben to another match with the district Under-11s. After the game, as I stood with Mum, a guy came up to us. He introduced himself. It was Pompey youth development officer Dave Hurst. He explained he was there to watch me as my Dad had called him. He had liked what he saw and asked if he could come round to the house for a chat about it.

I was in shock but delighted to sign when Dave popped into Oak Tree Road a few days later. The fact he saw something in me is a judgment I will always be grateful for. He said I had talent and loved the way I always tried to do the right thing: control, pass and move. That, although I was very slim, I had potential. I signed associated schoolboy forms with Portsmouth and Dad drove me to their training ground and back for an hour-and-a-half session every Thursday.

Pompey, it seemed, operated differently to Saints. My Winsor teammates, who were on Southampton's books, weren't allowed to play for their Sunday team any more if they wanted to carry on at Southampton. I thought that was terrible because we all enjoyed our youth club football. Ironically, none of them got an apprenticeship and they felt they'd wasted two years.

Thankfully for me, Pompey allowed me to continue playing for Winsor and then Totton Youth each Sunday. The training was good. And I was fortunate to receive advice from experienced people in the game at such a young age. What I really appreciated was the interest shown in the likes of myself by first-team manager Alan Ball. Where else would you see a first-team manager take 14-year-olds training on Thursday evenings? He might have been a World Cup-winner for England, but he really cared about us kids. He was so enthusiastic and put on some great sessions for us. I was so lucky to have him teach and train me at such a young age.

I also had coaching sessions with Peter Osgood, the former England and Chelsea striker who had played for Saints in the 1970s, and Dave Thomas, an ex-international who played on the wing for Pompey, QPR, everton, Wolves and Burnley. Both were excellent. Ossie taught me how to whip and curl the ball. To use the instep of my right foot to curl it with power when striking the ball. When I'd mastered it, I thought: 'Wow!' As I went on to become a winger, it became a big part of my game because I was able to deliver whipped crosses.

Pompey was great at first. But I didn't appear to set the world on fire and got fed up because they didn't seem to rate me. They thought I was a bit too skinny. Ossie thought I lacked physical strength. It came to a head when he kept me on the bench in a match against the Navy, concerned that the opponents were a lot stronger than me and that I would get hurt. Then he sent someone else on who was a lot smaller than me. I thought then that Ossie, God rest his soul, had been talking bollocks.

I walked back to the car with my Dad and told him: 'Sod this, I want to pack it in.' Driving back home, Dad told me that although it looked bad I would know in a month to six weeks whether I'd get an apprenticeship. I definitely thought I wasn't getting one, but he convinced me to stick it out.

By chance, not long after Alan Ball spotted me playing against the same Navy team. I had a great first half, keeping it simple by getting the ball and passing it. I was right midfield with Darryl Powell (who went on to be a teammate in the first team) at right-back. We linked up and passed the ball well between us.

At half-time, Alan Ball walked right round the pitch to tell my Dad, whom he knew as Ben played in the same Winsor team as his son Jimmy: 'Your boy has got a chance to be a player, you know?'

My Dad replied: 'Oh, really?'

After the game, when my Dad told me of this conversation, I was excited.

It all changed for me from that moment. That Thursday I went training and Peter Osgood was saying 'brilliant, Darren, brilliant' all the time. Before he had hardly mentioned my name. I thought: 'This is interesting!'

A couple of days later I got a phone call to say I'd been given an apprenticeship at a time when the first team was in the top flight, something that was put in writing in that letter from Alan Ball dated 23 February 1988. My Dad knew it was going to give me the chance to prove him right about becoming a hell of a player in my early 20s. Everyone respected Alan Ball's opinion. I certainly did. He had made the journey from Southampton to Portsmouth without suffering any brickbats.

Why should he have got any? He was a star midfielder with Blackpool, Arsenal and Saints and, above all else, he was man of the match when England beat West Germany to lift the World Cup, from what I've seen on video. Geoff Hurst might have made history by grabbing a hat-trick, but Bally's workrate, skill and desire from wide right was an example to all his successors in that position, including me. He was a wonderful coach. I believed in him. Everything he said I took on board and acted upon. He instilled in me things that stood me in good stead and I took with me through to the end of my playing career.

Bally advised us to do the right thing by keeping it simple. For instance, he told me and the others to pass the ball with the inside of the foot because it provided the biggest surface area to make a connection. Control, pass, move using both feet. Work hard. Be a team player. He told us they were things his father, Alan Snr, had preached to him. His motto was: 'Simplicity is genius.' He kept us on our toes! Dave Hurst used to tell us: 'Do the right thing because if you don't the gaffer will come down on you like a ton of bricks.'

I remember one time there was a lad there doing a passing skill and flicking the ball with the outside of his foot. Alan Ball picked him up on it and said to him: 'If you want to do it like that then you can f*** off to Spurs.' That remark is something I now find hilarious, given that is precisely what I ended up doing. Alan was very friendly, always had time for you and knew all the kids' names. A really nice guy.

Alan believed in the group of young players there. He and others at the club thought us a special crop. I don't believe they were thinking about me, more the likes of Darryl Powell, Mickey Turner, Micky Ross and Andy Awford, along with Kit Symons in the year above. All very good players.

A few years later we were on a golfing holiday in Spain and bumped into Alan Ball on a night out. My Dad and I sat and talked football with him for a few hours over a couple of beers. He loved talking football. Lived and breathed it. I was so upset when he passed away in 2007.

The first day I started my apprenticeship saw me moving out of my home and into my 'digs' in Portsmouth. It was so daunting for me. So nerve-racking. I stayed with a lovely couple called Phil and Christine. I shared with Mark Kelly, a Republic of Ireland international already at the age of 18 and being billed as the next George Best. He was a really nice lad who I looked up to and aspired to be as good as.

My first-ever day as an apprentice, in July 1988, was spent running down the beach at the start of pre-season. It was absolutely hell and I felt sick. I might have been a cross-country runner at school, but now I was ploughing through the sand and shingle with professional footballers.

I thought: 'This is my job, it is going to be tough and I've got to get used to it'. Within two or three days, I was all right and cruising through it. The stamina I'd built up while running as a Bitterne Park pupil was paying off. They took us off to HMS *Nelson* in the second week. We ran in the morning and the afternoon.

On the first morning we ran six miles with a PTI instructor from the Royal Navy, the last mile-and-a-half as quickly as we could because it was being timed. The PTI told us: 'Just follow me. I'll lead the way.'

I ended up running with him and, when I saw the finish, I ran past him. The next day the next PTI was out and racing me.

The lads loved it as the Navy would send out a new PTI each day to try and beat me, while they just jogged behind and took it easy. It was a cross-country challenge with a 'jolly' going on behind.

The next day we did a 3,000m run. John Gregory, who had been brought in by new owner Jim Gregory (they were together at QPR) as assistant to Alan Ball, knew I was a decent runner and said to me 'don't wait for them'. He sucked me in and off I went.

People started to take notice of me. Kevin Ball, the club captain, said to me: 'You're a fit lad. Can you play as well?' I told him: 'I'm OK.'

My first youth manager, Graham Paddon, who had played for Norwich and West Ham, had the same mentality as Alan Ball. He wanted me to do the right things too.

I'd been either a central midfielder or right midfielder, but not a winger as such up to that point. In Paddo's team, I lined up wide all the time in a 4–4–2. He encouraged me to take people on. He liked me as a player and thought I had a good touch. And my crossing became pretty good. I listened to Paddo because I trusted him. He encouraged us to cut out the flash stuff, insisting, like Alan Ball, that it was a simple game. Control the ball. Pass it. If you can do it in two touches then do it in two touches. And when you get in the final third, get your crosses in.

I wasn't a typical winger in that I didn't tend to burst past people. But I had the thing where I'd drop my shoulder, probably like David Beckham has done, and get my crosses in after gliding by people. In Paddo's side I always felt involved.

I didn't play in the youth team straight away. Second-year apprentices were given priority to give themselves more of an opportunity to earn themselves a contract. My first game as an apprentice was for Portsmouth Reserves, managed by John Gregory, at Petersfield. There was an injury and I got on at half-time. I scored with my first touch. I think it was with my hand, but it counted! The ball just hit me from a yard out. I was absolutely delighted I was playing with players such as Mark Kelly, Mike Fillery and Billy Gilbert. It felt fantastic. Two weeks earlier I had been at school, and now I was playing and scoring for Portsmouth Reserves. My confidence was so high. Everything was going great. I was enjoying training and playing, got on well with the lads well and in Paddo I had a coach who believed in me and was always full of praise.

Unfortunately it changed after a couple of weeks. I was playing for the youth team in another pre-season game in the middle of nowhere. Dad was there. I did a block tackle and thought I'd broken my leg. I was stretchered off and went straight to hospital.

Graham Paddon spoke to my Dad and said: 'Don't worry, he'll be OK. He has been outstanding and I love working with him. You should be really proud of him, Norm. He's been a revelation.'

When my Dad told me all that at my hospital bedside it was brilliant because I was so down. Those words gave me such a boost. I'd badly strained my knee ligaments and my leg was in plaster for 10 days. John

Dickens, the club physio, had me doing 20 laps of the pitch on crutches, while the team trained. I enjoyed the challenge of getting back to fitness. When I was able to, I did a lot of running and quickly regained it.

My first game back was as a substitute for the youth team. I came on at Ipswich when it was 1–1 and scored the winner in the last minute from 25 yards with my left foot into the top corner. I couldn't believe it. Paddo was buzzing. He said to me: 'I told you you'd be all right!'

We managed to reached the FA Youth Cup quarter-finals, where a Watford side, which included David James, beat us after a replay.

My first year as a full-time footballer could not have gone any better.

I went off on holiday to Dallas for a month in the summer of 1988 to stay with friends, Dave, Joe and Vic Roy and their wonderful parents Lou and Mary. I'd met them two years before when they put me up while being a host family for the Dallas Youth Cup in which my team, Southampton and District Schools, were taking part.

I'd got on well with all the Roys and loved the American lifestyle so much I couldn't wait to return. I'd saved up spending money and Dad paid my air fares. And I had a ball. Since then I've gone back every summer. On my first return trip, I even played in their indoor football league and we won the competition. If Pompey had found out they'd have been furious. We weren't able to go out to the bars then as we were under 21, but there were plenty of house parties at all these rich kids' places in Dallas. It was a great laugh.

The boys also introduced me to their idea of fun, which was to wrap bundles of toilet roll around the grounds of people's houses. Early in the morning, when the dew had settled, we would go round and inspect our handiwork as the residents tidied up the mess.

I carried on doing well in the second year of my apprenticeship at Portsmouth (1988–89). We didn't have a big reserve squad so I continued to play for them in midweek and the youth team on Saturday.

I was picking up good experience for the second team, playing at stadiums like Highbury and White Hart Lane and against opponents such as Niall Quinn and Martin Hayes (Arsenal), Gordon Durie (Tottenham), Steve Williams (Luton) and Frank McAvennie (West Ham). Steve, as you know, was an idol of mine from when he played at Southampton. He was a fearsome competitor – I didn't want to go anywhere near him. He was moody, but a hell of a player. All this helped me on the physical side. I was 16 and not the strongest and up against men.

Alan Ball was sacked in January 1989. He had got Pompey back in the top flight two years before but could only keep them up there for a season. He became Colchester assistant before being appointed manager of Stoke, where Paddo joined him after we had just beaten QPR 3–2 after being 2–0 down in an FA Youth Cup tie. I was devastated Paddo left. When I spoke to him as he was departing, he said to me: 'Don't worry, you'll be fine. Just keep doing the right things.'

Malcolm Beard, the old Birmingham player, took over from Paddo. He was a really nice guy and a good coach. He knew he had taken charge of a few good players, and we showed we were as our FA Youth Cup run rolled on. We beat Arsenal, who included Andrew Cole when he was just plain Andy, 1–0 at their place. It was a huge result because they had the best youth team around.

Then we went to Liverpool to face a side with Steve McManaman and Steve Harkness. I put us 2–1 up, but they equalised a minute later. It was an incredible experience to play at Anfield and draw with the mighty Reds. Our Cup run was capturing the imagination of the Portsmouth public. We were the talk of the town when Liverpool came to Fratton Park.

Even the kick-off was delayed because of the amount of people coming into the ground to watch it. What!? No one usually watched youth games, but a lot of people were talking us up, saying that we were a talented group of youngsters. I scored the opening goal with a 25-yard free-kick. Unfortunately, once again, Liverpool equalised immediately, sending the game into extra-time. However, in the last minute of extra-time I hit the winner with a cross-cum-shot which was deflected into the net.

In the players' bar afterwards, I was with my Mum and Dad and the boys wanted to go out and celebrate. I wasn't sure whether to but my parents said to go out and enjoy myself. Next day, I appeared on television for the first time with the local TV stations showing our big night. It was crazy.

The next round was a big let down. We lost 1–0 at home to Middlesbrough in the semi-final first leg in front of another big Fratton crowd expecting another great night. And then we went out after losing the second leg 2–1.

Despite Alan Ball and Paddo having gone, I'd built up enough experience and confidence through the help I'd been given to make me believe I had what it took to be a professional footballer.

4

Pompey Chimes

John Gregory gave me my first contract as a professional footballer. It was in the spring of 1989. He had taken over from Alan Ball as Portsmouth manager a couple of months before. I had been upset by that because of what Bally had done for me but, looking back, the writing was on the wall for him as soon as chairman, the late Jim Gregory, brought John in to be his assistant after the midfielder had announced his retirement as a player the year before.

Jim, I believe, wanted someone he knew in charge rather than a boss he had inherited on taking over the club in 1988, and John fitted the bill following their time together at QPR. I didn't appreciate it at the time, but John had one big thing going for him: he had served Terry Venables as a player when Terry was manager at Rangers. Terry had turned him into an England international footballer (a trick he was to perform with me). John, in turn, helped Terry's Second Division Rangers to the 1982 FA Cup Final, which ended in defeat after a replay to – you've guessed it – Tottenham. And who scored Spurs' winner that day? Glenn Hoddle, who was to go on and manage me on three occasions.

Under Terry's continued influence, John also helped QPR to promotion and a UEFA Cup place. But when Terry became El Tel on assuming the reins at Barcelona in 1984, John and Rangers struggled and, after a spell with Derby, he quit and took up the offer from Jim to give coaching and management a whirl at Pompey.

He might not have pulled up any trees with the first team by the time he was dismissed in January 1990, but John ensured that promising youngsters like myself were to be a part of the club's future. John often told me I'd done OK when I played for his reserve team but would never over-praise because he wanted to keep me on my toes. People told me they had heard him talk very highly of me, but he would never say it to my face.

Quite often John would cross balls for us youngsters after training, and I was told on Steve Wicks's first day as his assistant and reserve manager that he turned to his old QPR teammate and said: 'Wicksy, take a look at this kid's quality.' He appreciated technical ability and it was nice to know how much he did rate me, even though he wouldn't tell me himself. I'm grateful for the faith he showed in me. He's a nice guy who I still see occasionally. Some people don't know how to take him, but he says what he thinks and expects players to show their skills.

I signed a deal around my 17th birthday for the remainder of that season and one more. John Gregory brought me into his office with another young lad, Micky Turner, who had done well. I was told I'd get £150 a week for the first year and £175 for the second. I'd been earning just £35 a week on the YTS (Youth Training Scheme). I was over the moon. It was what it was all about. I'd wanted to be a professional footballer my whole life, and it had become a reality. From the following season someone was going to have to clean my boots!

The two years I'd had as a youth-team player I'll never forget. I owe the career I went on to have to the influences of people like Paddo, Malcolm Beard, Alan Ball and the senior Pompey players, who always had time for me. Now I'd arrived at the business end. After the way things had gone in my first year, I had expected to get a contract, but when it happened it was fantastic. The family was buzzing. A few of my youth teammates got a deal too, including Andy Awford and Darryl Powell.

With Kit Symons, who had got a contract a year earlier, we were the nucleus of Jim Smith's Pompey team which reached the FA Cup semi-final in 1992; players who went on to have long careers in the game. Micky Ross, along with Micky Turner, were the two other players to get contracts from my youth team, but sadly, even though they were very good players, they weren't as fortunate as the rest of us. What happened to them just showed the thin dividing line between making it and not making it. They didn't get that little bit of luck we all need along the way.

Life was changing and I had to adjust. As an apprentice, I had to do a lot of chores, like cleaning boots and changing rooms and pump up the balls for training. Doing them made me appreciate being a full-time professional when it happened. All I had to do as a full-time pro at the training ground was turn up half an hour before a session started and, with my boots already cleaned for me, go out and train, shower and go home. Youngsters often don't have to do those chores these days and can sometimes take things a little for granted if they are lucky enough to get a pro contract.

I had 'digs' in Portsmouth all through my apprenticeship, which the club paid for. Once I became a pro, expenses for them came out of my wages. I maintained my Pompey home base for emergencies, but mainly stayed at Dad's back in Southampton where I could hang around with my brothers, sister and our friends after training. There might be a near-four-year gap between the siblings, but we all still shared the same mates.

At this point, I still played small-sided games with them all. Seven or eight of us would bundle in the car and head off for the local sports centre for a match. I probably shouldn't have done it as I was now a pro, but I loved to play. I didn't want to do much else, although we did go into town to either walk around the shops or catch a film. And I also loved my golf. I remember squeezing in nine holes back in Southampton between two Portsmouth reserve games on successive nights. I was so fit it didn't bother me.

My Dad liked the idea of me playing golf because it got me away from football. He was a member of a club in the New Forest, called Bramshaw. Through his introduction, my brothers and I became members too. There was a nice country pub near the course which did decent food and was a place where we could relax after a round.

I kept clear of bookmakers, which a lot of my teammates probably didn't. The money I spent was buying my mates a Kentucky Fried Chicken and going to the cinema. I didn't start going out to bars and clubs until I was 19. And even then I only went to them on Saturday nights, mindful of the jaundiced view Saints supporters had of anyone with a Portsmouth link. I'd go out with a few of my teammates like Micky Ross, Graeme Hogg, Warren Aspinall and Shaun Murray, who lived in Southampton as well.

I got my first car, a Vauxhall Astra, for the journey into training. But I had a lot of trouble with it. Every morning I'd get up at 8.30, and pretty often it wouldn't start. On these occasions, I'd go to my Dad: 'You've got to take me in, the bloody car isn't working.' I ditched it after about three months and got a Vauxhall Cavalier, which was much more reliable.

My first-team debut was given to me by Frank Burrows, who had returned to the club for a second spell in place of John Gregory, with Portsmouth involved in a season of struggle in the Second Division.

With John and Alan Ball it was football, football, football. But with Frank it was totally different. He was old school. He wanted the team to play a direct style in which the players would get the ball forward as quickly as possible – the dreaded 'long ball' – and do a lot of running. I didn't either like or dislike him, but I will never forget the night when he decided to give me – as a raw 19-year-old – my first experience of playing for the club's first team.

It was against Cardiff in the second round of the League Cup at Fratton Park on 9 October 1990. I thought there was a chance I might be involved as I'd been playing well for the reserves, which was a good team with young and hungry players. Micky Hazard, the lone experienced performer, showed us the ropes! It amounted to us doing all the running and then giving him the ball to do his thing. Unfortunately for Micky, his style of play didn't suit the kick-and-rush game preferred by Frank Burrows. Micky, who became a teammate of mine at Tottenham, soon realised he wasn't going to be part of the manager's plans, but he enjoyed playing with us youngsters.

That reserve team was managed by Tony Barton, who was a real gentleman. He'd bossed Aston Villa to the European Cup and was a legend. We were lucky to have him. He was complimentary about me and always supportive.

An hour and a half before the Cardiff game, Frank named the team and I was on the bench alongside Awfs. I was nervous and so excited. I told Mum and Dad and they came down for the game.

Sitting there waiting to go on, there were lots of things going through my head. Am I going to get my opportunity? Are my boot laces tied up tight enough? Are my shin pads on properly? Then came the call I'd waited my whole life for as Frank bellowed my name and Awfs's from the dug out as we stretched down by the corner flag. As we jogged back, I thought: 'Is this it?' It was.

My legs were shaking as I came on at 1–1 to replace Darryl Powell. And Andy came on too. There were about 10 or 15 minutes to go. I got a couple of early touches, which settled me down, and I ran around full of energy. I was hoping for extra-time. I was absolutely buzzing and wanted to play as long as possible. I got my wish as the game ended without any further score and went into extra-time. Colin Clarke scored a couple to put us 3–1 up. Then, in the last minute, I was clean through on the left. Instead of shooting I squared it to give Colin his hat-trick. He put it over from eight yards, but I'd proven myself a team player.

The feeling that I was playing professional football was wonderful, incredible. I'd done what I'd set out to do from the age of seven. The fact that it went so well made me think: 'I can do this'. I was high on the adrenalin it produced for days.

The day after the match, the papers were full of Andy and myself and how we had changed the game. Frank's comment was: 'Don't get carried away.' That was understandable and kept our feet on the ground. For the next three or four weeks, I stayed on the bench because the team kept winning.

I got my full League debut when right winger Steve Wigley got injured, and I was named in the starting line-up against Wolverhampton Wanderers, a team I later played for, in a Second

Division fixture at Fratton Park on 3 November. It was a near-enough full-house. About 16,000 fans turned up instead of the 7,000 originally expected. The reason was nothing to do with me playing, it was the fact the club were selling tickets for our next League Cup game. After beating Cardiff, we'd drawn Chelsea, dug out a draw at their place and everyone was getting excited about the replay.

I'd played on the pitch so many times for the youth and reserve team, but I entered a different surreal world that day. It was a crazy atmosphere. Pompey fans were rated among the best in the world, and I got a real taste of just why. The noise and passion was amazing. But to be in that situation is the reason I wanted to play football. I loved it.

I was extra nervous, but it went fairly well and we drew 0–0. I had an all right game but nothing special. I did a couple of good things and wished I'd played better. But I'd started. I was on my hands and knees after I came off after about 70 minutes. I was shattered. The pace had caught me by surprise. It was clear the nerves had got to me too. In the end I played about 20 games that season with a squad which included Andy Awford, Kit Symons, Shaun Murray, who came from Tottenham, and Darryl Powell.

Halfway through the season, Frank called me in to talk about a new contract, as my current one was ending in the summer. He got frustrated with me because I didn't sign it immediately. He wanted me to commit to two or three years. I only wanted a year's extension. I believed in my ability and thought we could sit around the table and do it all again next year. I also had my good friend and teammate Warren Aspinall telling me what I should and shouldn't be signing for. He didn't want people to take advantage of me. I ended up signing for £400 a week and £200 bonus for every first-team appearance, plus a £20,000 signing-on fee. Frank wanted me to sign on the same terms for three years, but I stuck to my guns and put pen to paper on a 12-month arrangement.

Tony Barton replaced Frank Burrows in March with the team in trouble towards the bottom of the League. We stayed up with a couple of games to spare. It had been a tough start for me but felt good. We had survived and I'd made my breakthrough into the first team.

The following week we went to Wolverhampton for the last game of the season. There was nothing to play for and Warren Aspinall asked Tony the night before the game if it was all right if the lads could go out for a few beers. It was no problem so off we went. Micky Ross, Shaun Murray and me ended up in a night club until two in the morning. When we came back to the hotel, the door was locked. I phoned Warren, and he looked down from his window to see where we were. We knew we were going to be on the bench against Wolves. But it was clear we had

had too much to drink. He was in fits of laughter saying: 'I'm going to sell this story one day!'. Then he advised us to climb up the drain pipe. He eventually came down and let us in.

The next day someone got injured after 20 minutes and on I went. It was boiling hot and I felt awful. Shocking. I never drank the night before a game again. Not that I'd done it before that day. The fact Tony allowed us to go out might amaze people. But he was old school, from a time when managers allowed players out for a few beers before games because they didn't want them to think about the match too much, fearful they'd freeze. I read Brian Clough did it with Nottingham Forest in the European Cup before their first-ever tie in it, against serial winners Liverpool. It did the trick. Cloughie did it again before the 1980 Final against Kevin Keegan's Hamburg. He banned training, and ordered his team to chill out and sup a few ales if they wanted. Again it worked.

Tony appreciated that a point might be stretched, as there wasn't anything riding on this game. Nonetheless, it was a different mentality from the attitude of the modern boss.

It seemed that Tony would keep his job for the following season. Everybody was pleased about that and we went off for the summer. I visited my friends in Dallas. While I was away I heard that Jim Smith was coming in and Tony had gone. It was a downer for me and I felt disappointed for Tony. I was saddened to hear of his death in 1993.

Jim Smith's arrival turned out to be the start of everything going really well for me. Paddo had come back as Jim's assistant. I was really pleased. A new management team meant everything was starting afresh. From day one of pre-season for 1991–92, all the pros – young and old – were fighting for a place in the first team on the opening day of the season. At his first meeting, Jim Smith said: 'Everyone is on a level playing field. Everyone has a chance to prove that they are good enough to be in my team.'

There were plenty of experienced pros like Guy Whittingham, who went on to score a record number of goals for the club the following season, by which time I'd left for Tottenham, Colin Clarke, Martin Kuhl, Warren Neill, John Beresford and England winger Mark Chamberlain. Mark and Steve Wigley were two other very talented right wingers at the club – so I obviously had my work cut out. I was determined to give it my best shot and establish a regular place in the first team.

Pre-season went well, but I do remember one painful experience in one of our friendlies. Jimmy Case, the former Liverpool midfielder who had gone on to Bournemouth, elbowed me right on the nose. My teammate Gavin Maguire, who was a nice guy, went berserk and ran up to Jimmy, yelling 'What are you doing? He's a 19-year-old kid who used to idolise you as a player!' I don't know if it was deliberate, but I felt it all right. I was OK afterwards, though.

Things were generally working out well for me, and Jim was beginning to get an idea of how the team would line up for the first League game. He was developing a sweeper system with Kit Symons and Guy Butters as the centre-backs, Awfs as the sweeper, and Warren Neill and John Beresford as right and left wing-backs.

In one friendly, I ended up being tried at right wing-back, a position I went on to fill for England. I think my running ability made Jim and Paddo think I could handle the role. It went really well. I was able to get up and down the pitch and get crosses in and return to a defensive position when needed. My only worry was how I would get on against a tricky winger, because defending had not been my strength. The gaffer obviously didn't worry about that.

I had done enough. I was in the starting line-up for the first match of the season against Blackburn Rovers at Ewood Park. I was alongside other youngsters: Awfs, Darryl, Kit and Guy Butters as well as Chris Burns, playing his first professional game after signing from non-League Cheltenham. Jim had proved as good as his word from that first meeting.

Growing up as a Southampton fan, the first game of the season was one I always looked forward to over the close season; the expectation your team can do well. I'd enjoy watching Wimbledon tennis, but apart from that it always seemed a long summer waiting for day one of a new season.

Now I was actually going to be involved in such a match. I was so excited, especially with the prospect of playing Blackburn away as they were the team everyone had been talking about in their quest to reach the top flight. Blackburn's owner, the late Jack Walker, had started to plough money into the club and this fixture came just a couple of months before Kenny Dalglish took over as manager, guided them into the top flight and the 1995 Premier League title. They had the likes of David Speedie and Gordon Cowans; lots of good players. I felt so proud walking out in the August sunshine that day.

It got even better early in the second half when I put us 1–0 up. I took a short corner, the ball was knocked back to me and I whipped it in. Their 'keeper Bobby Mimms missed it when challenged by Chris Burns and it went straight in. It was my first goal in League football – and a very lucky one. I didn't care. I was over the moon, although unfortunately for me they equalised in the last minute from a corner. I should have been guarding the post where the ball went over the line.

That went down well! At the end I had mixed emotions. It had been hard work in hot temperatures, but overall the match had gone well for me and the team as we got a point no one expected.

The season continued in a similar vein the following Tuesday when I was the man of the match as we beat Gillingham in the first leg of our League Cup tie. I was still playing wing-back and things were going great. My confidence was sky high. In the second leg I scored again – this time there was no luck about it – as we went through.

I played a few League games but felt under the weather at Grimsby and missed the next match against Cambridge United when informed I had bronchitis and shouldn't play. As a result, the system was switched to 4–4–2 and the boys won 3–0. Warren Neill came in for me and played brilliantly at right-back with Steve Wigley putting in a 10-out-of-10 display in a role just off the front man.

I thought I wouldn't return, but Jim brought me back straight away, playing in front of Warren as a right winger, rather than as a wing-back, which pleased me no end. That was when my season really kicked off. The understanding I developed with Warren was probably the best I've ever had with any other full-back. He was an experienced pro and a clever footballer, the most underrated player I ever came across. He helped me unbelievably. When I came running back to help him defensively he would just say: 'No, no, just watch your full-back, stay up where I can give you the ball.' So I did and he supplied me with the ball constantly, whether it be to feet or over the top if I made a run. A lot of full-backs want protection from their wingers. Not Warren. My confidence went from strength to strength. He was a dream to play with.

We all got a taste of the big-time early on when we were drawn to play Manchester United after overcoming Oxford United in the League Cup at Old Trafford. I was up against Mal Donachie and had a really good game. Afterwards, there was talk in the press that Man U were interested in me. A sign of things to come! I was happy just to have played there, up against people like Ryan Giggs in his first year as a regular, Bryan Robson and Brian McClair. They went ahead, and we equalised with a wonderful lob from John Beresford before they went on to win 3–1. After the game, I saw my Dad and he said: 'This is where you want to play if you are ever lucky enough to get a chance. I'd love to see you play here.' I wish he'd reminded me of that three years later when I turned down a move to United (more on that one later)!

Portsmouth did all right in the League – we finished ninth – but it was in the FA Cup where we shocked everyone. And I made my name.

5
Cup Fever

The FA Cup competition in 1991–92 with Portsmouth was life-changing for me, so I make no excuses for going through it round by round. It is impossible to overstate its significance for me.

Third round

It began in the West Country. We played Plymouth in the League on New Year's Day and stayed down there for the third-round tie against Exeter City, where Alan Ball was manager, three days later. We relaxed playing golf at St Mellion and stayed at a nice hotel. We played the Grecians off the park, although we only went through 2–1 thanks to a last-minute Warren Aspinall goal.

Fourth round

If I had to pin-point one match that marked out my route to the top level, it was our fourth-round victory over Leyton Orient. It was a freezing cold January afternoon. Ice had the country in its grip. A lot of games were postponed. I didn't think our tie would escape because one half of the Fratton Park pitch was frozen. However, fortunately for me, the referee gave it the go ahead. With so many matches called off, there was more media attention on ours.

I played well in the first half. I remember being up against Glenn Roeder (who had returned to Orient after playing for the likes of QPR, Newcastle and England B). Glenn, a defender, had been compared to England's 1966 World Cup-winning captain Bobby Moore because of his class and calm on the ball in his younger days. And he was known for a brain-scrambling step-over trick. I managed to mesmerise him with a bit of skill of my own to get through, although the 'keeper saved my shot.

At the start of the second half came the moment when people began to stand up and really take notice of me. We were awarded a corner, which was headed clear towards me 25 yards from goal and I hit the sweetest of left-foot volleys, which flew into the top corner to put us one goal up. It was by far and away my best goal to date.

With about 20 minutes to go, I scored my second. Guy Whittingham turned on the halfway line and struck a cross-field ball towards me, which I nodded down into my path and hit with the outside of my foot from the angle of the box into the bottom corner.

That sealed a 2–0 win in front of a decent-sized crowd, and I was voted man of the match after capping my best performance that season with my two best-ever goals for Portsmouth. It was a wonderful feeling. And after the game all the media wanted to talk to me, including Mike Donovan, who has helped me with this book. I was to be headline news the following morning.

I went up to the players' lounge to receive the man of the match champagne. The chairman, Jim Gregory, who never normally came out of his own private room next to it, emerged to give me SIX bottles of bubbly, which my Mum and Dad swiftly took off me!

The joke then was that he saw some big transfer coming. In hindsight, that might have been true! He was good friends with Terry Venables, who had been a player and manager for him at QPR. He might well have been on the phone to Terry at Tottenham that very day.

I went out for dinner and drinks with my family and friends. I made sure I taped BBC TV's *Match of the Day*, which was broadcast that night, so as I could watch it the following day. When I woke up I also read all the papers. Mike had given me a big write-up in *The People* after the first of our many meetings, but all the reports were sizeable and complimentary.

After breakfast and my scouring of the papers, I went and watched my brother Ben's youth team, and people came up to me and congratulated me for my goals, which they'd seen on TV. Even during the live coverage of another tie, broadcast that afternoon, the pundits talked about my goals and performance and my piece of skill against Glenn. It was all very strange. You want to do well, appear on television and have people say nice things about you, but when it all happened to me I found it quite embarrassing.

I'd surprised myself with how well things were going. It was the emotion I always had whenever I went up a level. It was down to that lack of self-belief, I guess. I figured the only way to deal with it was to try and enjoy the moment and hope I'd have more of them.

I was soon brought down to earth a few days later when we played Bristol Rovers in the League at Twerton Park, a ground our hosts were sharing with Bath City after leaving Eastville and their city temporarily due to financial problems. I remember it was on the side of a hill and we lost 1–0.

Fifth round

In the fifth round against Middlesbrough, there was a big crowd at Fratton. Graeme Souness, then the Liverpool manager, was among the

20,000 spectators. Scouts had started to turn up from several clubs, including Tottenham, after reading about all these promising Portsmouth youngsters.

We knew it would be a tough tie. 'Boro were top of our division (the English second tier) and it was a very tight game. I managed to set up Guy Whittingham for the opening goal, but their defender Alan Kernaghan equalised late on to force a replay. We were all very disappointed as this now meant an eight-hour midweek coach trip to the north east. Lovely.

There was a good atmosphere at Ayresome Park. 'Boro were formidable at home and we expected a tough time on a freezing night – and got one. We were 1–0 down after five minutes. Colin Clarke had come in for Guy Whittingham, and I twice set him up for equalisers to make it 2–2.

Shortly after the interval we were awarded a corner. As I went over to take it, I was taking all sorts of verbal abuse from their fans. I scuffed the corner and the ball travelled low. A defender went to clear but completely missed it and the ball ended up in the net. I turned round to the fans and started laughing. We went on to seal the match when I scored our fourth goal after being set up by Darryl Powell.

We stayed over and Jim Smith made sure we all went on a night out to celebrate. He told us: 'You've just reached the quarter-finals of the FA Cup. Make sure you enjoy it.' There were a few hangovers flying about the following morning. I think Jim might have still been pissed! He was great fun, a real character.

Jim Smith was a great guy, a brilliant man-manager and often took the boys out. On the playing side, he was proving great for me and the other lads. He kept his training sessions so simple. He'd get the first XI to take on the reserves. He just wanted us to get used to playing together. The reserves tried their best to impress, but the first team started to pick itself. I was loving it. I was 19, a regular and people were talking about me as an up-and-coming player. That win at Middlesbrough increased the speculation that some leading clubs were courting myself and Awfs.

Sixth round

I certainly got a test of my potential when we faced Nottingham Forest in the last eight. Brian Clough was their manager, and they wanted to make up for the previous year when Tottenham had beaten them in the Final. They had some wonderful players, including Teddy Sheringham, whom I was to link up with for Tottenham and England, Roy Keane, Nigel Jemson, Andy Crosby, Brian Laws, Des Walker and Stuart Pearce, another future international colleague. It was a great team.

The tie was witnessed by another capacity crowd packed into our Victorian ground and was played in an incredible atmosphere. I'd been extremely nervous beforehand. Our right-back Warren Neill, who was a reassuring presence behind my right-wing position, told me on our car journey to Fratton to enjoy it and that it would be the sort of occasion I'd have to get used to. I hoped he was right.

Before the game, there was talk of Stuart Pearce marking me. The Young Pretender v The England Legend. Stuart was certainly capable of some bone-crunching tackles. Would I be able to reproduce my form against arguably the best left-back in the world and most certainly the best in the country? I did a few interviews saying I loved Stuart Pearce the player. It was reported that I was frightened of Psycho (Stuart's nickname). One back-page headline said: 'Psycho Scares Me to Death!' None of that was true, it was just the media trying to hype the game up.

I knew he would want to give me an early whack to let me know he was about – and I didn't have to wait long. I made my first run down the right in the opening minute and he came in near the corner flag and – bosh – scythed me down. We were awarded a free-kick. John Beresford crossed the ball in, Forest goalkeeper Mark Crossley dropped it and Alan McLoughlin knocked it in to make it 1–0.

Forest were good and showed us why they were one of the best teams in the country. They forced us to defend for the rest of the game. Roy Keane ran the whole game. He was awesome and I was up and down marking Stuart Pearce. But we held on. I got cramp for the first time and told Jim Smith how tired I'd got. He told me it was probably down to nerves, but that I had done well. It had been a magnificent performance by the team.

Semi-final
We came through to the last four with Liverpool, Norwich and Sunderland. All us players wanted Sunderland as they were the other team not in the top flight, even though they had managed to knock out Chelsea in the sixth round. The draw handed us the toughest test of the lot against Graeme Souness's Reds, who had overcome Aston Villa 1–0 to get there. It was to be at Arsenal's Highbury Stadium on 5 April 1992.

Interest in me from other clubs had been growing. I remember the week before the semi-final, we played Charlton in a League game and teammate Gavin Maguire giggled and said to me shortly before kick-off in the dressing room: 'They're all out there. I've never seen so many scouts. No pressure, Daz!'

The hype really kicked off in the days before the semi-final itself. It was such a high-profile match, and against a team who were reportedly interested in signing myself and Awfs. We were just two wet-behind-the-ears kids and had never had to deal with the media in an intense way. All that changed when we turned up for what we thought was just the normal golf day we had had before our previous ties. The press were everywhere: reporters, photographers, radio, TV. I spoke to Graham Paddon and told him: 'I don't want to talk to them.' He turned round and said: 'You're going to have to. Just enjoy it and say you are having a great time.'

The media kept asking about Liverpool and whether Awfs and I wanted to sign for them. When the press asked me if I would go to Anfield. I told them: 'No, I don't think I would. I'm happy where I am. I want to play at the top level but I want to get there with Portsmouth.'

While Awfs and I were having our pictures taken on the putting green afterwards I asked him: 'What did the press ask you?' He replied that he had been asked if he wanted to go to Liverpool and he had told them the same thing as I did. Thank God we were on the same page. The next day the papers were full of how me and Awfs had cold-shouldered the mighty Liverpool. Of course, I'd have loved to have gone on to play for Liverpool at some point, but I couldn't say so in the circumstances.

At the time, though, I was struggling to think how my life could be any better. Steve Wicks, who was now an agent and half acting for me, was unimpressed by my public pronouncement on not wanting to be a Liverpool player. He said: 'What do you want to say that in the press for?'

'What do you want me to say right before Portsmouth play Liverpool in the semi-finals of the FA Cup?' I replied. 'It's probably one of the biggest – if not the biggest – game in the club's history. Everyone's going to love me saying I want to leave – and I don't.' I had told Steve six months earlier that if a club wanted to buy me they could, but I was not going to ask for a transfer. I reminded him of that there and then. In fact, I never asked for a transfer in my career.

We travelled up and stayed at the Noke Hotel in St Albans, just outside London. It was a lunchtime kick-off, and I was as nervous as hell over breakfast. The papers that morning were talking about me playing at the ground that was to be my new home as they had also linked me with a move to Arsenal. I felt a lot of pressure. Being the way I was, I kept a lot inside. But Steve Wigley was a big help as we sat having breakfast together. Even though I had replaced him in the team, Steve, who has gone on to become a good coach, remained a friend and always offered words of advice.

He suggested if I was one-on-one with Liverpool goalkeeper Bruce Grobbelaar, that I should 'give him the eyes', a phrase widely used in football meaning 'look one way and put the ball the other' when there was a shooting opportunity face to face with the opposition's goalie.

We arrived at Highbury a couple of hours before the game. The first thing I wanted to do was take a look at the pitch, especially as it was such a renowned venue, the scene for the biggest day of my life. I had the chance to get through to the Cup Final which, as a kid, I thought was more important to win than the League. As I've mentioned, the Final had pretty much been the only live match on television I remember growing up and one you tried to picture yourself in with your mind's eye.

I tried to take it all in. Looking to my left, the Clock End was already rammed with Pompey fans, and it was still an hour and a half before kick-off. I thought to myself: 'This is what the big time is all about.' The supporters were singing and going crazy. They waved banners. A couple I saw from the recorded BBC television highlights stated 'The Bald Eagle has landed', in reference to follicly-challenged Jim Smith's nickname, and the slightly cruder 'Go shag 'em Shaggy', alluding to the moniker I'd picked up due to my adjudged similarity to Scooby Doo's owner in the American cartoon which was popular at the time. Another I noticed was 'Anderton walks on water' which had been done by my brothers and friends.

It was Pompey's Cup Final and everything I saw, smelt and felt as I took my sneak preview reflected it. Those incredible supporters surpassed themselves that day – even before a ball had been kicked. Back in the dressing rooms, I returned to my nervous state as I paced the heated floor of its luxurious changing facilities. The gaffer read out the team:

Goalkeeper: Alan Knight, a Portsmouth legend.
Defenders: Warren Neill, arguably the best right-back I played with; John Beresford, a great left-back, who went on to join Newcastle; Kit Symons, a top centre-back who went on to play for Manchester City in the Premier League; Andy Awford, another leading centre-back who was compared to the late great Bobby Moore.
Midfielders: Myself; Martin Kuhl, captain, a complete central midfielder, who went on to play in the Premier League; Chris Burns, a tigerish midfielder, gentle giant off the pitch; Mark Chamberlain, a former England international who could make a mockery of his full-back; Alan McLoughlin, Republic of Ireland midfielder, a clever player who linked play well.

Forward: Colin Clarke, our top striker whom I watched score his debut hat-trick for Southampton.

Substitutes: Guy Whittingham, a fantastic goalscorer who moved on to Aston Villa in the Premier League; Warren Aspinall, a real talent who had played for Everton and Aston Villa as a teenager.

When I now look at that team on paper I can see why we did so well. It had really good players, with most of them performing well at the top level in some part of their careers.

Liverpool started quickly and had a couple of half-chances in the first 10 minutes, with Ian Rush hitting the bar. We settled after that. Alan McLoughlin was playing off Colin Clarke up front, which meant we had an extra player in midfield and created some good opportunities. They had most of the possession early on, but we began to dominate for the rest of the opening half.

The Reds got back on top in the second half and we had to defend for most of it. There was a battle between me and Rob Jones, a young lad who had just started to play for England. I did OK, but didn't think I was playing that well. Neither of us got the better of the other.

We started to assert ourselves a bit more in extra-time and, after about 10 minutes, I went close to scoring. The ball came to me, I chested and volleyed it. It took the slightest deflection off Mark Wright, another England player, which took it wide. I don't think Bruce Grobbelaar would have got to it, but the referee gave a goal-kick anyway. I thought: 'That was my chance'.

However, two or three minutes later I got another opportunity and this time I scored. We won the ball in midfield after a loose ball from Ian Rush with Liverpool on the attack. I immediately spun round, screaming for a long ball from Warren Neill, underlining the understanding we had developed that season. As I ran in behind their defence, Warren hit the ball where I wanted it and I was one-on-one with Bruce Grobbelaar. I controlled it with the outside of my right foot – I wonder what Alan Ball would have made of that! – and that took me closer to goal. I had a lot of time to think about what to do. I recalled the words of Steve Wigley. Everything flooded into my mind about what it meant to the fans, the manager and my teammates.

I saw Mark Wright coming in after I'd taken that touch. I tried Steve's idea and looked at the far post and put it in the near corner. Bruce had started to read where it was going, but could only get back to his near post in time to get a touch on it and the ball trickled into the corner.

It was at the Clock End and the Pompey supporters went bananas. I jumped up and nearly fell over because my legs were so tired. They were on the point of buckling. I was saying to myself: 'Oh my God, we've done it. I'm going to an FA Cup Final.' There were only about 10 minutes left on the clock.

With less than four minutes left came the moment which changed the course of the tie. Liverpool's Steve Nicol had come out of the back four on a run and knocked the ball passed Awfs and, as my mate came in to challenge, went over him and down. Free-kick. The last minute of injury time, 1–0. John Barnes took the kick, and our 'keeper Alan Knight made an incredible save onto the post. Then everything went into slow motion as the ball rolled along the line and Ronnie Whelan tapped it in.

We were devastated. I couldn't believe it. I was dumbstruck. The players, staff and fans all were. The final whistle blew. We had drawn with the mighty Liverpool, but the result was tough to take. I'd scored in an FA Cup semi-final, but it had not been enough.

In the dressing room, Jim Smith and Paddo tried to lift the lads. They told us how we'd drawn with one of the best teams in the country, in Europe, and deserved to beat them. That we'd done well. That we had another chance to beat them on another big occasion. I was interviewed after the game with everyone wanting to talk to me after scoring. But I felt flat with Liverpool equalising so late on.

I was interviewed by television outside the Marble Halls of Highbury still feeling down, saying we'd played well but disappointed we had given a goal away so late. We went back to the hotel where we had a good few drinks before getting on the coach the following morning for a League game at Tranmere the following day. We were shattered and lost the fixture against a near neighbour of Liverpool's.

Our best opportunity to make the Final had been missed. In the replay at Villa Park on 13 April, Alan McLoughlin hit the bar in the last minute of normal time, which ended 0–0. There was no score in extra-time and it went to penalties. I was fifth penalty-taker, but Liverpool had netted enough to beat us 3–1 in the shoot-out before my turn came around.

It was one of the most difficult defeats of my career to take because I had been playing alongside guys I'd grown up with like Awfs, Darryl Powell and Kit Symons, and the experienced pros who'd helped turn me into a player that had everyone linking me with to imminent transfer to a big club. I didn't believe the Wembley dream was ever going to end as we got through each round.

I remain convinced that had we got to the Final against Sunderland we would definitely have won the Cup. It was such a disappointing way for our run to end – and we still had six games to go in the League. The Cup defeat finished us in terms of promotion as the campaign petered out. There were a lot of exhausted young lads in their first year as a pro like me. I needed the season to end sooner than it did.

I played in almost every game – we had nearly 60! – and found first-team football was played at a completely different level to what I'd experienced in the reserves and youth teams. It was so much more demanding. I struggled with a groin problem in the last few games and couldn't run freely. I had pains in my lower back as well. My body was still growing. Paddo told me not to worry, and that I'd had the most incredible season. It was certainly one I will never forget, but it was hellish too.

I went to see a doctor in London to find out whether I had a hernia. He told me I was fine. But I wasn't – because I had to have an operation on it three or four months later, by which time I had moved to Tottenham. It proved to be not the first misdiagnosis of my career.

6
Earning Spurs

During the FA Cup run speculation had been building about my future. People were telling me what I should and shouldn't do. Steve Wicks, who had become a players' agent with First Artists, said he'd look after me. Steve was a real diamond guy. He had given me so much confidence with encouraging words when he was my Portsmouth Reserves manager. I agreed to go with him, but when he sent something to sign I didn't autograph it. He would phone me up fairly regularly. One afternoon, he called to tell me there would be something in the papers the following morning. He said Liverpool and Tottenham had spoken to Pompey about wanting to sign me and Jim Smith was likely to call me in into his office to discuss it. So I went in to training believing the manager would tell me I was being sold. Jim didn't pull me in or say anything about it and there was nothing in the papers. But what Steve had said screwed with my mind.

There were other agents, like Eric Hall, talking about me getting this that and the other through a transfer. I got fed up with that sort of thing and found it hard to deal with. I didn't know what was true or not. My head was in a continuous spin. One day, I spoke to my accountant Leon Angel, who was looking after my pension and had been introduced to me by Steve when Steve was in charge of Pompey Reserves. Leon mentioned how well things were going for me. I told him how I was feeling about the rumour mill around me, and that Steve Wicks had been on the phone the other day saying Liverpool and Tottenham wanted to sign me, but I didn't know what was going on and didn't know what to believe.

Leon told me that he was doing Tottenham manager Terry Venables's accounts and knew him very well. He said he'd ask him whether Spurs' interest was genuine. He did just that and Terry told him I was his number-one summer target, which pleased me no end. Leon also said that he himself was registered as an agent. It wasn't his main job, but he fulfilled the role for Tony Dorigo (Leeds), Gordon Durie (Tottenham) and Gary Pallister (Manchester United). They were all top players. I asked if he'd act for me and he agreed. That was it. I was relieved to have someone I knew well in charge of matters, and after all the anxiety I'd been through I could now concentrate on playing football.

Leon invited me and my Mum and Dad to a Tottenham game. I thought that was great. Spurs had won the FA Cup the year before, which qualified them for the European Cup-Winners' Cup, a trophy they won in 1963. We saw them play Feyenoord in the second leg of their quarter-final at White Hart Lane on 18 March 1992. It was a goalless draw and meant Spurs went out 1–0 on aggregate, but I was busy taking in this big stadium and the atmosphere of a big European night. I loved it.

Afterwards, we went into a lounge and through to another room. Terry Venables was sitting down. He saw me and said: 'Hi, Darren. How are you doing?'

I was in shock. My mind went back to when Portsmouth had played his Tottenham side the year before en route to Spurs lifting the FA Cup. I had been climbing some steps at Fratton Park and noticed Terry stood in a doorway at the top. I was awestruck. When I reached him he put his hand out. We shook hands and he said: 'Well played, son.' I had been a sub and had only got about 20 minutes on the field, but I was delighted he'd been aware of my performance in a match dominated by Paul Gascoigne.

Terry remembered our meeting too and said that he had felt, even though I was a skinny 18-year-old, that he had seen enough of me to believe I could turn into a good player. He told me I reminded him of Chris Waddle. He had been following my career and been impressed. He asked me what I thought of the atmosphere in the stadium and I told him. I was also introduced to Alan Sugar, the club chairman.

There was nothing untoward about the occasion. I'd just gone to watch the game with Leon, who happened to be a Spurs fan. But somehow Jim Smith found out I was there. He said: 'I know you're just a kid, and love watching football, but be careful. People might get the wrong idea if you put yourself in that situation.'

As he drove me and my parents back to his house in north London, Leon said that Tottenham's interest in me had heightened further. He thought they would want me to go there in the summer and said we should discuss what sort of money I would want to go there. I laughed and said: 'It really doesn't matter how much.' I didn't believe the move would happen.

The transfer that put me on one of football's biggest stages came after a fun end-of-season trip to Tenerife with about nine or 10 of the Pompey lads, including Awfs, Daryl Powell, Kit Symons, Guy Butters and Warren Aspinall.

Darryl kept telling me I was definitely going to Spurs. I didn't think so, because I hadn't finished the season that well. But when I got back I got a phone call from Jim Smith. Tottenham had come in for me and the club had accepted the offer. I asked him: 'What do I do now?'

'You should go and talk to them,' he told me. 'You'll be fine. Terry Venables is a great guy. He'll make you a better player. I don't want to lose you, but you've had a good season and the club need the money. I'm glad I've been able to help you on your way.'

Jim knew I was petrified and suggested I took my Dad along when I went to see Spurs. Dad and I drove to Leon's and discussed the contract he had been speaking to Tottenham about. I would have been happy regardless of what the offer had been.

We met Terry at the Royal Garden Hotel in Kensington, West London. Terry had an aura about him. He was 'The Man' as far as I was concerned. He told me that although he wasn't the team manager any more, he would be overseeing everything with a new management team in place for the following season, made up of Ray Clemence and Dougie Livermore.

He told me how much he thought of me and how well I'd done during the season. I plucked up the courage to ask him how much he had paid for me and he responded: 'The whole lot.'

'How much is that?' I asked.

'Two million,' he replied. 'That's how much we think of you.' I looked at Dad and just smiled. I could tell my Dad was thinking: 'F**k me!'

The fees that had been suggested in the press had been about half of that. It was a hell of a lot of money. To put it in context, England and Southampton striker Alan Shearer signed for Blackburn in a British transfer fee record of £3.3 million that summer.

I was offered £3,000 a week on a four-year contract, rising by £1,000 a week each year with a £200,000 signing on fee. It wasn't bad for a 20-year-old! They threw in a BMW as well. I signed subject to a medical, which I passed before walking out onto the White Hart Lane pitch with my Mum and Dad. It was then that it sunk in. I would get to play on this pitch all the time. Mum gave me a big hug and said: 'I'm so proud of you.'

I was able to enjoy the moment. It felt absolutely incredible that such a thing had happened to me. I was like the little kid who'd worn Tottenham replica kits growing up pretending to be Glenn Hoddle when I asked the kitman Roy for some up-to-date versions to give to my American friends who I was visiting a couple of days later.

Spurs told me they had to delay the announcement for a couple of weeks because, I think, they were completing the move of their striker Paul Walsh to Portsmouth – which went through. It was tough not to be able to tell anyone about it, but I was now a Spurs player.

My American mates Dave, Joe and Vic Roy, who had moved to Washington DC with their parents Lou and Mary, were delighted with the Tottenham kits I brought them. So were other friends out there, like Bert Schilling, who lived next door to the Roys with his sister Marlee (who is now married to Vic) and their parents Bob and Brenda.

It was bizarre. I wasn't even old enough to drink in the United States, but I'd just moved to one of the top clubs in England for £2 million. I'd always told my friends how I was doing, but they really weren't sure how good I was. They hadn't even heard of Portsmouth! But they certainly knew who Tottenham Hotspur were.

However, when the significance of the switch from the second division to the top one sunk in I got jittery. It was such a jaw-dropping leap. I was also scared stiff, with self-doubts again eating away at the back of my head with my having moved up so much in class.

I was frightened not to be going back to Portsmouth. People might say the fee didn't matter, but I'd only had one full season in professional football. And that was in the second tier. Now I felt I was expected to be a good player, ready made to play at the highest level. I might have only been 20, but Spurs hadn't bought me to play in the reserves for a couple of years.

While I was out in the States, my Mum called, saying that the fixtures for the inaugural Premier League season were out, adding: 'You'll never guess who you're playing in the first game. Southampton away!' It was amazing. My dream as a kid was to play for Saints, and now I was going to their ground to perform as an ex-Pompey player with a top, top club.

There were adjustments to be made in all areas of my life. I'd starting seeing a girl, Kerry, and wondered whether it was the right thing to invite her to come and live with me in London. In retrospect it was probably the wrong thing. She and Mum started looking for flats to rent while I was away in the States with pre-season training six or seven weeks away. I let them get on with it and ended up in a block of nice apartments in Stanmore, a residential suburb in north-west London. We didn't really like it. There was one nice older couple we got on with, but the rest of the neighbours were horrible, complaining about the noise we made, although we were relatively quiet. Fortunately for me – and not for Kerry – I was out of the flat a lot once pre-season training began.

As it was the build up to the first Premier League season, I was caught up in its promotion. Sky were big backers of the new division, and I appeared in their original advertising campaign. I was filmed doing sit-ups and appeared in a montage alongside established top-flight players.

I thought it was just part of playing for a big team after a big transfer but, in fact, it was a whole new ball game for English football. The Premier League was a one-division revolution, a breakaway from the Football League by the elite after 104 years. It was difficult for me to appreciate that at first. Leaving Portsmouth had been a step up for me anyway, so I didn't see the difference between the old First Division and the Premier League. It was only in the next couple of years that I realised how quickly things were changing in terms of television coverage, wages, crowds and stadia. Everything was getting better.

Growing up, I'd been used to seeing the FA Cup Final and perhaps a semi-final live on television. But the start of the Premier League marked the start of live matches screened almost daily from around the world by Rupert Murdoch's global satellite giants. Looking back, I was part of history in the making.

My first day at Spurs was like the first day at school. The first person I remember meeting was midfielder Steve Sedgley. Steve just started taking the piss out of me, speaking with a traditional Hampshire accent. It was his way of welcoming me. He was a great lad and a great character. He was absolutely nuts! He would eat anything: worms, grass, paper, mud... He would have me in fits of laughter, always playing practical jokes.

The first week of pre-season was the toughest. It gave me the chance to show my running ability. After one week I couldn't believe how well I'd settled in with my new teammates. They were so down to earth. No 'Big-time Charlies'. I remember that in training Vinny Samways was the player who impressed me the most. He could receive a ball in any situation and deal with it; controlling it and passing to a teammate. He never gave the ball away.

I wasn't the only player Terry brought in that summer. There was Neil 'Razor' Ruddock from Southampton, Dean Austin, a young full-back from Southend, Jason Cundy, from Chelsea, who had been on loan the previous year, Gerry McMahon, from Glenavon in Northern Ireland, and Peter Beadle, a young striker from Gillingham.

I was playing all right in the friendlies and got a hat-trick in one at Sunderland. Everything was going fine in the new job.

My competitive debut for Tottenham came on Day One of the Premier League: 15 August 1992. It was a boiling hot one as we faced Saints in front of a packed 15,000 crowd at the compact Dell. It was nerve-racking. I felt weird having supported Southampton. The game was awful and finished 0–0. Every time I touched the ball I was booed. It was my first insight into the scrutiny and pressure you are under playing at the top level. People tried to put me off my game. I remember going to take a throw-in on the far side right where I used to sit in the front row. And people were sat there booing and shouting abuse. I smiled to myself and I thought: 'I've seen more Saints games than these muppets!'

Strangely, though, I enjoyed the occasion apart from the added negative of being elbowed in the last five minutes by Francis Benali, which left me needing about eight stitches across my eye. That pleased Southampton fans no end. Francis is a nice guy off the pitch, but on it he always seemed to try and kick lumps out of me.

Four days later I made my home League debut against Coventry City. It was under floodlights, but we were far from bright. The team didn't play well and we lost 2–0. It was a terrible result. Given the occasion, for me it was bitterly disappointing. Straight away I sensed what playing in the Premier League was all about. There was pressure with every game. You get beaten, the crowd aren't happy. Simple.

At the weekend, I played well at home to Crystal Palace, but we drew the game 2–2 and should have won. Then we got thumped 5–0 at Leeds. Eric Cantona ran riot for them. It was panic time. We had started the season poorly and didn't win until our sixth match when we beat Sheffield United 2–0, with Teddy Sheringham scoring on his home debut after joining from Nottingham Forest, where Brian Clough had called him Edward.

I didn't feel right but played in the next League game, against Everton. I did OK but came off after an hour when we were losing 1–0, struggling with my groin. I got in the bath in the dressing rooms. I felt a bit sorry for myself, wondering whether I could really cut it. I felt out of my depth. I didn't know if it was because I had a physical problem, or because I just wasn't good enough. Moving up to London had been tough. At Portsmouth I could always just go home. But I couldn't now. I had to settle in a new environment, away from where I was brought up. I had so much self-doubt.

As I lay in the bath thinking all these thoughts, Terry Venables came in – with the game still going on – and said: 'Don't worry, it'll be fine. You're only 20. This season is just a bedding-in period. I bought you for next year and beyond. You've signed a four-year deal and you're going nowhere. I think the world of you. You're going to be a top, top player. The physio [Dave Butler] tells me you've got a hernia problem that is limiting what you can do so we'll send you to see someone.' He was so understanding. And the fact he'd come in to speak to me while the game was still going on highlighted what a caring boss he was. Spurs went on and beat Everton 2–1 after I'd come off. I was pleased for the team, but it didn't help my confidence. It seemed the team were better off without me.

I was scheduled to make my England Under-21 debut in Spain the following midweek and Terry advised me to go and enjoy the experience of a different environment. He said it would be good for me. I took his advice and went off with the England squad. I met Paul Gascoigne for the first time during the trip. He'd turned up at the airport to support the first team, who were also playing the Spanish the following day. He'd had a terrible injury, sustained in the 1991 FA Cup Final win over Clough's Forest, but was over it and enjoying his football in Italy with Lazio. He'd got to hear that I was 'Dazza – the young big-money signing' and was winding me up about it, in a nice way, joking: 'Dazza, my arse.' It had been 'Gazza – the young big-money signing' a few years earlier when he joined Tottenham. He could identify with me over it. Gazza was nice and full of life. Good fun.

Spain was a booster. I loved it. Awfs was there, and it was good to see him again. We won 1–0, and I scored the winner in the last minute. I came back confident, feeling good about everything, but things were still not right.

I played a couple of more League games, away losses to Coventry and Sheffield Wednesday. I also managed my first Spurs goal in a League Cup win over Brentford. In between, we had a friendly against Lazio in Rome's Olympic Stadium, organised because of Gazza's transfer to the Italian club. On the flight home, Teddy Sheringham came and sat next to me and asked how I was feeling after my move to Spurs. I told him I was struggling. He said: 'You played bloody well tonight, but you love to moan on the pitch when you don't get the ball, don't you?' I just laughed and said: 'Yeah, you're spot on!' He had me sussed, just like my teacher Mrs Starks. From then on, he always looked out for me and I looked up to him.

Something, though, had to be done about my nagging physical problem. I didn't know exactly what was wrong and spoke to physios Dave Butler and John Sheridan. They thought the problem was in the groin and advised me to go and see Dr Jerry Gilmore, the Harley Street surgeon who was the expert who recognised the syndrome in kicking sports now known as Gilmore's Groin. Dr Gilmore had risen to fame when he operated on Gazza's groin and got him fit within three to four weeks to face Arsenal in the first-ever FA Cup semi-final at Wembley in 1991, when Gazza scored *that* goal, a 35-yard free-kick that beat David Seaman. I nearly went through the roof when he touched the tender spot and told me I had a hernia and it needed to be sorted as soon as possible.

Terry said I should get the hernia operation done because, although I could play on it, there was no point in carrying on if it was uncomfortable and affecting me adversely. He thought it would give me a good break and an opportunity to get fully fit. He always kept an eye on me and was a real father figure. Later, Gazza told me Terry had been the same way with him when he came to Tottenham from Newcastle at a young age. I guessed he made Gazza feel like that by employing different tactics. After all, Gazza was a little crazier than me! With me, Terry's style was like someone putting an arm around my shoulder and telling me not to worry about it and that it would turn out all right. He was always complimentary and made me believe in myself.

Terry knew how to treat everyone, no matter what they were like. His man-management was so good. That's what has made him so popular with players. He was a people's man. Terry had charisma. He didn't demand loyalty, he just got it.

I had the operation and spent a few days at home. It coincided with Kerry and me moving from the flat we hated in Stanmore to a decent-sized house on a new estate in Hemel Hempstead, in a cul-de-sac with friendly neighbours. My new teammate Dean Austin, who was from the town originally, had recommended the area. My Dad, having been in the removal business, helped us move. Because I'd just had surgery, I got out of doing any lifting. Not that I'd have been of much use, judging from my efforts for my Dad as a kid.

When I went back to the training ground after a week I started jogging and then running with physio Dave Butler. I could feel my fitness coming back straight away. He soon got me going, and before I knew it I was back to full training and feeling great.

I made my first Spurs appearance for more than two months at home to Chelsea on 5 December. I got on for the last 10 minutes with Sol Campbell, who was then still in the youth team. We lost 2–1 and Sol scored our consolation goal. I was relieved to be back in the fold. However, it was on Boxing Day that things really picked up for me again. The match was a goalless draw against Norwich at Carrow Road, but I felt great; much better within myself than I'd done since I started at Spurs. I hadn't appreciated just how badly the injury had affected me until I had the operation. Now my confidence was back and I played well.

I put in another couple of decent performances, and the team started to play well together. We had some good players, like Teddy, Ian Walker, Nicky Barmby, Gordon Durie, Gary Mabbutt, Nayim, Erik Thorsvedt, Vinny Samways, Paul Allen, Steve Sedgley, Dean Austin, Justin Edinburgh, David Howells and Razor. They were all great lads, and my first season in the top flight was starting to go as I had dreamed it would.

I maintained my form and had a good game at home to Sheffield Wednesday, even though we lost. Their team included the former Spurs and England player Chris Waddle, who I hear commentating on the radio a lot these days. He said to me: 'Keep it up, you're playing well.' That was nice to hear from someone whose opinion I respected.

We beat non-League Marlow 5-1 in the third round of the FA Cup, setting up a clash against top-of-the-table Norwich City, whom we beat 2–0 at Carrow Road. The match was broadcast on television, and the pundits were talking about how well I had played, along with the team.

I scored my first goal in the top flight on 7 February 1993. The fact that it was against Southampton was the icing on the cake. We were playing Saints live on Sky at White Hart Lane. We'd dominated the first half, yet went in at half-time trailing 1–0. But we scored four times within about five minutes soon after the restart – including my debut strike, a cross from Vinny Samways that was half-cleared by their 'keeper straight to me. I controlled the ball on my chest and smashed it into the roof of the net from eight yards. I didn't know what to do, so I just ran behind the goal and started high-fiving all the fans.

The following week we played in front of the television cameras again at home in the fifth round of the FA Cup. I scored the first goal as we beat Wimbledon 3–2 in a match that was full of crunching tackles. I remember Terry told me to stand right on the touchline in front of Vinnie Jones, known as a hard man, as he took his long throw-ins. As he picked the ball up for his first throw, he looked at me, pointed at his elbow and said: 'This is going right on your f***ing bugle, little boy!' I slowly retreated.

It seemed the Midas touch was with me as I scored and made four as I helped England Under-21s beat San Marino 6–0 in another Euro qualifier at Luton's Kenilworth Road two days later. I got some international experience with Spurs shortly after that when Terry took us out to Spain for a friendly against Real Zaragoza, with Gus Poyet, who joined me at Spurs, in their team.

After the game we had a night out involving plenty of drinking. Nicky Barmby ended up being sick and then Steve Sedgley decided to pick a chunk of chicken out of the puke and started to eat it... he really would eat anything! The following day we went to Barcelona, where the lads were going to stay for another night on the town, although myself and Nick Barmby had to go home as we'd been selected to play for England Under-21s.

Terry was flying home with us, and as we walked through the airport we discovered what a legend he was in the Catalan capital. Everyone made a fuss of him. They loved him – and with good reason. In the 1980s, he had guided Barca to the Spanish Championship and Cup and the European Cup Final, losing it to Steaua Bucharest on penalties, with former Spurs striker Steve Archibald in the side. He then signed Gary Lineker, who went on to join him at Spurs, and Mark Hughes from Manchester United for the Nou Camp outfit.

I returned to Fratton Park to help England Under-21s overcome Holland 3–0 in a European Championship qualifier. I managed another goal in front of those wonderful Pompey fans, which was a fantastic feeling. In the meantime, Spurs continued the FA Cup run to the semi-finals. Nayim got a hat-trick for us when we beat Manchester City 4–2 at Maine Road in the last eight.

I was delighted to make the last four for the second successive season. The fact that it was against Arsenal at Wembley Stadium added to the occasion. Spurs had beaten the Gunners two seasons before at the same stage in the first semi-final to be staged at the national stadium, largely due to the brilliance of Gazza and that magical goal, which he conjured up to help Spurs towards lifting the Cup for an eighth time.

Sadly, any dreams of a ninth victory were dispelled as my second successive semi-final appearance ended up much like the first. Tony Adams got the only goal as the Gunners claimed North London bragging rights, but I believe we deserved to go through. After that the season fizzled out and we just missed out on a UEFA Cup place for 1993–94.

However, things had continued to go well for me. I must have set up goals in nearly every game from the New Year until the end of the season. Myself and Teddy seemed to be developing an almost telepathic partnership, and he finished the season with 22 goals, which made him top scorer in the Premier League's first term after he'd got the first televised strike in it for Nottingham Forest in a 1–0 win over Liverpool.

My self-esteem was high, with people saying nice things about me and the fans so supportive. They even voted me Spurs' Player of the Year. It all made me believe I really belonged in the elite of English football. Everything was wonderful in my new world as I finished my debut season at Tottenham, but just three or four days later everything was turned upside-down.

I was preparing to take part in a testimonial at Enfield in the evening when I learned from the Spurs press office that Terry had left the club. He and the chairman had had a bust-up and Terry had been sacked. Terry tried to get his job back through the courts, but Sugar got his way.

I had been on such a high because over the previous four months I'd turned my season around thanks to Terry. I had grown up so much and was able to deal with everything connected with my move after struggling and being unable to cope. It was all down to his efforts. He was the reason I came to Spurs in the first place. It didn't make sense to me to get rid of the main man. I felt it was a crazy move by the chairman.

There were reasons why it happened, but as a 21-year-old kid I didn't care about the whys and wherefores of what had gone on behind the scenes. I just cared about Terry. The way Terry oversaw joint first-team managers Ray Clemence and Dougie Livermore was perfect. Why change it?

I was so angry, especially after what Terry had done for me and everything he had done for the club. He'd been proved right to bring in the staff and players he did. The team was a good one and had played with style. I wondered whether the chairman had actually been watching the team play. We were looking so good for the next season, and it was all down to Terry. Now I feared that all we had worked for would get ripped apart.

When I played the testimonial, all the Spurs fans were there screaming and shouting verbal abuse against Alan Sugar. Dougie Livermore wanted to keep me away from it all and advised me to keep my own counsel. He said he knew I was upset but there was not a lot I or anyone could do about what had happened, and if I spoke to the press they would only twist what I wanted to say. He said that I should go off and have a week's holiday before my summer matches with England Under-21s.

My head was spinning, but I bit my tongue and went away to Ibiza with Kerry while the fallout went on back home. I read that Razor and his missus had chained themselves to the gates of the chairman's house. Neil said he'd never play for the club again because of what happened with Terry – and he didn't, which was a shame. What a player he'd been for us that season! It was another example of the natural loyalty Terry provoked.

In contrast, of course, Alan Sugar became a hate figure. The fans were going doolally from what I read. The backlash clearly got to him a little, as one newspaper quoted him as saying: 'I felt as if I'd killed Bambi.'

But to be fair to the chairman, he moved swiftly to limit any damage.

7

Terry-picked

I came back from my break and went straight to a St Albans hotel, where I was getting together with the rest of the England squad to play European Under-21 qualifiers against Poland and Norway before heading off to compete in the Toulon tournament. There were some good players there, including Awfs, Chris Sutton, Lee Clark, Gary Flitcroft, Richard Hall and Jamie Redknapp, who went on to be a teammate of mine at Spurs.

The late Ray Harford was the coach and a fantastic one at that. His knowledge of the game and the sessions he put on were great, really enjoyable and the lads got a lot out of them. The manager was Lawrie McMenemy, who was also assistant to Graham Taylor in the senior set-up. Lawrie had been in charge of Saints when I used to watch them as a boy, and I was thrilled that he was working with us.

After I arrived I was immediately asked – along with Gary – to get measured up for a suit to wear for the full England squad. Graham Taylor's squad had World Cup qualifiers against Poland and Norway and we were put on standby for the American tour which followed, a trip planned to familiarise England with the nation hosting the Finals the following year. I thought: 'Oh my Lord, this is all happening so fast'.

Our Under-21s did well, winning 4–1 in Poland, where I scored my fourth goal in four matches for the team, and holding hosts Norway 1–1, but Taylor's team drew 1–1 with the Poles and were stunned 2–0 by the Norwegians. Neither side looked certain to make the finals of their respective competitions – and so it was to prove.

Instead of a trip to the States that summer – perhaps to call in on my American friends between commitments – I was in France to help the England Under-21s win the friendly Toulon tournament, sealing it with a 1–0 win over the French in the Final after beating Portugal and Scotland and drawing against the Czech Republic and Brazil.

Back at Tottenham, Alan Sugar brought in Ossie Ardiles for the beginning of 1993–94 after Terry Venables' departure. Fortunately all the upheaval did not affect my confidence on the pitch. The Spurs supporters were a big part of that. I had just played the best four months of my career so far and was earning praise after a difficult start during which I'd had criticism, largely from the media. Reports had said I wasn't good enough, and that I wasn't worth £2 million. Whenever I was substituted they said it was because I was terrible.

The press also knew Tottenham fans could get on the backs of certain players at times, so they wrote stories about how the White Hart Lane faithful were giving me stick. But the truth is the Spurs supporters were always great to me through thick and thin. Not once did they boo me. It would have been a worry if they had, because all I was ever aiming to do was do my best and hope that people thought I was a good player.

Ossie coming in helped me too. His football philosophy of all-out attack suited me down to the ground. It enabled me to keep flourishing. I knew a little about him before he joined Spurs. He had managed Newcastle before Kevin Keegan and guided West Brom to promotion the previous season and, of course, had been a wonderful player for Spurs and part of Argentina's 1978 World Cup-winning team.

At first, I was guarded with him because I was still unhappy Terry had gone and didn't want to accept another manager, no matter who he was. But Ossie was great to me immediately. He told me: 'I just want you to get on the ball and get the team playing and create chances.' As an attacking player, he was fantastic for me. It was gung-ho with Ossie. The only thing I found strange about him was that he insisted on smoking in the dressing room.

The stall was set out early. In pre-season matches, we played something comparable to Holland's Total Football. There was no long ball. It was pass, pass, pass. Ossie brought in Colin Calderwood and Jason Dozzell, while Razor had gone. But the base of the team was much the same as in my first season at the club.

The team started out well, but it all went wrong when Teddy injured his knee. He was supposed to be out for a couple of weeks, not five months, which is how it turned out. We struggled to score without him – although he did manage 14 in the 19 League games he did play – and were conceding goals by the bucketload. We went on a losing run of seven games in the middle of the campaign, the worst of any Premier League side that season.

The second half of the season was a real struggle. In the end, we were lucky to survive in the top flight. We had to win at Oldham in our second-to-last game of the season to stay up. Fortunately we managed to beat them 2–0. Personally, though, I had a good season with Ossie giving me a lot of freedom. I played on the right but could switch to the left to get on the ball. This campaign helped secure me my full England debut.

Terry Venables had kept a close eye on my performances despite Spurs' battle to avoid relegation from the top level for the first time in 16 years. He was appointed England coach in January 1994. His first match was a friendly against Denmark at Wembley two months later, on 9 March, and there was plenty of speculation about who was going to be in his first squad.

Ossie took us away to Spain for a week's training before a big game against Chelsea on 27 February. We trained on the beach in the morning and played golf in the afternoon followed by dinner and a night out. The post-dinner sessions were quiet, though. We were the only people in the bars, so the senior players asked Gary Mabbutt, the Spurs captain, to tell Ossie we wanted to go to Puerto Banus in Marbella because it was too subdued where we were.

Mabbs did and Ossie agreed. He always liked looking after the boys. It was much more lively in Puerto Banus, which pleased the lads. I remember one night Steve Sedgley diving into the marina fully clothed. What a clown! It was a good trip and great for team bonding.

I remember playing golf with Teddy and a couple of the other players. Teddy was driving our buggy all over the fairways near the greens. We were warned not to by the officials. He did it again, went over the brow of hill and ended up in a bunker. The official was right behind us. We just looked at each other and said: 'I think we're off!' We laughed, got out of the buggy, grabbed our clubs and walked back to the clubhouse. That was the only time I've ever been kicked off a golf course.

One lunchtime, after a training session, a few of us, including Mabbs and Teddy, were having lunch in the port. We were talking about who Terry was going to choose for his first squad. All the boys thought I would be selected. I was flattered, but didn't agree.

We returned home to finish off our preparation for the Chelsea game at the club's then training ground at Mill Hill in North London. On the day before we took on the Blues, we'd just finished our session when I heard a commotion from a nearby pitch. My little brother Ben, who had been on a week's trial with Spurs, had broken his leg during a match. I went to see how he was and could see a lump in his leg, which was a mess.

Ossie and coach Steve Perryman were fantastic and made sure the club looked after him. My parents came up and stayed at my house in Hemel Hempstead. I was with them rather than at the hotel with the rest of the Tottenham squad. At the hospital, it was discovered Ben had fractured the fibula and tibula of his right leg. It was a bad injury.

I had to go off from home to meet up with the lads at the team hotel in West London. They were concerned about Ben and the rest of my family. But I had to put it all to the back of my mind to concentrate on the game that afternoon. It turned out to be a ridiculous match. We went 2–0 up but were then 3–2 down by half-time. We got back to 3–3, scoring a penalty, and missed a spot-kick to go 4–3 up. We ended up losing 4–3 when they scored with a penalty of their own in the last minute. It was a massive blow as we were deep in the Premier League danger zone.

After the match, Dougie Livermore, now a coach after running the side with Ray Clemence, said to me back in the dressing room: 'I think you might get some good news tomorrow.' He was right.

I'd returned to Ben's bedside the following day when a call came through from Irene, a secretary at Tottenham, who gave me advance warning that I was in Terry's first squad, to be announced later in the day. As England had missed out on qualifying for the 1994 World Cup in the United States under Graham Taylor by then, it was all doom and gloom. Everyone wanted Terry to lift the mood, and he had become the white knight, coming in on his charger to rescue our national team and lead the gallop to a bright future. To be a part of a new era from day one, and led by a man who had brought me into the big-time at Tottenham, made my inclusion extra special.

It was supposed to be one of the biggest highlights of my life – and it was – but seeing my brother lying there as I took the call made me feel weird. What had happened to him was the other end of the spectrum. This was what football was all about: highs and lows aplenty.

Ben had impressed during his trial and the club had told him they wanted him back the following week. We could have ended up playing alongside each other for Tottenham. But the injury meant that any professional football career was out of the question. It might have been different these days, with the improvements they've made in medicine. But back then Ben had a rod put in his leg for 18 months, and when he tried to come back a couple of years later it proved too late.

The media knew all about what had happened to my little brother and wanted to interview me as an England new boy. They obviously thought it was an even bigger story because of Ben, and I asked if he wanted to do interviews with me. I thought it might cheer Ben up if I involved him. It worked: he liked doing his interviews, but it was all a bit strange.

The following Sunday, I met up with the England boys. I was as nervous as hell. I almost didn't want to go. I didn't know how I'd fit in with all these megastars, being a quiet lad. I was driven to Burnham Beeches Hotel in Buckinghamshire, where the squad were based, by John Coberman. Terry had got John to chauffeur and look after me when I first arrived at Spurs feeling unsettled and wet behind the ears. He'd got him to do the same thing for Gazza when he'd arrived from Newcastle at a young age.

As I walked into reception, Michelle Farrer, who was the FA player liaison officer, introduced herself and got me checked in. I looked through the double doors to the bar where I could see experienced England players Tony Adams and David Seaman having a drink. Tony walked out to me and said: 'Come and have a beer with us.' So I put my bags in my room and came down to have a few drinks with them and other players joined us as they arrived. They were all so friendly and welcoming. It broke the ice. I'd been petrified because, again, I felt I didn't belong. I always struggled with new surroundings and meeting new people because of the way I am. They were all great lads and got me out of my shell and settled.

It helped that there were a couple of other younger players involved, like Rob Jones, from Liverpool, and Graeme Le Saux, who had moved from Chelsea and was to be part of Blackburn's Premier League title success the following year. We trained on Monday and Tuesday mornings, watching TV, playing video games and generally relaxing in our down time.

Terry called a meeting on the Wednesday morning with the match that evening. He told us: 'I'm going to name the team now, so you can go upstairs and make your phone calls to let people know and we'll leave in 20 minutes for training.'

He might have had me in mind, as I'm sure the experienced guys would have organised for their families to come to the game already. Anyway, I was in the team he read out. I was thrilled and stunned. I had just wanted to play some part in the game and be able to say I'd played for England. And get a cap. That was as far as I'd dared imagine because I was in the squad for the first time. Now I was going to realise my ultimate footballing ambition.

I phoned Mum and Dad to give them the news, and they were beside themselves with delight. Their reaction made me feel good for them. I had the rest of the day to wait and think about the match under Wembley's floodlights. We had a light training session, practising free-kicks and corners and set plays, and went back to the hotel for lunch and a sleep in the afternoon. I was surprised I was able to drop off, but I did. That was probably because I hadn't slept the night before as I was nervous about whether I'd be playing or not.

At about 4 or 5pm, Gazza came up to my room and asked for a shaver. I could barely shave so he probably knew I wouldn't have one. He just wanted a chat. He started talking to me, saying: 'You're good enough to be here. Terry brought me to Tottenham and he did the same with you because he rated both of us. He knows what he's doing. Have belief everything will be great and enjoy it. You'll be fine. This won't be your only time with England, but make sure you take it all in because it's your debut. That only happens once. I let mine pass me by.'

Gazza was someone I'd admired. I'd watched him play for England in the 1990 World Cup in Italy on television while visiting my friends in Dallas. I remember his tears on being booked in the semi-final against West Germany and knowing it would have put him out of the Final had we not lost. That tournament had really captured my imagination, with the way Gazza and Chrissie Waddle turned on the style, and manager Bobby Robson got the team to play with five at the back. Just four years later, I was in an England team with Gazza! Not only that, he wanted to make sure I was all right.

What he said and how he was with me really helped. It gave me so much more confidence than I would otherwise have had. Gazza's a top man and I'll always be grateful to him for what he did for me that afternoon. However, despite everyone's help, the question that came into my head as I sat there in the dressing room before kick-off was: 'Are you good enough?'

I was very nervy to start with, but determined to keep it simple when I did get on the ball, just like Alan Ball had taught me. I had a couple of early touches and they helped settle me. One of them came against Michael Laudrup. He was one of the leading players in world football, playing his club football for Johann Cruyff-managed Barcelona before switching to Real Madrid the following season. And he tried to prove it as he went to go past me.

I slide-tackled him and dragged the ball back into my possession and the crowd roared. Wow! To me it was just a tackle, but I sensed this mini victory over a Danish sporting hero had got the crowd on my side.

We went in 1–0 up at half-time thanks to a David Platt goal. I didn't really do anything wrong in the first half and that gave me great lift going into the second. When I came back out and looked up at the crowd I thought 'I belong here, I love this'.

Soon after the restart – when we were 1–0 up against the European champions – David Platt laid the ball into my path. I took a touch and saw I was one-to-one with Peter Schmeichel, the great Manchester

United goalkeeping legend, and dinked it over him. I executed it exactly as I'd wanted to. Perfect. I thought 'goal'. All of a sudden, one of Schmeichel's defenders came running round and kicked the ball off the underside of his own bar and out. A goal would have been the icing on the cake.

Another time I flicked the ball over one player and, as the next one came in, I lobbed it over him. It was a party piece and the whole stadium went crazy. I was growing in confidence and felt great. I'd played at Wembley the year before in the FA Cup semi-final against Arsenal. That was an occasion. Playing my first game for England's senior side in front of a full house with the team playing well put it in the shade.

I took Gazza's advice and took mental snapshots of everything. I appreciated how special it was. It was just six days after my 22nd birthday. Only a couple of years earlier, I'd been playing for Pompey in the second tier. Now I'd just won a cap in an era in which they did not hand them out for fun. Squads were generally smaller than they are now.

It was the best I ever played in terms of what was on my mind, the nerves I felt and the fact it was my full England debut. It is a game that is always a highlight when I look back, I couldn't have wished for it to go better. I ran my socks off, covered every blade of grass, showed a few bits of skill and was named man of the match as we won 1–0. In the changing room, Terry said to me: 'Well played, different class.' Gazza turned round to Terry and said: 'Cor, he's not bad is he?' Terry smiled and agreed before reminding me of that moment when I had sat in the bath feeling sorry for myself during the Everton game and he had come in to lift my spirits, adding: 'I told you you'd be all right!'

I looked around at my teammates, Alan Shearer, Paul Ince, Tony Adams, David Platt, Gary Pallister, Peter Beardsley and, of course, Gazza among them. I was pleased I'd played well in that sort of company. They were top, top players, ones I'd looked up to. Terry knew they were the right players for me to have around. I'd repaid Terry's faith in me without a doubt.

I didn't have anything else to prove to myself. I had the whole of my football life ahead playing for England and Tottenham. It was the ideal platform for me to play in the world's biggest international tournaments. Everything was exactly as I wanted it to be. It was tick, tick, tick.

Terry spoke very well of me after the game. The media wanted interviews and I did a lot of them. It was great because it was off the back of me playing well for England. I felt I had been representing family, friends, club-mates, everybody, but at that level there was extra pressure to do well for myself. I was concerned about what people were going to think. You always want them to say nice things. And now they were going to.

I went into the players' lounge after it all to be with Mum, Dad, Gran and my brothers and sister. It was so nice to share the moment with them. Being young and a little naïve, I had been carried along. I had been fortunate to have surrounded myself with people I could trust like Alan Ball, Jim Smith, Graham Paddon, Leon and Terry. But the biggest and most trustworthy supporters had been my parents.

I was absolutely buzzing and went with my family to celebrate at Planet Hollywood, the West End restaurant owned by Arnold Schwarzenegger, Sylvester Stallone and Bruce Willis. We were like typical London tourists. It was gone midnight and when we got to the eaterie it was closing! But they kept it open for us when they recognised me from the game and said: 'It's on the house'. That was something I could get used to. It highlighted, in a small way, the difference between doing well for your club and doing well for England.

As my international career developed and I did well, even Arsenal fans would come up and congratulate me on my performances for my country. That's not bad for a Spurs player! I still got stick from Southampton fans over my Portsmouth link when I faced Saints, but it did subside a little because of my performances for England.

I managed to score in my second game for England against Greece a couple of months later. It was at Wembley again in another friendly. My goal gave us the lead and we went on to win 5–0 with David Platt getting a couple and Peter Beardsley and Alan Shearer chipping in. Five days later I bagged my third cap in another home friendly which we drew 0–0 with Norway. I was enjoying myself, and Terry's efforts seemed to be bearing fruit. The defence looked particularly solid, keeping three clean sheets.

England might not have been in the World Cup Finals in the United States that summer, following the failures of Graham Taylor's team, but I did get out to see my friends in Washington DC. As it happened I went to a few World Cup games – all with Norway involved. My Tottenham teammate, goalkeeper Erik Thorsvedt, was playing for them and got tickets for me and my friends. We went out to a couple of Irish bars afterwards and the Irish fans were singing my name! My friends said 'Wow, you are quite famous!'

When I returned for the 1994–95 season with Spurs, three of the stars from the global extravaganza became my teammates.

8

'No' to Fergie

As I prepared for the 1994–95 season with Tottenham, I had settled into Hemel Hempstead quite well. Life with Kerry was fine at first. She had moved up for my sake when I'd joined Tottenham. But she was only 18 and acted like she was more grown up than she was. Kerry enjoyed the lifestyle and the fact her boyfriend was playing for Tottenham. She got too big for her boots. My American friends Dave and Joe threatened not to come back to visit if Kerry was still around after she took them into the players' lounge once and left them in the corner while she went off to socialise with others in the room.

Kerry didn't like me going on 'boys' nights out' with either teammates or friends. Once my brothers and a group of friends came up from Southampton. We'd planned to go out, but Kerry said she wasn't feeling well and wanted me to stay in with her. As our visitors had come so far I decided to have the night out with them. But Sam, the girlfriend of my mate Gavin Dobson, who stayed in with Kerry, told us the next day that as soon as we'd gone out, Kerry had jumped up and said to her: 'Let's go out and follow them and see where they are going.'

I knew our relationship had to end. Two years had proved long enough for both of us. She moved out and my brothers moved in, along with Southampton friends Ian Parker and Gavin. Gavin was in the Army and posted nearby while Parker, who was in Ben's class at school, came for the weekend and stayed four years!

I didn't think any of us could cook and used to treat them all to dinners out. But then I discovered that Parker had chef qualifications, and when my Dad found out he pulled him up on it and said: 'If I hear Darren has spent another couple of hundred quid on dinner for you lot again, you're out!'

So Parker got put in charge of meals. We were like a proper little family sat around the dining room table with Parker serving us up our dinner. I remember broccoli figured in a lot of them. Very healthy! The house wasn't that big and I hadn't hired a cleaner, so I got Parker to do the housework as well – there was no chance my brothers were going to help him. I figured he could earn his keep. But he did get some time off from slaving away over the kitchen oven and pushing the vacuum cleaner.

We had great neighbours, Fanny and Jason and their kids, Stephanie and Andreas – who were from Greece – and they often provided us with either home-cooked meals or an invite to join them for a barbecue. We would also visit a nice Italian restaurant we knew called Radio Days, where the manager Kamilo went on to become a very good friend of ours. I loved Italian food and still do. All our neighbours, including Wilf Rostron, the former Arsenal player who was coaching at Watford, were tolerant of us five boys.

By this point, I was fortunate enough to have a sponsored car from Honda, which was arranged by the car company's Bushey dealership, not far from where I lived. It was managed by Tim Dibbs, who is now such a good friend that I'm godfather to his and wife Lisa's daughters Katie and Emma.

One day at training, when I had left Parker in the car in the car park that overlooked the training pitch at Mill Hill, my mate John Coberman, who had driven me around when I first arrived at Tottenham, came into the canteen to say I needed to speak to Parker.

'No chance,' I said.

'No, no you'd better,' he replied.

'What's he done now?'

'I'll leave him to tell you.'

'Just tell me, John!'

'He's crashed your car.'

'What do you mean? He can't even drive!'

So I went over to the car park, where Parker stood with his bottom lip quivering. He explained that he had wanted to turn the car to face straight at the training pitch instead of turning his head slightly. I said: 'You lazy f***ing tosspot. What is wrong with you?'

He had never driven before, and the car was an automatic. When he put it in gear it had rolled forward and he panicked. He tried to slam down on the brake but hit the accelerator and crashed into a young pro's car. Off we went to Bushey to see Tim and, as we entered his office, I turned to Parker and said: 'Go on then – tell him what you've done!' Parker was like a little schoolkid. Tim said: 'What are you like, Parker?!' And then he gave us another car and added to Parker: 'Leave this one alone, please!'

Parker, though, was and remains one of my best friends. He's like my PA because he makes a lot of business and personal arrangements for me. I have become godfather to his partner Michelle's sons Jake and Carter. Jake is such a cool kid, although, for some reason, he's a Liverpool fan. I think it is because of Fernando Torres!

Back on the pitch, it was clear Tottenham had to improve on 1993–94 in the forthcoming season. Ossie's first term in charge had proved almost disastrous. It had shown Spurs needed a bigger squad, especially when Teddy Sheringham was injured. Ronnie Rosenthal had been a stop-gap replacement, but it turned out we needed someone longer-term with Teddy sidelined for so long.

Ossie and Alan Sugar acted decisively by taking a leaf out of Keith Burkinshaw's book and boosting the playing staff with stand-out World Cup performers Jürgen Klinsmann, Illie Dumitrescu and Gheorghe Popescu. Keith had flown to South America in the wake of Argentina's World Cup success of 1978 and returned with Ossie Ardiles and Ricky Villa. Ossie proved the better choice, as he earned legendary status among all Spurs followers, but Villa, although a more erratic performer, put himself into the club's hall of fame with his mazy FA Cup Final winner in the replayed Final against Manchester City at Wembley in 1981.

Now it was the turn of one German and two Romanians to try and emulate the Latin American duo of yesteryear. Jürgen had shone in USA '94 as he scored five goals (one short of the Golden Boot) in guiding Germany to the quarter-finals four years after helping his country lift the Cup, sealing it with a victory over Diego Maradona's soccer Pumas. He was later to captain his country to glory at Euro '96 and hit the target three times in the 1998 World Cup Finals; two tournaments I was destined to play in.

Alan Sugar went over to Monaco to seal the deal for Jürgen and was pictured on the back of his boat in the principality's harbour with him. The lure of London and a classy, traditional club that everyone knew attracted him. Tottenham suited a player who had played at the top level in several European countries.

Ilie Dumitrescu and Gheorghe Popescu had emerged as global stars as they helped Romania reach the quarter-finals in the United States. There had already been plenty of hoopla as Spurs' profile was high, but with the arrival of such great names, it went through the roof.

The Romanians were well known, but Jürgen was a superstar. Everyone knew who he was. I was in awe of him. But straight away, after the first day's training, you knew he was as normal as the next guy. He arrived in a little VW Beetle, although I'm pretty sure he had a Ferrari locked away in his garage that he didn't let anybody see! He always mucked in as one of the boys; he just wanted to be one of us. He was a real nice guy and a true gent. Although he generally looked after his diet and prepared himself for games in the right way, he would always join us down at the local greasy spoon for a fry-up whenever we did a warm-down at the stadium.

What a player Jürgen was. He knew what he wanted, what was right and won the Footballer of the Year award while always having time for everybody. He proved popular with players as well as the club staff and supporters. Even though we looked up to him as a footballer, we considered we had made a good friend that season. We were all together on tour at the end of the season in Hong Kong and Jürgen was due to fly home to Germany the following day. He put his credit card behind the bar for the lads to have a drink. It was a nice touch.

The pre-season friendlies were great fun. Everyone wanted to watch us. It was fantastic. Jürgen made his debut against Watford. There were 15,000 packed into Vicarage Road, the first of a season of sell-out crowds. Even the kick-off was delayed. It was a bright, sunny day and the crowd's reaction to Jürgen was incredible. It was Klinsmann-mania. You couldn't get off the pitch after the warm-up with people trying to get his autograph. It was a friendly and yet everything was crazy. This gave us a taste of what was to follow, with all our matches sold out and everyone wanting to beat us because he was in the team.

They were exciting times and great for all of us. We were now a part of a team that everyone was desperate to watch. We were on a world stage. It was fantastic.

We went off for a short tour of Ireland. Teddy, or perhaps David Kerslake, came up with an idea for Jürgen that would win over those cynical towards him because of his reputation as a diver. Before we played League of Ireland side Shelbourne they said to him: 'If you score you've got to dive!' It was a great idea and would have been wasted had he found the net that day. However, the new goal celebration was to make a hell of an impact once we'd started the season. It was part of a love affair Jürgen developed with most supporters of the English game.

Klinsmann might not have been the first foreign player to come over to play in England, but his arrival did seem to spark the major influx we have seen since then. He was to prove a big influence on all us players. He taught us to look after ourselves better in areas such as diet and general lifestyle, despite our love of transport cafes!

Although the punishments were later revoked and replaced with a £1.5 million fine after Alan Sugar challenged them, we kicked off the 1994–95 season with a points deduction and no place in the FA Cup after being found guilty of financial misdemeanours in the 1980s.

The first game was against Sheffield Wednesday at Hillsborough, which was filled to the rafters following a lot of media scrutiny, particularly of Jürgen, and the fact people knew we played an attacking style of football. We had a lot of good players. Ian Walker was in goal, while Sol Campbell and Stuart Nethercott were the centre-backs with David Kerslake and Justin Edinburgh full-backs. Colin Calderwood sat in front of them, while the rest of us – dubbed the Famous Five for our adventurous play – included myself and Dumitrescu on the wings with Teddy and Jürgen up front and Nick Barmby just behind them. It was all-out attack.

Within 20 minutes against Wednesday, we were 2–0 up. Teddy got the first and I scored the second. We were playing great football. Passing it to death. They couldn't get near us. When the second half started they scored a goal out of nothing. Then it was panic stations for some reason. And Colin put through his own goal. But we stepped it up again. Nicky put us back in front and, after about 30 passes, the ball came to me and I crossed for Jürgen to score his first goal for Spurs. Cue 'the Dive'. The fact that Jürgen showed himself capable of laughing at himself swept away every cynic who had given him stick for seeming to be blown over by a feather in the past.

The fly in the ointment was a late Wednesday goal – which left the scoreline 4–3 to us – that seemed to be a sign that the previous season's pattern of conceding too many goals might repeat itself.

We played Everton in the following midweek and Jürgen scored two, one an unbelievable overhead kick. Three goals for him, two wins for us. People were saying 'What a team this is. Ossie's a genius'.

We played Manchester United at White Hart Lane on the Saturday and lost 1–0 to a Steve Bruce goal. We played well and deserved something from the game. Teddy missed a penalty, Jürgen had a goal disallowed for offside that wasn't and we more than matched them.

We beat Ipswich 3–1 at Portman Road and could have been 10-0 up at half-time. It was frightening how good we were. After a couple of League defeats, we produced a 6–2 win over Watford in the first leg of our League Cup tie after they'd gone 1–0 up within 20 seconds. We were annihilating teams.

Before the return leg kicked off at our stadium on 4 October, I put pen to paper on a new four-year contract in Alan Sugar's office for £7,000 a week, plus a signing-on fee and a clause that said that if another club offered £4 million for me I would be able to move on.

A few months earlier, Chris Sutton had signed for Blackburn for £5 million to become the most expensive signing in British football, and this made me think a £4 million buy-out clause was cheap considering I was an England international and Chris wasn't. When I left the room,

Alan Sugar asked Leon to stay and said to him: 'Keep that clause quiet and, if anyone offers more, Darren can have half of whatever it is above the £4 million.'

Unfortunately, things took a wrong turn a couple of hours later when I tore my groin – an injury which put me out for three or four weeks – and the team lost 3–2.

We went four more games in a row without a win. During this period we suffered a shock 3–0 League Cup exit at lower division Notts County and a 5–2 loss at Manchester City in the League. Teams had figured ways to play against us.

We beat West Ham 3–1 in the Premier League on 29 October, but by then the decision had been made to sack Ossie. I thought 'Here we go, another manager coming in at a time when I've got injury troubles. Will he like me?'

I'd just started back in training the day before Gerry Francis arrived as my new boss, with Roger Cross as his assistant. He'd done well with QPR, but other than that his coaching career was a mystery to me, although I obviously knew him as an England international midfielder.

Our first conversation gave me encouragement. I told him my groin felt sore and stiff after training. He said he wasn't surprised as he'd heard I'd torn it badly. Then he stunned me. It was a Wednesday and he said: 'See how the groin feels on Friday because I want you to play against Aston Villa on Saturday.' It was what I wanted to hear. I was happy because I knew then that he rated me – and I played in his first match in charge.

By half-time we were 3–0 down. Oh my Lord! We hadn't played that badly, it was just they scored with every chance they had. Our defensive frailties were quite evident. We came out and scored immediately and got back to 3–3 before they hit a last-minute winner. What a sickener! We had a different manager, but the same problems.

Gerry, who was superb, started to get it right. He was all about teamwork and he did a lot of work on the training ground. We went back to a solid 4–4–2. He brought Mabbs back for Stuart Nethercott, who had done really well as a youngster in a team that only concentrated on attack. Under Ossie, whenever anyone asked what we should do when we lost the ball defensively, he would reply: 'You're good players, you shouldn't give the ball away.' Mabbs was the club captain and a leader and made a huge difference.

We had the players who were always going to create chances and score goals, but we had to make ourselves solid defensively. Gerry had Dean

Austin and Justin Edinburgh as the full-backs. Mabbs and Colin Calderwood were the centre-backs. We played four in midfield with myself and Nick Barmby wide and Gheorghe Popescu and David Howells in the middle. Teddy and Jürgen were up top. The team under Gerry and Roger, who was a great bloke and great to work with, was balanced.

The manager believed in his teams being fit. Tuesday was a running day. We called it Terror Tuesday. We sprinted box to box, having a few seconds rest in between. It was hard work, although it got easier as our fitness levels rose. And there was no doubt it helped us in games. The training sessions on tightening-up also paid off. We had one spell in which we didn't concede a goal for six games.

Fortunately we still we were able to score goals. Gerry turned us into a very good side and we played well until the end of the season. Nicky and I got up and down and creating things. Popescu and Howells would just sit there, keep us ticking, breaking up lots of the opposing attacks and protecting the back four. Up front Jürgen and Teddy scored goals for fun. My understanding with Teddy was at its peak. One example was a corner routine we did which produced three goals in three games. Teddy moved to give himself some space and I would hit a low ball to him, which he hit first time.

Many teams have tried to emulate it over the years. Even Manchester United tried it when Teddy went there. But he and David Beckham never achieved the same success.

Spurs ended the League season seventh, but had we shown consistent form before and after Gerry's arrival we would have been second.

We had a fantastic run to the semi-finals of the FA Cup in 1994–95. There was a third-round win against non-League Altrincham Town and we blew away Sunderland 4–0 before drawing Saints in the next round. They held us to a draw at White Hart Lane and then led 2–0 after 15 minutes in the replay with the tactic of Stuart Nethercott man-marking their star player Matt Le Tissier not working too well. Gerry changed things just before half-time, with Ronnie Rosenthal coming on and scoring twice to force extra-time before completing a hat-trick. They were all brilliant goals. No one expected that from Ronnie! We ran out 6–2 winners. I got a goal, and so did Jürgen and Nicky. It was just before my 23rd birthday, so I had a double celebration that night, although I made sure I didn't rub any Saints' fans' noses in it and went to a bar out of town.

In the FA Cup quarter-finals we were drawn away to Liverpool. It was a classic match. We were the form team and Liverpool were on fire as well with Jamie Redknapp, Steve McManaman and Robbie Fowler playing great football, and John Barnes running things from midfield for them.

By this point I'd been moved into central midfield and Gica (Gheorghe Popescu) having picked up an injury a few weeks earlier. I absolutely loved being completely involved, running all over the place. It was a real battle with me and Howellsy, who I loved playing with centrally. He was so underrated. Technically, David was one of the best I played with. He would sit and allow me to have freedom to get forward and wide, where I could still deliver my crosses. We went up against Barnes and Redknapp and finally came out on top with a last-minute goal from Jürgen. What a moment! The lads were buzzing and we had a good night out.

Everton was the semi-final draw we got, with Manchester United taking on Crystal Palace. Their manager Joe Royle had his side pumped up, and they launched balls into our box left, right and centre from set plays and we lost 4–1 at Elland Road. We were awful. We were big favourites to win the game but didn't perform on the day. It was my third semi-final loss in four years. It hit me hard.

After that the season just petered out. We had a chance of getting into Europe, but missed out on a UEFA Cup place by just a point to Arsenal.

At the end of the season, Jürgen went home when he decided to invoke a get-out clause and move back to Germany to play for Bayern Munich. I understood his reasons. He had played his career all over Europe and just wanted to go back to his homeland. Alan Sugar was furious and said live on TV that he 'wouldn't even wash his car' with the shirt Jürgen had personally signed for him. I thought to myself: 'Like you wash your car!' Jürgen's decision no doubt provoked a tirade from the chairman against high-earning foreign players in the English game. He took to referring to those players as 'Carlos Kickaballs'.

This was probably the best of my 12 seasons at Spurs in terms of performance. I played well and felt things were getting better for me every year. The bonus was a great team spirit. The backbone of the side was English, but the foreign boys were good guys too. We'd all go out together for either a drink or dinner most weeks.

In the meantime, I had played three times for Terry Venables's England in friendlies. Two were straight-forward ones at Wembley. I helped us beat the United States 2–0 (Alan Shearer getting both goals) – with my invited American friends looking on, and I was man of the match as we drew 0–0 with Uruguay at the national stadium. They were enjoyable experiences, but routine in comparison to the one in between.

This was a friendly against the Republic of Ireland at Lansdowne Road on 15 February 1995. There were 46,000 packed in – but the match only lasted 27 minutes. The Dutch referee Dick Jol had no choice but to abandon the match because of crowd trouble. It was a bit worrying.

There were five of us Tottenham boys involved: myself, Teddy Sheringham, Sol Campbell, Ian Walker and Nicky Barmby, but I was the only one to start. We went one down to a David Kelly goal and the game was just going along fine. Suddenly there was this uproar behind us and all sorts of big wooden objects coming on to the pitch. What was going on here? The ref told us to get off the pitch. There were sticks coming down and chairs being ripped up as we made our way to the dressing room. I hoped it wouldn't escalate. I didn't want to be part of a disaster.

As a kid I saw that sort of thing on television but had never experienced it, and I felt safe with the security around us. I thought we'd get back out soon, but obviously it was a lot worse than I thought because the match was called off. It was the only professional match I ever played in that was. It was bizarre. We felt a bit strange as we left the stadium for our flight home in the early hours because of what had gone on.

Funnily enough, I had a scarier time as a youth player with Portsmouth at a tournament in Belgium. I was only 16 or 17. We were playing a team from the Middle East, I think they were from Saudi Arabia. It only took one bad, waist-high foul – I think by Darryl Powell with his gangly legs – and it all kicked off. All their bench joined their team on the pitch and they were all spitting and kicking us. Their goalie ran off, picked up the corner flag and was trying to whack us with it. Their subs went into the woods behind the pitch and emerged with wooden sticks to hit us with. It was a melée. We stuck up for ourselves. It was a full-on riot of a reaction from them, but we were ushered away and asked to leave the country. Somehow we were blamed for it. I believe it was because the authorities were sensitive because the Heysel Stadium tragedy involving Liverpool and Juventus fans had occurred in Belgium just a couple of years before.

It was while playing for England during the Umbro Cup after the end of the 1994–95 season that I found out Alex Ferguson, four years before his knighthood, wanted to sign me for Manchester United.

I scored my second senior international goal and was named man of the match for England in a 2–1 win over Japan at Wembley on 3 June. Five days later, I scored what was probably my best-ever goal for England in dramatic circumstances at Elland Road, Leeds. We'd gone 2–0 down, then 3–1. David Platt pulled one back with a minute left, then I stepped into the limelight in injury time. A long ball from Graeme Le Saux was headed on by Teddy and back by Alan Shearer for me to half-volley home off both posts to give us the draw.

As I relaxed over a few beers with the players afterwards, I found out what Fergie thought of me. I was in the middle of a game of snooker with Gary Pallister, the Manchester United defender who was in the England squad, and he told me: 'I think Fergie thinks a lot of you, he might want you.' I said: 'Really?' I didn't know what to think.

By the time we played Brazil at Wembley three days later – and lost 3–1 to finish second in the competition – it was clear there had been a bit of interest in me from United. And, of course, there was that clause in my Spurs contract that said that if a team offered a certain amount, I could go. But all I was thinking about was flying out on holiday to the United States the following day. It had been a long season.

My agent, Leon Angel, was at the Brazil game and when I saw him afterwards, he said: 'We've got a meeting with the chairman Alan Sugar.' I said: 'OK, I'll be back in about three weeks.' He said: 'No, tonight!' I said: 'Really?' He said: 'Yeah, he wants to offer you a new deal and wants to speak to you about it.'

I had a couple of drinks with my family and friends, then off I went with Leon. It was so exciting. My season had certainly finished with a bang, and this was another explosion. We turned up at Sugar's mansion in Chigwell. Gerry Francis was there. Gerry said he was chuffed with how I'd played in the three Umbro Cup games. We all sat down and had a chat about whether I wanted to stay. Gerry was desperate for me to do so as he had lost Jürgen and Gica to Bayern and Barcelona, with Hull-born Nicky Barmby also thought to be homesick in London.

I said I wanted to stay and so it was decided that they would offer me a deal when I got back from the States, with Leon negotiating on my behalf while I was away. By this point it seemed obvious United were going to come in for me, and I'd guessed Alan Sugar was trying to get me to sign a new deal without *that* clause.

At the airport the following morning the clerk at the check-in desk said to me: 'Good morning Mr Anderton. How would you like an upgrade to first class?' I replied: 'Really? That would be fantastic.' It was another example of the perks that came with playing for England. While enjoying the flight, the stewardess said to me: 'The captain would like you to join him in the cockpit for the landing.' I replied: 'Yes, please.' It was great. I really enjoyed it and was invited to do the same on many more occasions prior to 9/11.

America was great fun. We went to basketball's NBA Final in Houston. I enjoyed plenty of nights out in New York, Washington DC and Philadelphia. I spoke to Leon on the phone several times while I was out in the States. There was lots of talk back home of United, champions Blackburn and Kevin Keegan's Newcastle all wanting to buy me. Blackburn wanted me to fly back and sign for them. I told my mates we could fly back on Concorde, sign and then fly back. But I decided that if I was to move on it could only be United. Fergie came out in the press saying I was the only player he wanted to sign that summer.

We had our last night out before I headed home. My mate Joe Roy was drinking all sorts of shots while 'toasting' my move to United. He overdid it and ended up passing out and having an ambulance take him to hospital. We picked him up in the morning before I headed off to the airport. It was a fun and crazy summer.

Gary Pallister called me the day I got back and asked: 'Is it all right to give the manager (Ferguson) your number, he wants to speak to you?'

I said: 'Um…I guess so.'

I then went off and played golf. When I got back my brother Scott said that Alex Ferguson had called me. He told me: 'I shit myself when I heard Fergie's voice. I didn't know what to say to him. I think he's going to call back.' About an hour later he did and explained he'd had a problem with his current right winger, Andrei Kanchelskis, who wanted to move on. He told me Manchester United were the best club in the world and said I should come up and have a look around. I said: 'Maybe I will.'

He'd heard there was a 'buy-out' clause in my contract and asked me what the figure was. I said I didn't want to say, but the prices being quoted in the papers should give him an idea. The figures being quoted were around £6 million, which of course was actually £2 million higher than the clause actually said. It was obvious United were prepared to offer well above what was needed. When I came off the phone, my head was spinning. I didn't know what to do.

The following lunchtime, I had arranged to have a meeting with Alan Sugar, Leon and Gerry Francis about my future and my new contract. When Leon and I arrived at Alan Sugar's house, I went and had a chat with Gerry. He obviously knew the situation and, possibly, that United had already made an offer that day. He explained he was desperate for me to stay and that the chairman would give me a dream deal.

He also spoke of how, if I went to United, I would be playing as a winger again and he wanted to build his Tottenham team around me in central midfield. He said that I had had a fantastic season and he loved working with me. Manchester United were in transition. Mark Hughes and Paul Ince had gone, Mark to Chelsea and Paul to Inter Milan and, of course, Kanchelskis was on his way. David Beckham, Gary and Phil Neville and Paul Scholes had not yet developed into the top players they became at Old Trafford.

I told Gerry I didn't want to leave, that I was happy where I was – but that United were United after all, a world-famous club. Having someone like them interested in you is enough to turn anyone's head. And they had probably the greatest manager of all time, who had guided them to trophy after trophy. But in my mind I knew I wanted to stay.

We went back in to rejoin Alan Sugar and Leon, who had been negotiating. Leon told Alan Sugar I didn't want to go, but he had to look after my interests. He also stated that Manchester United and Blackburn were offering £6 million, which would give me a £1 million bonus if I accepted either of them following the earlier agreement.

Alan Sugar told him: 'We could do a £4 million swap deal with Kanchelskis, which obviously stops that bonus.' Leon then said to him: 'Well, if that is the case, and if you want Darren to stay, then you pay a £1 million bonus on top of what you are offering him.' Sugar agreed! And he even got out the champagne.

He had pulled out all the stops, telling me how much he wanted me to stay and that I'd been fantastic for the club. It had been a real charm offensive. He made me one of the top paid players in the country, if not the top. Happy days.

The REAL truth of it was, however, that I never wanted to go. I'd only been at Tottenham three seasons. The fans and everyone at the club had been fantastic right from the beginning. I thought I should show loyalty. I loved playing for Gerry Francis and loved playing for Tottenham. I was having the time of my life. Why change it? On top of that, there was Euro '96 coming the following summer.

As it turned out, I didn't win as much with Spurs as I would have liked. And Fergie built another team of champions that I could have been part of. I might have even stood in the way of Becks and superstardom as he would have been behind me in the pecking order for the right-wing berth at the Theatre of Dreams.

Regrets? Not then…

On New Year's Day in 1996, I walked down the stairs to the main entrance at White Hart Lane against Manchester United (a match Spurs won 4–1). Fergie was walking up the other way. As we passed each other I said 'Hello'. He just carried on without a word. I guess I'd pissed him off the previous summer by saying 'no' to him.

9

Injured Party

My confidence was sky high when I returned to Tottenham for pre-season training in July 1995. I was as happy as Larry. I had my new contract in my pocket, having played the football of my life for Spurs the previous term, attracted the offer from Manchester United and earned praise for my Umbro Cup performances with England. The following summer my country would be hosting Euro '96, the biggest football tournament to be staged in England since the 1966 World Cup, which, as most know, provided the biggest moment in the host nation's history since it invented the sport.

There was, however, a physical price to be paid for my experiences over the previous year: an aching groin. If I'd have completely rested instead of extending a long season by playing those three Umbro Cup games I might not have been lumbered with it.

Whatever, it had to be dealt with. There was a chance it could be a hernia on the other side to the one I'd had operated on when Terry Venables was at the club. On the second day back I thought I had my answer. The troublesome area felt really sore, just like the previous occasion. So I went and checked it out with the physio, believing it was a hernia. But the physio, Tony Lenaghan, did not agree. He thought it was probably just a groin strain and that I'd be all right after a few days if I iced, stretched and rested it.

I accepted his advice, although I wasn't convinced. I struggled on for a further three or four weeks, not really knowing what the problem was. I even played a couple of friendlies. It was as sore as hell after each of them. The more it dragged on the more I was convinced I had another hernia problem. Just before the season started, I told Gerry I wasn't right and wanted to see Dr Gilmore, the hernia specialist, I'd seen before. He agreed to allow me fix up the appointment with him.

A couple of days later the physio told me about another guy who could operate on me if it was a hernia. He said that he had a new procedure using 'mesh technology' which meant I'd be back in 10 days to two weeks rather than four to six weeks. Medicine was developing all the time and it would suit me to get back quicker. So I agreed to see him. The guy confirmed it was a hernia which needed to be done. He said that he had done the operation on an Aberdeen player who had got back playing in two and a half weeks, and that the mesh was stronger and better and that I wouldn't have any problems with it.

The physio might have been trying to get himself off the hook after holding things up with his original decision by suggesting this guy, I don't know, but I didn't mind as long as the new surgeon could bring forward my return with his new methods and there would be no ongoing problems. I had the operation about a week before the season started and felt fine. I missed the first three games, in which the boys drew away at Manchester City before losing home games to Aston Villa and Liverpool.

I came back for the next match, which was at West Ham. Gerry put me on the bench and I came on with us losing 1–0 and we ended up drawing 1–1. I returned to the starting line-up as we defeated Leeds 2–1 at White Hart Lane and beat Sheffield Wednesday 3–1 at Hillsborough. I was playing well and there was even paper talk of Fergie coming back in for me with a £10 million bid.

On 25 September we played QPR at Loftus Road. It was a Monday night and live on Sky television. We won 3–2, but it marked the recurrence of the hernia problem I thought had been solved. The moment I realised something was wrong came when I felt something go as I whipped in a corner. I went in at half-time not feeling great and came off 10 minutes into the second half. I was thinking: 'I've had this different kind of surgery and it hasn't worked'. I told the press guys just that afterwards. It was on the back pages of the papers the following day.

Immediately, the physio panicked and asked me why I'd said what I'd said. I simply told him I'd done so because I felt the operation had not been a success and I was fuming. He took me back to the same surgeon who told me the hernia was fine, that I'd just got a small groin strain and would be OK in a few days. Tony Lenaghan phoned Alan Sugar to tell him everything was all right. The chairman then called me to say how pleased he was about the 'good news' and say that the physio had said I might be able to play against Wimbledon at the weekend. Sugar had looked at me in a good light after I'd signed the new deal and always phoned to see how I was. I appreciated that. It was a nice thing for him to do. But I wasn't too sure about being fit to take on the Dons. Obviously, as we'd won four out of four with me back in the starting line-up, he wanted me back playing as soon as possible.

After a couple of days, my troubled area still felt sore. And Gerry insisted he didn't want to risk me and the lads went out and beat Wimbledon 3–1 without me.

I tried to get fit, but it wasn't getting any better. A couple of weeks later, I went and saw another doctor, Dr King, who told me that there was a lot of scar tissue in there and he might have to operate. He suggested an injection might do the trick.

I had it and needed to rest for five days. I asked Gerry if I could stay off as I was fed up and didn't want to drive back and forth to watch the lads train. He said that would be fine and I told him I was going to fly to America for a few days. He questioned it, saying a long flight might not be ideal. I replied: 'I'll go on Concorde!' He laughed and said: 'Go on then, relax and enjoy yourself.' So I called my travel agent and he got me on the Concorde flight that night. It was an incredible experience. You could actually feel it speed up when it hit Mach Two. The plane was narrow and not overly comfortable, but the service was fantastic and the flight was only three and a quarter hours instead of the eight hours it had taken me on my previous trips to the States.

I had a great few days in Washington DC and went back feeling refreshed and confident. I thought I would be OK as the groin felt good. I went back into training and did some running with the physio. No problem. Then I kicked a few balls. It was OK. But the more I kicked the stiffer my groin got. I was frustrated and the more I kicked the more I prayed the pain would disappear. It didn't. It got worse. I told Tony: 'Shit, it's no good.'

He replied: 'OK, Let's go back in and ice it.'

The following day we went back to see Dr King. He said I should have the operation to remove the scar tissue. I agreed. After the op, the doc said it had been a success and had most certainly needed to be done as he also found a cyst which he removed while performing it.

I felt better and confident once again I would now be able to get back to fitness. The first thing I asked was: 'When can I play again?' The doc said: 'Maybe four weeks. See how you go.'

After three weeks of rest, I went out on the training pitch and started jogging and felt good. The physio then asked me to kick a ball. I did, but felt one of the worst pains I'd ever experienced. I'd obviously torn my groin. I hadn't had any bad injuries before and so didn't know anything about rehab. If someone takes a big hole out of your groin muscle it needs to be built up with weight training The muscle was as weak as hell. I was devastated. I thought: 'Oh no, not another balls-up of an operation!'

So that was me out for another God knows how long. I tried to get fit, but it didn't happen. Each time I came back the problem flared up again and didn't seem right.

I could do running in a straight line, at 50 per cent pace. Whenever I tried to step it up I couldn't. I was unable to run in curves or twist and turn. I spoke with the medical staff and had a scan done. The physio said everything was fine so carry on. That was good news to someone who just wanted to play football. A couple of weeks later, however, I was still not fine. I caused myself pain each time I tried to increase my pace.

The season was running out when I spoke to Terry Venables, who asked me how I was doing. I told him: 'Not great'. He suggested I went to see Dave Butler, who had been the Spurs physio when I first joined the club and had rejoined Terry in the role in the England set-up.

Dave lived in Bushey, near me in Hemel Hempstead. He had a little practice at his home and when I told him he said to 'come on over and we'll have a little look'. I explained I had an ache and couldn't sprint. He examined me and said I had a big indentation, a hole which showed I might have an old tear from a few weeks before. He said I should ask to see a report of the scan I had had done about a fortnight before.

Back at Tottenham I popped into the treatment room and saw Tony's second-in-command Ali Beattie. I told him I was concerned about what I thought might be an old tear at the top of my leg/groin, and pressed down on the area explaining I could feel a big hole. I asked him if he could check the scan and report. Ali went off and returned with the scan and I asked him if an old tear showed up on it. He thought one did. But he said he couldn't find the report. This was not normal and he phoned Tony Lenaghan to find out what it said and where it was.

Two minutes later Tony rang me. He told me to take it easy. Don't do this, don't do that. Just rest and it'll be OK. I asked him: 'Did the scan show a tear?' He didn't answer. He just kept going on about me having to rest, where previously he'd told me to keep running with it. When I came off the phone I asked Ali: 'Was there a tear?' He confirmed there was. I was furious.

A tear would explain why I'd been unable to run beyond half to three-quarter pace, had no spring in my step and couldn't turn. If the physio had told me there was one there I'd have dropped back on my efforts and treated the problem and got it right instead of carrying on as we were. It made me lose belief in Tony's abilities. It also left me feeling that I couldn't trust Tottenham. And led, in part, to me being dubbed 'Sicknote'. In hindsight, perhaps the tag would have gone away if I'd gone public over the 'scan scandal' and revealed what the physio and the club had done to me.

Privately, of course, I wasn't happy and told my Dad how angry I was about what had happened. He inadvertently told the press after a journalist rang him up to talk to about what he thought of the situation 'off the record'. He verbally abused Tottenham. Totally slaughtered the club. Next thing we knew it was on the back page of a tabloid. I told Spurs he'd been stitched up, that he didn't say what they'd printed. My Dad was banned from talking to the press after that.

Many people said to me at the time: 'You should sue.' I told them: 'I could never sue Spurs after all they've done for me.' Besides, I felt the scan business was just one of those things that can happen, that Tottenham were my team and I didn't want to drag them through the mud. I kept it in-house and settled for letting Alan Sugar know what had happened and my feelings about it.

If Tony Lenaghan was sat opposite me now I'd blame him as he has to take responsibility – but only up to a point. I don't hold any grudges against him. He meant well, but perhaps the job was too big for him. And after all it was Tottenham who employed him. The word was that he'd answered an advert in the *Evening Standard*, the London evening newspaper. He'd worked in hospitals, never with a big football club like Tottenham where he had to deal with a lot of injuries. I believe he felt pressured from Alan Sugar to get me back fit as soon as possible and took chances with my fitness because of that.

I think the chairman was on his back the whole time as he was very unhappy that I had hardly played since signing the new deal in the summer. It was quite believable that Sugar's approach to the treatment room would be similar to the one he adopted in other areas of the club. Alan Sugar was in the dressing room before and after games to see Gerry Francis. He even came in at half-time. He wasn't picking the teams, but he was very involved.

There was the time he even asked me to go on the bench for a game to 'give the fans a lift' after I'd been out injured. It was a bit cheeky of him. I phoned Gerry to tell him Alan Sugar had phoned me and he just shrugged it off as a well-meaning chairman jumping the gun, putting it down to the fact his action was motivated by how much he rated me and the thought that it would do the club a bit of good if I was involved.

I am convinced Tony Lenaghan should have been strong enough to tell the chairman when I was unable to play because of the injury. Instead, I think he told Alan Sugar what he wanted to hear. That I'd be back in two weeks. I told friends and family I'd be back in a fortnight for SEVEN MONTHS. It drove me crazy. It was why I stopped talking to the press about it. People close to me suffered from the frustration I felt.

I was, through my livelihood, used to running, getting the blood going. Exercise made you feel so much better. But when you get a bad injury that isn't possible. And, although you don't realise it, the inactivity affects you mentally because you are unable to get a lot of negative thoughts out of your system. It is not until you get back out there jogging that you start to feel positive. What made it worse for me was I had an injury that was just dragging on and I didn't know how much longer that situation would exist.

I always had friends and family around, which really helped me cope. I wasn't a monster but would express my frustration by being snappy, short-tempered. That's how it is with people in all walks of life. I carried on socialising with my friends and neighbours, but in the back of my mind my physical ailments were getting me down. I was just desperate to be playing. People might think you don't care because you were getting paid, but you care more than anything when you are unable to do what you love – play football.

When I eventually spoke to Alan Sugar in depth about what had happened to me over the scan scandal, the chairman played down Tony Lenaghan's role. He described his physio's role as one of a 'lorry driver', a term I guess which meant he was a lowly employee rather than an executive. He said that a specialist would have looked at the scan and told him how to treat me, and that it was not Tony's job to decide on what that treatment was.

I said to the chairman that if that was the case, I should have been told what the scan revealed and should definitely not have been told there wasn't a tear. Alan Sugar has to take the responsibility, along with Tony, for the whole episode, because he employed the guy. It all boils down to the fact it doesn't matter what you earn or how good you are, if you are not fit, you are not fit. Simple. These days physios, managers and owners understand that better and players get the treatment they need. The game has improved in that way, thank goodness. It's too late for me, of course!

I remain angry about the treatment I received from Spurs that season and how it led the public to believe I was always injured, a perception underlined by the media calling me 'Sicknote'. It was a label which had first come about when I'd been ill with a migraine at Portsmouth and missed a game. When I came back into training, Andy Gosney, one of the goalkeepers, joked: 'Have you got your sick note?' It was nothing, but someone must have heard it and dug it out for a story. And it stuck. I've had a few nicknames, like 'Shaggy', but 'Sicknote' emerged top of the list. I tried not to worry about it because I felt the more you talked about it, the more you brought it to people's attention. But it implies I was a skiver, that I was just content to sit on the sidelines and pick up my wages. I got kicked all over the shop and played with all sorts of injuries. I was no soft touch.

Although it often made the injuries 10 times worse, I always wanted to play. I should have been held back by the physio if I wasn't right, but the squads weren't as big as they are now. Tottenham might have had quite a few internationals, but only three or four top ones that they needed to play every week. I was one of them.

Nowadays players are stretchered off on a Tuesday and back in training three days later. These days the game is more athletic and physically demanding, but there's nothing heroic in doing that. It just shows they didn't need the stretcher in the first place and that they were acting like lightweights. I was brought up in an era where players were more honest in situations like that, because we just wanted to play.

My nickname doesn't reflect the reality because I still managed to play getting on for 600 games, which I think is a more than respectable figure for a professional footballer, especially at the level I achieved. Even so, I still get called 'Sicknote'. Ninety-five per cent of the public are respectful, happy to shake my hand and tell me I had a great career. But then there are a few idiots. Football has a lot of rivalries and when a few blokes are drunk they can start behaving like fools. I was on a plane to Spain with my fiancée Katie not long ago when there were a few behind us chanting 'Sicknote'. I sat there and ignored it. On the bus from the plane to the terminal we ended up standing right next to them. They wanted to talk to me – in a nice way. I just blanked them. Simple.

A little while later, I was with my sister Kelly walking her dogs through a park in Southampton when a guy who was on that very flight came up to me and said: 'I don't know how you didn't react to those blokes on the plane, fair play to you. I almost got up and whacked them myself!'

I was at the races with some friends and one of them got involved with a guy and it ended in violence after he'd taunted me with the usual 'Sicknote' thing. If I'd have waded in there might have been all sort of repercussions: headlines like 'England World Cup star in punch-up'.

I was sitting in a restaurant having breakfast recently with Katie, near her parents' home in West London. There was a guy in there, and it was obvious he wanted to say something but was a bit nervous. Eventually, he came over and said 'How are you doing, Sicknote?' I just said 'What! Do you know how disrespectful that is?' He explained he was a fan and loved watching me play. But it was clear to me he had no idea about how rude he had been.

Normally I am pretty good in dealing with this thoughtless type of person, although sometimes I feel like telling them to f**k off. Katie tells me they don't know they are winding me up, just that they've seen it in the papers and think I am known – and want to be known – as Sicknote. Bizarre.

10
Football's Coming Home

I decided the best way to get fit for Tottenham and England was to run regularly with Dave Butler in the evenings after doing rehab at the club during the day. It was a killer of a schedule, but I wanted to return to playing as soon as I could after missing so much of the 1995–96 season. I knew how keen Alan Sugar and Gerry Francis were to have me back for the remaining Premier League games. I was also aware, of course, that Terry Venables wanted me to be available for Euro '96.

My plans looked like they might be upset when someone got hold of a picture of Dave and I out jogging. Tony Lenaghan saw it and gave me grief over it, insisting he was in charge of my rehab, not the England physio. I used some diplomatic skills to smooth things so I could continue with Dave, who was proving such a big help in getting me fit, by telling Tony I had just happened to meet up with Dave at our local sports centre and now we went out running together. Thankfully, Tony accepted it.

I finally got myself fit three weeks before the end of the season, returned for a reserve game against Bristol City and lasted the whole 90 minutes. I felt good, even though I knew the muscles were still weak, and pleaded with Gerry to give me a place on the bench in the next first-team match. It was against Arsenal at Highbury on 15 April. I was desperate to be involved. After all, it had been nearly seven months since my last appearance for the first team, that fateful night against QPR at Loftus Road. I nagged Gerry for a week. He was a good guy and wanted to look after me. He told me: 'I don't want to mess you up here. You've been out for a long time and I don't want you to have any more setbacks.' I got the right hump, thinking he was going to ignore my wishes.

Then, on the night before, he phoned and asked: 'Are you sure you're OK?'

I said: 'Yes, I am. You've got to put me on the bench. I'm desperate to be involved.' He agreed.

I was buzzing. I got an unbelievable ovation from the Spurs fans when I took my place among the subs that night It was 0–0 and deep into the second half when Teddy Sheringham called over and shouted 'get him on'. It was nice to think someone of Teddy's stature felt I could make a difference, even though I hadn't played since the previous September. Gerry brought me on for the last 15 minutes and I did all right. But the Spurs fans went crazy in their support of me – what a feeling!

A big deal was made of whether I had enough time to prove myself fit for Euro '96 with just three games left of the season. To be honest, I didn't believe I would be after the next match 12 days later. It was against Chelsea at White Hart Lane. I played the whole of the 1–1 draw in boiling hot temperatures and finished on my last legs. I was shattered. I thought to myself: 'There is no way you are going to be fit for the European Championships'. It was a horrible feeling because fitness was a big part of my game.

After the game, I was in the players' lounge with my Mum, Dad and brothers, sipping a Coke, when I was told the press were downstairs and wanted to speak to me. I really didn't want to because I felt so awful. But I always tried to speak to the media if I could, so I went down.

I told them my fitness wasn't great, but I was so happy to be back. The next day they hammered me, saying there was no way I should play in Euro '96. If that's what they thought, they could have just written it anyway. They didn't need me to talk to them about it. I'd given them my time when I was feeling terrible and then they did that. I was absolutely fuming.

My groin was really stiff when I went in for treatment the following morning and trained the next day. A game against Leeds at Elland Road was three days away and I didn't think I'd be able to play. I was still struggling. Even when I travelled up with the team 24 hours later I still didn't feel that great.

On the morning of the match, I took part in a little five-a-side – something Gerry Francis always used to put on before an evening game. I felt better. After resting up for the rest of the day, I joined the lads on the coach to the ground in good spirits. I was able to start.

We went one down in five minutes but came back to win 3–1. And I played well – and scored two goals. I nearly completed a hat-trick. The press wanted to speak to me after that, but I told them to piss off, apart from Steve Stammers of the London *Evening Standard*, who was a nice guy. He was always fair, and I treated him like a friend.

The next day the press were saying I had to be picked for Euro '96 because I had played well and looked so fit. That it was as if I'd never been away. It was amazing how quickly their opinion changed!

Oldest sibling: Ben, Scott and Kelly with me.

Prize guys: Scott and I after winning a five-a-side competition.

Saints alive: My favourite Southampton shirt.

Home: Mum, dad and us kids at Oak Tree Road en route to a holiday in Canada.

Leading from the front: A schools cross country win.

Kitted out: Me in my first Spurs kit, with Scott in the all red of Liverpool and Ben.

Me, Dad, Mum and Kelly on holiday in Devon.

Having a Ball: Being presented with a trophy by Portsmouth captain Kevin Ball, before I went on to clean his boots as a Pompey apprentice.

Knobbly knees: Celebrating scoring the winning goal for Bitterne Park Rangers.

Courting couple: Mum and dad with their dog Lisa.

What have I taken on here? Dad with us 'monsters'.

Juggling: Obsessed with keepy-up.

All smiles with Windsor United Under-14s (second from left, front row).

Christmas present: A ball!.

Nice cuppa: My favourite Spurs mug.

Oh brother: Ben with Alan Ball, who gave me an apprenticeship.

PORTSMOUTH

FOOTBALL COMPANY LIMITED

Registered Office:
FRATTON PARK, PORTSMOUTH, HANTS. PO4 8RA

Tel: 731204

AB.PE
23rd February 1988

Mr and Mrs Anderton

~~blurred~~

Southampton
Hants

Dear Mr and Mrs Anderton

I am pleased to inform you that Darren will be offered an apprenticeship with Portsmouth Football Club on leaving school.

I will be in touch with you in the near future to discuss the arrangements and the starting date.

I look forward to seeing you both in the near future.

Yours sincerely

A Ball
Manager

Chairman: B. J. DEACON, C.B.E. *Vice-Chairman:* J. R. PARKHOUSE
Directors: G. G. GAUNTLETT, D. K. DEACON, S. W. SLOAN, Mrs. J. DEACON
Secretary: W. J. B. DAVIS

Registered in England No. 123460

CLUB CALL
0898 12 11 82

The Apprentice: Copy of the letter from Alan Ball telling me I was to get an apprenticeship with Portsmouth.

Eye on the ball: Playing for Portsmouth. (Action Images)

Goal: Scoring for Portsmouth against Liverpool in the 1992 FA Cup semi-final at Highbury after giving 'keeper Bruce Grobbelaar 'the eyes'. (Action Images)

Volley good: Wearing Tottenham's second strip. (Action Images)

Celebrating my best Spurs goal: Against Leeds in the FA Cup. (Action Images)

As good as his word: Jurgen Klinsmann told me he would send me to his doctor. (Action Images)

My favourite playing partner: Teddy Sheringham. (Action Images)

We faced Newcastle at St James' Park three days later on the last day of the season. Our hosts were hoping to clinch the title. They had led the race from Manchester United by 12 points after we had beaten Alex Ferguson's team 4–1. However, the Magpies had faded, with Fergie playing some mind games which led to an emotional televised outburst from Newcastle manager Kevin Keegan in which he stated how he would 'love it' if United tripped up. Now Keegan's side had to beat us and United lose against Middlesbrough on the final day of the season to win their first title since 1927. We held them to a 1–1 draw as United sealed the crown with a 3–0 victory.

I did OK in front of the Toon Army, nothing special. But I'd played three full games in eight days. I hadn't done that since the start of the season. It proved enough to get me back involved with England, because a few days later I got a call from Terry Venables. He told me I was in the squad to face Hungary at Wembley 13 days after the end of the League season.

In my absence, Terry had kept England busy with friendlies, with Steve Stone coming in for me and playing very well. The press thought he might keep his place even if I returned to fitness. I believed that if I was fit I would play, though, as I had taken so easily to international football.

There were Wembley clashes against Columbia (0–0), Switzerland (3–1), with Teddy Sheringham on target, Portugal (1–1), Bulgaria (1–0), my future Spurs teammate Les Ferdinand banging in the winner, and Croatia (0–0). Terry also took the team out to Oslo for a goalless draw with Norway.

Thankfully, my return to the fold could not have gone any better for me. On 18 May 1996 I scored my only goal double for my country, either side of a David Platt effort, as England won 3–0, the team's best scoreline since Terry had taken over.

I was a bit knackered at the end, though. Terry had these bright tactical ideas and one of them was to play me as a right wing-back. It is a role in which you have to work like a dog, running forward and tracking back the whole time, a role I'd played for Jim Smith at Pompey for a few games at the start of the 1991–92 season. As I'd been out for most of the season, it was far from surprising I was so exhausted by the end of the game.

I flew out with the national squad to the Far East for a brief but eventful trip which completed the Euro '96 preparations. Five days after beating the Magyars, we took on China in Beijing in front of 65,000. We won 3–0 thanks to the Spurs connection. Nicky Barmby, by then at Middlesbrough, claimed a couple and Gazza, by then at Glasgow Rangers, was also on target. From a selfish point of view, I played well and was involved in all three goals. I felt tired because of the humid conditions, but everyone was in a good mood and we had a quiet night out with a few beers.

We went on to Hong Kong for an exhibition game against the Hong Kong Select XI. Terry Venables pulled me aside during training for the match and told me I had proved my fitness by completing the three games for Tottenham and doing likewise against Hungary and China. He thought I'd been great, but he didn't want me to overdo it, and would give me half an hour at the end against the Select XI to keep me ticking over. That's when I knew I'd be in England's Euro '96 squad.

The game was rubbish. We only won 1–0 and got a slating for it. Afterwards, all the players had to attend a dinner function with local dignitaries. Our captain Tony Adams, on behalf of the players, asked Terry if the players could have a night out together. Terry told him it was OK to go after we'd finished our starters, as long as we behaved ourselves. He understood team bonding was very important. All the lads got on and we looked forward to a fun evening.

It was the day before Gazza's 29th birthday and we went to a bar to celebrate. The people in there were very nice to us and provided shots of drinks for everyone. I had a few. One or two were consumed in what was dubbed the Dentist's Chair, where the contents of the glasses were poured into the open mouths of the players. I had my turn sitting in it. We were all up for it. It was a great night.

I remember panicking when I woke up the next morning. I looked at the clock and saw it was 11am and thought 'Oh my God, I'm missing training!' I phoned Walks (Ian Walker), one of the other Tottenham players on the trip, to check it out. He told me not to worry, that training had been cancelled. It was a massive relief. I don't think anyone would have made it downstairs anyway.

Terry Venables had used common sense in letting the players have a night out. We hadn't done anything wrong, just had a few beers and shots. There were no games left on the tour. But someone took pictures of us all in the bar, and an image of Teddy Sheringham, sitting in the Dentist's Chair in a ripped £5 Umbro T-shirt, was plastered across the papers back home. We were slaughtered for that. Yes, we'd had too much to drink, but we did not cause any trouble and Euro '96 was a long way off.

The media found another stick to beat us with over our return journey. After a day's shopping in Hong Kong, we boarded a late-night plane bound for home. We sat around on the top deck either playing cards or sleeping for the 14-hour flight. Everything seemed normal. But some of the radio media guys on board with us had sent reports through that the England team had smashed the plane up. A big thing was made of it. By the time we arrived back at Heathrow the media was out in force, ready for a feeding frenzy on the England 'wrecking crew'. They were definitely on our case!

The whole thing was based on one cracked television screen, which had been accidentally damaged and which the players offered to pay for. It was something dealt with quietly by the squad as a whole rather than individuals taking any blame, and would have remained in-house but for those reports.

All this, however, was just part of being in the public eye. It was intense when we played for our clubs, but it was a different ball game when it came to England. I am very patriotic and was so proud to represent my country. You are – in a sporting sense – going to war for your country and, if you do it right, the people will love you for it. It was such an honour. It always gave me a massive buzz to put on the shirt with the Three Lions crest, but being able to do it as part of a squad in such a big tournament gave it an added dimension.

The fact that Euro '96 was part of the Cool Britannia thing that was going on made everything even more special. The movement was a renewal of British pride through its culture, just like the time of Swinging London in the 1960s. The *Football's Coming Home* song, recorded by comedians Frank Skinner and David Baddiel with musician Ian Broudie of the Lightning Seeds, emphasised that we were at the centre of it.

I was made very much aware of this when we set off for Wembley to play Switzerland in our opening group game on Saturday 8 June 1996. I sat there on the coach with Teddy Sheringham next to me looking out of the window and fans lined the street all the way from our Burnham Beeches hotel in Buckinghamshire. How they knew our exact route I didn't know, but I didn't care. It was fantastic they were there.

Alan Shearer put *Football's Coming Home* on the CD player when we came in sight of the Twin Towers, which are now, sadly, no longer there. The lads got right into it when they heard that song. If we didn't already feel patriotic and proud enough, that swelled our chests even more.

It was like Groundhog Day each time we played in the tournament, with the supporters out on the streets and Alan acting as DJ, with the 80,000 crowd adding their version of Skinner and Baddiel's song when we stepped into the arena from our dressing rooms to taste the atmosphere. It made the hairs on the back of my neck stand up each time I looked up from the tunnel where we stood before getting changed.

I tried to keep things as normal as possible in the dressing room, have a massage and remain subdued. I didn't want to get too over-excited before playing a huge game at Wembley. You could not have got bigger matches than the ones we played there during the tournament. To be in this situation was everything I'd wished for growing up. Everything.

I was one of a few quiet youngsters in the room, although overall it was noisy. There were a lot of characters, like Gazza and Paul Ince. They were absolute lunatics and really up for it. Incey was a great person to have in your team as a leader. He wanted to get out there and win tackles – not kick people. He was one of several capable of carrying the team. Tony Adams and Stuart Pearce were immense men. There were top internationals like Alan Shearer, Teddy Sheringham and David Platt, players I'd watched and had so much respect for. I felt like a raw-boned kid. Steve McManaman and I were the youngsters charged with playing the worst role in the world at wing-back, having to get up and down the flanks.

I was inwardly thinking that although I had got myself in my dream situation, the reality of flying the flag of St George on the biggest of football stages was daunting. After all, it was bloody important. The nation was expecting us win the competition, just like the Boys of '66 had theirs.

Terry Venables was a calming influence in the dressing room. He didn't shout and scream. Terry knew how to get the best out of people. He certainly did with me, instilling self-belief by telling me to 'be the player that you are'. He filled me with confidence and did the same for the other players. What really made him a good coach, each time we readied ourselves to open the door and walk up that world-famous tunnel, was his ability to make you feel at ease, which was exactly what I needed.

It was a blistering hot afternoon when we kicked off the tournament against the Swiss. There was an opening ceremony beforehand, something I'd never experienced. It was like a circus show. Then we came on as the star attractions. We were supposed to saunter through the match against a side which included defender Ramon Vega, who was to join me at Tottenham the following year.

The week leading up to the game had been a long one because we were champing at the bit to kick-off the tournament after all the build-up. A big deal was made out of the fact Alan Shearer hadn't scored for about 12 matches. I never doubted him, though. He was an absolute goalscorer. Selfish. His main aim was always to hit the back of the net, and he wasn't happy unless he was succeeding in doing that. He had that mindset, one any top striker has to have.

Typically, Shearer netted when it mattered against Vega and Co. We had created a few chances before Al put us in front midway through the opening half with a great finish. We could have added to it before the interval.

The whole stadium became very edgy during the second half when the Swiss began to get a bit of possession. What made nerves jangle even more was the weather. It wasn't nice for players more used to cold weather than hot. We laboured as the sweat dripped off us. The heat also ensured the pitch was sticky, which meant the ball did not run nicely. We usually played our internationals at Wembley in the evening, when there was a bit of dew on the ground, which allowed the ball to zip around.

Before you knew it, we'd conceded a penalty with just a few minutes left. Stuart Pearce was adjudged to have handled, although I don't think it was intentional. Kubilay Turkyilmaz beat David Seaman from the spot.

A 1–1 draw was not good enough for a lot of people. The feelgood factor surrounding England turned to feelbad. I didn't play well. I'd obviously got out of bed the wrong side and my fitness was not what I had hoped for. It was all probably due to nerves, but it didn't excuse my display. It was my worst performance for England.

It was the first time I thought my place in the England team was in jeopardy. But eight or nine of us must have thought the same thing. Lots of people didn't play well. We went to pieces. We sat back in the dressing room devastated. Terry told us: 'That was 45 minutes of hell. You were nowhere near good enough. You don't need me to tell you that. You've got to be better than that. It was baking, but you were giving the ball away too much. You need to keep it. Simple. We can't do anything now so go off and relax, behave yourselves and we'll start again Monday.'

When we met up at the hotel on Monday lunch time, I went up to Teddy's room. We just sat there and said to each other 'What the hell happened there?' It was almost unbelievable that the team and we as individuals had played so badly. Embarrassing. We both sensed that we had got worse and worse when the crowd turned against us. They had been looking forward to the tournament for so long and felt let down and cheated. We gave the ball away, looked unfit and couldn't string two passes together. It was horrible.

When we were one up, our confidence was high and the spectators were buzzing, thinking we were going to go on and win 3–0 or 4–0. The fact that we didn't upset all the players too.

The press immediately brought back up all the stuff about the Dentist's Chair and the 'wrecking' of the plane as well as, rightly, panning our performance.

Sol Campbell and Teddy Sheringham had been pictured coming out of a nightclub in Gants Hill, Essex after the Swiss game and the media asked: 'What were they doing out after such a bad performance and result?' Even though it was a week before we played again! Whatever we did, it seemed the media were against us. It was a good thing for team spirit because it strengthened our bond, but it meant we had to be careful what we did and said.

Terry used his common sense again, explaining that if he gave us time off again overnight the media would come down on us like a ton of bricks no matter what we were doing. So he wouldn't be able to do that again. He decided that on the days after games we could go and meet family and friends for the day, but had to be back in the hotel by 10pm. The boys understood and respected him for the way he dealt with things like that.

We wanted to put things right straight away after a nightmare game, but had to wait another seven days before getting the opportunity. It was a long week stuck in a hotel. In our down time, we ended up either playing computer games in our rooms or being on the phone to family and friends. The boredom was lifted when other games were on. The lads would have a bet on via our local bookies of Platt and Shearer. None of us could wait for the next match so we could blow away all the negativity.

That was our mindset as we stepped out against the auld enemy, Scotland, in another afternoon date at Wembley the following Saturday. Terry could have panicked and made four or five changes, telling players they were useless. But he kept the same team and told us it was still one he thought good enough to win the whole thing. He reminded us that we hadn't got beaten by Switzerland, although we were poor. The previous Saturday was history. It was onwards and upwards.

11

Feelgood-bad Factor

I felt the feel-good factor at Euro '96 return for England when the whole team repaid the faith Terry Venables had shown in us by defeating Scotland on Saturday 15 June. It convinced the players and staff we could follow the Boys of '66 into our sporting history books. And the rest of the nation was united in the same belief. Everyone sensed that football was coming home.

A victory for the hosts over its auld enemy brought the tournament alive in blistering sunshine on an afternoon in which we refused to wilt. After our second-half rollover against the Swiss the previous week, anything less and we knew the bubble would be burst beyond repair. All of us involved in the squad would be hung, drawn and quartered and laid out to dry. And Cool Britannia would become decidedly uncool. There was so much at stake. The pressure on us was intense.

I knew what Terry wanted from me: get on the ball, pass it and cross it into the box – and get up and down the pitch. I'd done it all for him at Tottenham. He knew what I was all about. I didn't feel I had to go out there and prove anything to him. I always loved to play for him because I knew he believed in me.

There were plenty of pre-match nerves as we looked out at the pitch before the game. I was chatting to my Tottenham teammate Colin Calderwood, who was going to be on the other side that day. My Mum and Dad were there. It was weird for Dad because he was Scottish but, as I've said, there was no question of divided loyalties for him. He just wanted the side I was playing for to win, but he was chuffed when I gave him the Scotland shirt I'd got off opposing midfielder John Collins afterwards!

I spotted Mum in her posh seat during the National Anthem before kick-off. As we stood there respectfully, she was waving her arms around and pointing. I wondered what her eccentric and embarrassing behaviour was all about. Then I realised the singer Rod Stewart, a big Scotland football fan, was sitting directly in front of her and she wanted to show me. My Mum loves Rod Stewart. Whether she was watching him or the game after it kicked off, I'm not sure.

It was more like a Premier League game than an international. Lots of hustle and bustle. The soaring temperatures didn't suit either side early on. The quality of the football wasn't good and we weren't playing that well. We went in at half-time at 0–0. It had been a terrible half.

At half-time we brought on Jamie Redknapp and he immediately made a difference as we started to pass it around a lot better. A few minutes after the restart, Alan Shearer gave us the lead. Off the field Alan had a dry sense of humour and liked to have a good time, but on the field he was all business, such a winner. And he had already put himself about, crashing into Scotland defender and Blackburn teammate Colin Hendry. If you see your centre-forward doing that it inspires you to step up and close down. Alan got his reward for his part in lifting our spirits with his goal. A nice move saw Steve McManaman feed Gary Neville, who crossed to the far post for Alan to head the ball in. Cue Alan's trademark right-arm-up salute as he wheeled away in celebration with me and the others chasing after him. It was fantastic. The stadium went crazy. We started to dominate. I shot narrowly over and Teddy had an effort saved as our game flowed confidently after the goal.

However, Scotland upped their performance and played better than we thought they would. They started to test us and got a penalty when Tony Adams was adjudged to have fouled Gordon Durie. All the bad memories from seven days before came flooding back. Fortunately for us there was no equaliser for our opposition this time. Gary McAllister hit his shot straight down the middle, and luckily for us it hit David Seaman's thigh and flew over the bar. The relief I felt then was incredible. The stadium erupted. It was as important as us scoring a goal.

A couple of minutes later I helped make the final score 2–0. Teddy Sheringham brought down the ball from a goal-kick by David and knocked it out to me on the left. I saw Gazza make a run and played the ball over the top first time, straight in to his path. He flicked the ball over Colin Hendry and smashed it past Scotland goalkeeper Andy Goram. The fact Andy was a Glasgow Rangers teammate made the moment even sweeter for Gazza.

Given the grief we had all got in Hong Kong, Gazza mimicked drinking in the Dentist's Chair as he celebrated. It was absolutely brilliant: the best goal celebration ever. It was just typical Gazza and an iconic moment in English football folklore, which has been rerun more than any other when Euro '96 or Gazza have cropped up in retrospectives on television. Terry, who, as we know, had been a mentor to Gazza like he had been for me, was so happy for him.

Although we hadn't played brilliantly, we'd done OK. It had been all about beating Scotland. We weren't allowed home but had a quiet few drinks to celebrate in the bar of the Burnham Beeches Hotel, which we had to ourselves. The burden of the nation's disapproval at our perceived misdemeanours and opening-day performance had been lifted. The public were back onside and that made us relax.

We now needed a draw against Holland in our final group game at Wembley three days later to make sure of getting to the quarter-finals. It was no easy task. The Dutch had been a force in world football since their Total Football team of the 1974 World Cup, led by Johan Cruyff. Each player could fill in the role of the others in a fluid system developed by Cruyff's first club side, Ajax. From what I've seen on television, video and DVD, it was some side and they should have been world champions that year.

I've viewed the start they made after the kick-off in their final against West Germany; a 13-pass move with Cruyff forcing a penalty from which Johan Neeskens put them in front. The Germans hadn't even touched the ball. Amazing. The Dutch side, still to be feared even without Cruyff, might also have lifted the Cup four years later, again losing in the Final, to Argentina.

With Marco van Basten and Ruud Gullit, the Flying Dutchmen proved worthy successors to their 1970s equivalents by winning the 1988 European Championships. Dennis Bergkamp inspired them to the semi-finals of the 1992 Euros, and the quarter-finals of the World Cup two years later. Bergkamp, at the start of a phenomenal career with Arsenal, was still around to bolster a strong Dutch team against our side.

Holland also included Patrick Kluivert of Ajax and later AC Milan and Barcelona, Edwin van der Sar, the Ajax 'keeper who joined Manchester United in 2005, and Johan Cruyff's son Jordi, who signed for Manchester United two months later from Barcelona. They were no slouches, that's for sure. They had been held to a goalless draw by Scotland and beaten Switzerland 2–0.

A win for either side would decide the group winners, and fortunately for us we proved the time was up for the team dubbed Clockwork Orange (after Anthony Burgess's novel because of the colour of their shirts) as far as that ambition was concerned. The vibes were good for us in the wake of our victory against Scotland. When we went out for the warm-up 40 minutes before the game the stadium was beginning to fill. Ten minutes later it was packed with 80,000 singing *Football's Coming Home* once more.

We produced probably the best performance of any team I'd played in. Everything clicked. Everything Terry had wanted us to do and had preached for two years we did. Everything just fell into place against one of the pre-favourites for the tournament.

The unofficial anthem, words penned by a couple of patriotic comics, rang around the stadium non-stop through the second half. It was an incredible environment and one I had never even dreamed of being in. You couldn't hear yourself think. It gave me goosebumps. The hairs on the back of my neck actually stood up. We were 4–0 up (the SAS team of Shearer and Sheringham each scored twice, with Teddy's second coming after Edwin Van der Saar had spilled my long-range shot), against one of the world's better teams at Wembley under the lights, and there were 80,000 people singing their hearts out. It was the stuff that dreams are made of. Of course, all my family and my friends were there.

I was extra proud to be English. I ran around smiling, without a care in the world. The fact it was at night certainly suited us more than a hot afternoon. We didn't like playing in the heat, as we'd proved at this very tournament. The only blemish on the evening came when Kluivert scored a late goal to put his side through at the expense of Scotland. It would have been nice for my Dad if his homeland had been represented in the quarter-finals. Still, given the traditional animosity between us and the country north of the border, I'm sure a lot of those waving the white-and-red flag of St George would have been delighted that the white-and-dark-blue colours of St Andrew had been lowered.

We faced a bloody good Spain team in the quarter-finals on 22 June at Wembley. The Spanish had not lost in 19 games since the 1994 World Cup. They also had the great Real Madrid defender Fernando Hierro and Miguel Angel Nadal, the uncle of current tennis ace Rafa and known as the Beast, because of his beefy, physical style for his country and club Barcelona.

Again it was a Saturday afternoon, but fortunately it was cooler than the two previous matches played during the tournament. As we were a decent side too, we cancelled each other out. There were a few half-chances for both sides. I had one in the second half after I picked up a ball from Alan Shearer and shot wide. It couldn't have been the best match in the world to watch. It went into extra-time and tension was in the air. It looked as though we were headed for a penalty shoot-out.

I remembered how England had come undone in their last major spot-kick drama at a major international tournament when we lost to West Germany in the semi-finals of the 1990 World Cup. Gary Lineker had forced extra-time with a late equaliser and we had to face up to the ordeal from 12 yards. Gary, whom Terry had brought to Spurs before I was with the club, Peter Beardsley and David Platt netted. But Stuart Pearce had his saved and Chris Waddle, who had left Spurs for Marseille the year before, shot over before the Germans sealed their place in the Final. It was agony watching it on those television screens in Dallas. I felt so bad for Stuart and Chris.

We were determined history would not repeat itself when it was confirmed we had to face a nerve-shredding shoot-out against Spain. I had gone off for the last 10 minutes as I'd run myself to a standstill. Watching as my brave teammates stepped up to the plate was torture. I thought: 'Oh my God, this tournament could be all over for us in the next 10 minutes. We've got to win the shoot-out.' When would we get the chance to win a major title in our own country again? The feelgood factor from Wednesday would melt away and become meaningless.

I knew we had good penalty-takers. Alan Shearer and David Platt scored their penalties before Stuart had to deal with his demons from six years earlier as he prepared to take the third. You could cut the tension with a knife. I didn't turn away, keeping focussed on Stuart. The next second he'd thumped the ball home before racing to the crowd, clenching his fists and roaring like a lion in his Three Lions-crested shirt. It was another iconic moment. What bottle. What character! Gazza guided in the fourth. Hierro had missed his shot for Spain, but it wasn't until Nadal had his effort saved by David Seaman that it was over. Getting through on penalties was good for our confidence.

Four days later, on Wednesday 26 June 1996, came the moment of truth under the lights at Wembley, a balmy evening after a sunny day. The whole country was up for it. The Germans had a good team, with Andy Moller, Matthias Zammer and Stefan Kuntz, and two players who would go on to be Tottenham teammates, Christian Ziege and Steffen Freund. But we felt we were not going to be beaten by anyone.

We had developed into a side playing in the keep-possession style you associate with top international football teams, rather than the high-tempo tradition of the British Leagues. We had one change from the win against Spain with Paul Ince returning from suspension in place of Gary Neville, and we kicked off passing the ball for fun. Teddy came deeper to get more involved, and we scored after just a few minutes.

Gazza hit a short corner for Tony Adams to flick on at the near post for Alan to head home his fifth goal of the tournament. Everything was going to plan, then a few minutes later they snatched a freak goal. They had a shot which deflected right to Stefan Kuntz, who slipped it into the net. It was a goal out of nothing. They certainly did not deserve it on the balance of play.

We continued to play well. I had a good time against Christian, who was marking me, and got in a load of crosses. It seemed like only a matter of time before we scored. They held out until half-time and both sides played lots of good football. In the second half, there were a few half chances, but none were converted and the game went into extra-time. And it was in that 30 minutes that I came within the width of a post of putting my country into the Final.

The Golden Goal rule had been introduced to the competition for the first time, which meant that if a match went into extra-time the first or 'golden' goal would decide it. My almost-golden moment arrived from a Steve McManaman cross just a couple of minutes in. He'd been put through down the right and I made my run into the box as I could see he was free. I anticipated he would pull the ball back to me a fraction sooner than he did and was almost too far in when the ball came across slightly behind me, with Steve trying to avoid 'keeper Andreas Kropke getting to it. I got a touch as I stretched back to hook the ball goalwards, but was unable to squeeze it into the goal.

Instead, it hit the post and bounced into Kropke's arms. Oh my Lord! It was heartbreaking. I could have been a hero. A celebration had been planned in anticipation of a winning goal where we'd all just run straight down the tunnel. And I would have led it.

Then Alan Shearer volleyed a low cross for Gazza, who just hesitated and missed the ball by the width of a stud as he slid into an empty net. Again the celebration was put on hold as we went to penalties for the second match in succession.

It was probably one of my better performances for England. I felt great in myself. It was my fifth game at the tournament and I was now at peak fitness. The only thing I was short of was practice at taking penalties. I didn't figure in the first five of our takers, who had worked on theirs between the past couple of games while I rested from training, struggling with my back and hamstrings. It was planned that Gareth Southgate would take the sixth, if it was needed, and I volunteered for the seventh. I wanted the opportunity to do something about our situation if I was needed, even though I was certainly no expert, with Teddy our regular penalty-taker back at Tottenham.

The quintet – Alan Shearer, David Platt, Stuart Pearce, Gazza and Teddy – all scored. But the Germans' top five were also successful, as the rest of us stood going through the all the emotions on the halfway line. We were fortunate to have so many top class penalty-takers.

Gareth, not a regular penalty taker, struck his spot-kick well, but unfortunately Kropke went the right way and saved it and Andy Moller ensured that Germany went through when he beat David Seaman a minute or two later. Who knows whether I'd have done any better than Gareth? The 'keeper dives one way and you get it right or wrong. Everyone consoled Gareth. It was awful for him. Players don't think badly of others if they don't score from the spot. You know it is easily done. You can hit a penalty well and the 'keeper will save it, or you can mis-hit it and see the ball bobble over the line. There's no magic formula. You need a bit of luck in those situations – and we did not get any.

The fact remained that we were out. It hit me hard. It was so disappointing. I knew we were the better team. I walked around the pitch applauding the fans who had been so fantastic at the end of our draining semi-final. The season was over and we were either going home or on holiday to recharge. No one wanted to go home. No one wanted to go on holiday. Not until after the Final. My mindset was one of disbelief. I couldn't take it in. I'd convinced myself we were set for the Final.

It was a long night. We got back on the coach. People were everywhere. It might have been midnight on our last journey back to the hotel, but the fans were on the streets cheering. They were so good to us and I felt so bad that myself and my teammates had been unable to give them what they wanted. God knows what they'd have been like if we had won!

The Germans went on to beat the Czech Republic in the Final. It was my old Spurs teammate Jürgen Klinsmann who received the glittering prize from Queen Elizabeth II as their captain. Jürgen's team were the favourites and justified that position (they went on to adopt *Football's Coming Home* as they celebrated on their return to the Fatherland), but we too would have been fancied to beat the Czechs.

Time's a great healer, so they say, and when I look back on Euro '96 I feel privileged to have been a part of it because it meant so much to the nation. I'd played very well against Holland, Spain and Germany.

The difficulty of playing international football is that you don't have an understanding with most of your teammates. But that understanding with my fellow England squad members came quickly that summer. Terry had collected some top, top players. Tony Adams was the captain, but there were loads of skippers in the squad: Stuart Pearce, Alan Shearer, David Platt, Paul Ince and Teddy Sheringham. I learned so much from them and others.

Alan Shearer taught me what self-belief was all about. He had so much of it. His confidence was not arrogance, but you knew he knew he was top dollar. And of course, he showed himself to be a great goalscorer. If you gave him good service he would hit the back of the net. Stuart 'Psycho' Pearce, who had whacked me into touch in that FA Cup tie when I was a raw beginner with Portsmouth and he was lining up for Nottingham Forest, displayed so much strength of character, especially with that penalty against Spain. And I loved every second of playing with Teddy in such a prestigious tournament. Of course, I had the advantage of him being my teammate at Tottenham. He was someone I connected with when he had joined Spurs shortly after I did. We just clicked on and off the pitch. When we played we had an almost telepathic thing going. I knew when he was thinking of making a pass and vice versa. If I knocked it 40 yards, he'd be right there, control the ball and knock it off to the winger. It was almost like a pattern of play, but it wasn't something we practised. We just knew what the other was thinking. It was instinctive. He was a clever player. We were on the same wavelength. It was so easy. I was saddened he left Tottenham for Manchester United from a playing point of view, but we remained friends. I was delighted for him when he helped United win the 1999 Treble and that he got one of the two late goals which completed it in the Champions League Final win over Bayern Munich.

Gazza showed me how important it was to use individual ability, which he had by the lorry load, for the side as a whole. He wore his heart on his sleeve, as we all knew from those tears back in Italy in 1990, a time when I felt he was the best player in the world. Gazza was a real larger-than-life character, often at the centre of some media frenzy over his public and private life, upsetting managers and the FA, while being adored by the public along the way. He was a one-off. But as a footballer, he showed throughout Euro '96 that he was the complete team player. Nothing else mattered but serving the side. That's what made him a true superstar. It was all about football for him. He was great to have around the squad too. Every one of us loved his company. Gazza was so genuine. No side to him. He was what he was. Such a nice fellow. He had continued to put himself out for me; to give me advice and morale boosts since that time just before my England debut against Denmark two years earlier. It was incredible to get the opportunity to play with him.

I learned the most from Terry Venables: how to cope, how to play, how to behave. Part of my motivation for wanting England to win Euro '96 was to give something back to the manager who meant the most to me. We knew the end of the tournament meant the end of his reign. He had told us the previous December that he would not be renewing his contract with England, which expired at its conclusion. We got the impression that some of the suits inside the governing body's headquarters were far from committed to backing the best manager our country had had since Sir Alf Ramsey. All the players – to a man – were choked that Terry left. Life can be full of 'if onlys'. But I can't help wondering what difference Terry – who only lost one of 23 matches in charge – would have made to our showing at the 1998 World Cup had he carried on.

Euro '96 for me was an incredible experience. I was so grateful to have got myself fit enough to have taken part. It's left me with memories I will never forget.

I'd played my 10th full match in one day short of two months, three with Spurs and the rest with England. I felt ready to play a season of football. Instead I had to get ready to pack my bags for a summer break until the 1996–97 campaign got underway.

I booked a holiday for myself and my new girlfriend Kate in Antigua. Within two days, however, the breezes were whipping up into something far from balmy. More like barmy! There was a weather warning. I had a word with the people at the hotel who told us it would be fine. Then we asked some locals, who told us it wouldn't be. They said it would be raining for two weeks solid and the winds would get stronger. We decided to cut our losses, called friends in Washington DC and immediately flew out to visit them. Two days later a hurricane hit Antigua. We only just escaped one in Florida this year. I've done well to steer clear of them – so far.

Three weeks after the end of Euro '96 I was back at Tottenham for pre-season training. I hadn't had much of a rest. I didn't need one, though; I was buzzing and champing at the bit to get a full season under my belt.

12
Faith

Alan Shearer, my teammate for England at Euro '96, was big news in the wake of the tournament. He joined hometown club Newcastle United from Blackburn Rovers for a British record £15 million and went on to top the Premier League scoring charts.

Unfortunately for me, the 1996–97 term saw the start of a return to the dark days of the previous campaign. Far from enjoying a full season again, I had an early indication that I might have some more problems when I came off just over an hour into the opening League fixture against a Blackburn side dealing with the big hole left by their ace marksman. We might have won 2–0 at Ewood Park that day, but I was preoccupied with a groin problem. It felt terrible.

I played in our first home match of the campaign against Derby. We were cruising it until they got a last-minute equaliser and I had to come off with the wretched groin injury. I struggled on for a couple more games before seeing Dr Gilmore, the groin and hernia surgeon, in Harley Street. He told me the 'mesh' treatment I'd had the previous season hadn't worked and that I needed another operation. I had been right with my comments after the QPR game the previous season – the operation had been a failure.

I decided to put off the op and try to play on, but struggled in the next couple of games before my Dad said to me: 'Stop f***ing about and get it done. You're not doing yourself any favours continuing with it.' I took his advice and the operation went well with Dr Gilmore. The only trouble was that the rehab ensured I was sidelined for almost a month.

When I came back for a 2–0 home win against Sunderland, I felt fine. Sadly for me, that did not last. The club looked into finding out what was causing the problems I had had and sent me to a so-called expert. He studied my gait on a treadmill and concluded that one of my legs was shorter than the other. He fitted me with orthotic insoles to 'balance' them out. As I found out later, the diagnosis was wrong and my legs only appeared uneven because my back was out when they measured them.

After a couple of months I started playing again before I suffered my first major hamstring trouble against Leeds at White Hart Lane on 15

March 1997. I had put us in the lead and we were en route to completing a 1–0 victory when, in the last minute, I felt something 'pop' as I went past their Republic of Ireland full-back Gary Kelly. I wondered what the hell it was at first, thinking it might be cramp. The physio thought it might be too. But it turned out I'd torn my hamstring. That was me done for almost another month. I believe the fact my backbone was not in alignment due to the orthotic insoles caused it. It was something I subsequently tried to blank out of my mind, but recalling it has made me appreciate what a horror story it was. The orthotics really did me a big favour – not!

I attempted to return at Hillsborough, where we lost 2–1 to Sheffield Wednesday, and the hamstring cramped up again. It got into a pattern. I returned just over three weeks on from that when we took on Liverpool at Anfield and – after I scored in what turned out to be another 2–1 reverse – the muscle seized again early in the second half.

I was a glutton for punishment, it seemed, because the setbacks never stopped me coming back for more. It was another depressing period of not being able to find a solution to a problem. This was my career here. I didn't know whether I could find a way to continue at the top level. Again, my friends and family were a great crutch for me.

Finally, I went and saw a specialist in Sweden, whom Tony Lenaghan found. The guy told me my back and hamstrings needed strengthening. It was at this time that Glenn Hoddle asked me to go and see faith healer Eileen Drewery as he felt she would help me recover from the injury. Faith-healing was something I didn't believe in and I told him I'd seen a specialist in Sweden who had already told me what I needed to do over the summer.

The 1996–97 season had been a disappointing season for the club and for me personally. We lost early in the FA Cup and League Cup. And finishing 10th was our lowest position since Gerry Francis had taken over, and brought calls for him to be sacked from some fans. Perhaps if I could have played more I might have been able to ease the pressure on him, but it was just not possible.

I went to America to see my mates in the summer of 1997, and while I was there worked daily in the gym building up the weak areas in my body that had been diagnosed by the Scandinavian expert.

One night when we were there, we had a night out I'll never forget. Me and my mates Joe, Dave and Bert were in a group that visited some bars in Philadelphia. We went to a club which you entered via a lift to the eighth floor.

Dave nearly fell asleep at the bar because he had been out coaching all day in 100 degree heat, and the drink had obviously gone straight to his head. A bouncer came over and grabbed him and said: 'You're out!'

Joe replied: 'OK, we're just leaving. Let us grab our credit card from behind the bar to close our tab.'

Another bouncer turned up, grabbed Joe and now both brothers were being marched over to the lifts. I got my credit card back and went to grab our other friends who were on the dance floor, but I stopped in my tracks as I looked over to the lifts to see Joe's head being smashed against the doors continuously by this bouncer. I headed over there and said: 'What the hell is going on?'

As I said it, the doors opened and I was shoved inside the lift with Dave and Joe and the bouncers. Next thing I knew we were being clubbed with batons. I just tried to protect my head. When the doors opened at the bottom, Joe was on the floor with blood pouring out of his head. He got up and we all walked out. As we got outside, Dave turned round to the bouncers and said: 'You f***ing arseholes. You could have killed my brother!'

With that, they chased him and he tripped. They started clubbing and kicking him in the head in front of the many people hanging around outside. It was like watching the video of the Rodney King incident in 1991, the one which saw police charged with brutality against the young black man after using batons and which sparked riots in LA when the officers were acquitted the following year.

What happened to us was awful. The bouncers didn't care who was there.

Dave went off in an ambulance and had a CAT scan. Thankfully, he was OK. Joe had stitches in his head. I was lucky and just got a black eye and a bruised ear. We went to the police station and pressed charges. The boys sued and got a settlement.

With my stop-start season I'd missed out on England's 1998 World Cup qualifying matches under Glenn Hoddle. Moldova were beaten in Chisinau in Glenn's first game in charge and Poland and Georgia were dispatched home and away. But Italy beat us at Wembley with a Gianfranco Zola goal on 9 November 1996.

I remember going to the game with some of my American friends. We fancied a bite to eat and a drink after it and went to the Atlantic Bar in London, a regular haunt for us. I was at the bar ordering drinks and a bloke, from two yards away, said to me: 'You Spurs wanker'. I ignored him, just thinking to myself: 'What an arsehole'.

Five minutes later the same guy came up to me and asked whether I wanted a drink. I said: 'No thanks,' and carried on my conversation with my friends. He persisted.

'Why don't you want a drink?

'Because firstly I already have one, and secondly you just called me a wanker,' I replied.

I sat down with my friends, had dinner and forgot about it. Later I went to the toilet, making sure one of my friends came with me. It was something I always did when I was out in London, in case some idiot had a go. While we were in there the guy who had called me a wanker came in and started complaining I hadn't accepted a drink from him. As I stood in front of him, he decided to head butt me. A security guy, who must have been alerted to what was going on, came in and the stranger denied the head butt. As he did so, a red mark appeared on his forehead! I started laughing as I pointed the mark out to the bouncer. He was then thrown out.

When we went back to the table, the mate who was with me, Dave, told the story. On hearing this, Scottie, a friend in our group from New York, went outside and asked the bouncer to identify the culprit, who was climbing into a cab.

Scottie removed his jacket, walked over, hit the guy about four or five times, put his jacket back on, shook the guard by the hand and rejoined us. It was classic! So cool. No bullshit! The New Yorker had seen me unmolested on my countless visits to America – he wasn't around for the Philly incident – and could not accept what the idiot had done.

Obviously, it was all part of being a professional footballer. Something, as I've said, I learned as a former Portsmouth player when visiting Southampton, where fortunately one of my friends, Dave Fudge, who used to work as a bouncer in the city, knew the current doorman of the club we used and would always ensure we were warned of potential trouble.

Unpleasantness was something I always tried to avoid, and in the end I started having nights out in Bournemouth rather than my home city, which was not a problem because my new girlfriend Kate came from there. Also, by that time, I had a house in the area.

While in America in the summer of 1997, I was happy to sweat it out in the gym in the belief I'd be available to my club and country through the season leading up to the World Cup Finals. My optimism dissipated on my return. The first morning back at pre-season training for the 1997–98 campaign went well. But my mood changed after I went off to see a specialist that afternoon to check the strength of my hamstrings on a Cybex exercise machine. I got onto it and tried to push to my max. The results showed that I had obviously done plenty of work in the summer.

I went to the cinema that night and started feeling discomfort in my hamstrings as they stiffened. It was absolutely dreadful. That was it. I was back to square one with the hamstring trouble I'd picked up in that moment with Gary Kelly. My summer in the gym had been wasted by one day of pre-season.

Once again the tale of my injury woe was in all the papers. Glenn saw a copy of one at the airport as he was waiting for his flight to go on holiday and gave me a call from the terminal. He said: 'Is it true what the papers are saying?'

'Yes,' I said. 'My hamstring feels terrible.' This time he was more insistent when he said

'Please go and see Eileen. You have nothing to lose and I think she will be able to help you.' I agreed to go and he gave me her number.

My Mum believed in that sort of thing. She was also convinced it was unlucky to cross on the stairs and cut your nails every day. I used to tease her about these superstitions by calling her a witch! But she told me I should go and see Eileen Drewery. However, I remained very sceptical.

I wasn't alone. Glenn had suggested all the players should visit her if they had problems. Not many bothered to find out if there was any credence to the claims Glenn made on Eileen's behalf. At this point, I didn't know what else to do. So I called Eileen to arrange a meeting and went round to see her later that day. I'm glad I did.

I remember going to her pleasant little house out in the country around Bracknell in Berkshire. I rang Eileen Drewery's doorbell wondering if I had made the right decision. Was she a crackpot, as she had been portrayed in the press? I found her to be a lovely lady, who was very welcoming and very caring. I went into a room and sat on a chair. I explained how my hamstring kept seizing up and not allowing me to run for two weeks afterwards. I sat on a chair and she placed her hands on my head. Next she put them on my back and hamstrings.

She told me that I had a contracting muscle in my lower back and that both of my hamstrings needed to be manually stretched, otherwise each would tighten up every time I tried to exercise. Eileen obviously didn't understand anything about the body medically speaking, but she told me the solution had just come to her.

It was bizarre, but the first time I left her I felt like a different person, one who was convinced this woman had resolved what had been ailing me for so long. And she was proved right, providing me with the opportunity to devise a simple and effective stretch which I used for the rest of my career. My hamstring still tightens if I don't have a manual stretch now, even if it is just for a short run over the park, but as I'm retired I don't care if I have to walk around as stiff as a board for a week.

Back when I was playing, of course, the stretch was crucial and, without exaggeration, saved me from packing it in. From the moment I discovered that Eileen's idea worked, the physios at my clubs and country complied with my wishes and helped me extend my career to 18 years. The media might have ridiculed Eileen Drewery, but I had not seen myself getting fit before she laid her hands on me.

As I hadn't believed in what she did before I went to see her, I never pushed any players to go to her. But I did receive calls from many – including England teammates – asking for her number. What Eileen was able to do definitely worked for some. I did feel for her with the bad press she got. It was all blown out of proportion. That might have been caused by Glenn putting too much emphasis on her value to the set-up. He wanted her to travel with the squad to the World Cup Finals in France. It seemed as though he thought she was the difference between us winning the World Cup and not winning it. Obviously not everyone would agree with his opinion. The accepted wisdom was that to win a World Cup all you needed were the players, management and coaching staff. Not many were willing to use their imagination and accept that something beyond our ken might make a difference. All I know is that what Eileen Drewery did worked for me.

In the meantime, Teddy had left Spurs for Manchester United in June – to replace the legendary Eric Cantona, no less – after turning down a deal from Alan Sugar. As Teddy was my best friend in the game, we kept in touch. And he phoned me one night to let me know how much Alan Sugar had offered him, which was the same amount I was earning. To replace Teddy, Les Ferdinand was brought in, along with another summer signing, David Ginola.

Unfortunately, I had to wait a couple of months for my first game of the season due to injury. It came after that call I mentioned earlier from Alan Sugar, in which he asked whether, due to injury, I would go on the bench to give 'everyone a lift'. I was close to a return and scheduled to play in a reserves match, but I was only too happy to be involved against Sheffield Wednesday at White Hart Lane on 19 October 1997; the game Alan Sugar had referred to in our telephone conversation.

I sat there for most of the Premiership fixture as we cruised to a 3–0 lead, but came on for the latter stages after Wednesday had pulled back two goals back. It was 15 minutes of hell, to be honest, because I didn't want to do any damage. Thankfully, I didn't.

A couple of weeks later we played at Liverpool in my first start of the season. It was a nightmare. We lost 4–0. This proved to be Gerry's last game as he'd decided to call it a day. I was devastated. It was a strange time for me, very upsetting. I'd got on well with Gerry. He was one of the main reasons I stayed when I could have joined Manchester United. He was one of my favourite managers. I had been desperate to play for Gerry as well for my own sake. He was such a hard-working and meticulous manager who so wanted to be successful with Spurs.

I believe he left QPR for the challenge and not the amount of money he would earn. He'd always banged on about the Alex Ferguson philosophy of leaving nothing to chance in preparation. And there were hopes we could clinch a place in a European competition for the following season. But it wasn't going to plan. Gerry had lost Teddy, of course, our chief source of goals since he came from Nottingham Forest five years before, to Fergie at Old Trafford. And my being out for the first couple of months of the season hadn't helped matters.

David Ginola might have arrived with 'Sir Les' from Newcastle at the start of the season but, just as at the end of the previous term, things were not looking great for 1997–98.

I might now be able to play my part at last, thanks largely to the help of Eileen and the physio willing to do the hamstring exercise prior to each match. But we were in the relegation zone and Alan Sugar received more hostility than he had ever done from the supporters. It was evident that something needed to change.

The following morning, after the Liverpool game, while I was in bed watching TV, Alan Sugar was on talking about how he'd tried to convince Gerry to stay on. For some reason, he also started talking about Teddy and Les Ferdinand, saying that Les had signed for the same contract offered to Teddy. As there was a clause in my contract in which I had to be the top paid player at Tottenham by £5,000 a week, I thought: 'You cheeky f**k!' I called Leon and asked him: 'Are you watching this?!' His reply was: 'Yes, good news. I'll be calling Alan first thing tomorrow.'

Leon called Alan the following day to say we obviously needed to change the figures in my deal because of what he had said on television. Alan Sugar was livid, saying that I'd hardly played since signing the deal in the summer of 1995. I then had a meeting with the chairman in which there was plenty of effing and blinding. He said he had paid me a fortune and I'd hardly been fit and that Les Ferdinand's deal had been structured differently.

I said to him: 'I've been loyal to you and stayed here when I could have gone to Manchester United. I've hardly been fit because of the physios you've employed.' This was when I told him the story of the scan and I added: 'Don't you dare have a f***ing go about me being injured with that sort of thing going on.'

He said to me: 'The physio is just a lorry driver who does as the specialists tell him.'

I replied: 'That's ridiculous. I understand your frustration with my injuries, but believe me they are nothing in comparison with my frustration at the situation. I signed a contract which stated that clause and I believe you are an honest man and that you should stay that way.'

It was an interesting conversation! I totally understood what he was thinking, and he was fair and we renegotiated a new deal. After a few weeks I signed it on the Friday before we played Barnsley pre-Christmas.

In the meantime, though, the new manager was trying to find his feet.

13
Klinsmannship

Alan Sugar brought in Christian Gross as manager when Gerry Francis quit in November 1997. The chairman had been impressed by Christian's record: two titles and a Cup in four years at Grasshoppers Zurich in his native Switzerland. I also think his reputation as a disciplinarian who focussed strongly on his players' fitness appealed to the chairman. Alan Sugar was paying good money and wanted everyone to be earning it. He thought this guy would come in and train us day and night and get the best out of us. But I assure you, that most definitely wasn't the case.

He was a nice enough bloke and had a good way about him but, boy, was his way eccentric. His nine months at Spurs were a debacle. He did things so strangely; very different from what we had been used to. For instance, he insisted we came in on a Sunday morning for a warm-down. It meant we were unable to unwind by either going out for dinner or having a few beers on Saturday nights. The Sunday morning warm-down might be commonplace now, but back then it was a change we players didn't like.

We would have the Monday off and be in for training Tuesday morning and afternoon, Wednesday morning, Thursday morning and afternoon and Friday morning and then play on Saturday. It made for a long week. We had been used to training just in the mornings and having a day off in the middle of the week.

I was a substitute for Christian's first match in charge, a 2–0 win at Everton. I was not happy to be on the bench. He didn't even speak to me about it, although I would have understood his reasons as I wasn't fully match-fit. I'd only played my first game of the season the week before.

We experienced Christian's weekly training regime for the first time leading up to his home debut, against Chelsea. And he added another twist to the preparation. We had to meet up at the stadium at five o'clock the night before the game to be coached to a hotel in Cockfosters, on the outskirts of North London, for an overnight stay. We certainly hadn't done that previously. At about eight to 8.30 the following morning, we did some training, including sprints, in the hotel car park. I remember looking back down the coach as we travelled to White Hart Lane for the game and there were about five or six players asleep!

We actually played OK in the first half against Chelsea, but ended up losing 6–1 – and I had to come off the bench again. The following week we played Coventry City away and I was back in the team. We got beaten 4–0. His methods weren't working, that's for sure.

Christian was stats mad. The morning after the Sky Blues turned us over, we had a debrief and he verbally abused me during it. He asked me: 'How many times did you get into the opposition's box?' I said: 'No idea.' He replied: 'Maybe once or twice.' I looked at him in amazement and said: 'Well, OK, how many times did the ball go in their box? I'm not going to run into their box when the ball is in the other half.' He muttered some stuff which I considered bullshit. The guy seemed clueless. I couldn't believe he was now our manager. I thought to myself: 'Nice appointment, Mr Chairman!'

The media got on Christian Gross's back from the day he arrived. He had travelled by tube from Heathrow Airport to his introductory press conference and produced a London Underground ticket and was quoted saying: 'I want this to become my ticket to the dreams.' He was ridiculed by the press for that.

It did not look good for him. And it was soon not looking good for me.

Friday 19 December 1997 started off well when I signed the contract that had been sorted out with Alan Sugar after Les Ferdinand joined the club. Unfortunately, it turned sour. After putting pen to paper, I got injured, tearing my groin in training. It was an unwanted déjà vu for me as something similar had happened after I'd signed deals in 1994 and 1995.

I was practising free-kicks and corners before the home game against Barnsley the following day. I tried one free-kick and felt something go and immediately thought 'Oh God, that's bad'. I went to the physio as well as the club doctor Mark Curtin and said 'I think I've torn my groin here'. They said: 'OK, let's us see it and we'll see how it is in the morning.' I iced it for the rest of the day, praying my instincts were wrong.

I stayed overnight at the Cockfosters hotel as it was a home game and got up for a run around the car park at about 8.30 and started our training session. I said to the doctor, a nice guy, that it was no good. He then went up to Christian Gross and told him, adding that in his opinion it was something that needed to be sorted out and that he didn't think I'd be able to play later that day. Gross said 'No, no. It'll be fine.' Then he turned to me and said: 'You've got to come through this. It is all in your mind.'

I looked over at the doctor and said: 'What's going on here?' The doc replied: 'It's up to you. The manager can't make you play, but he seems to think you can.'

I ended the discussion by saying, through clenched teeth: 'Fine. I'll play. It is a torn groin, but I'll play with my left foot. Not a problem!' I played for an hour against Barnsley at home and when Christian Gross brought me off as we were leading 3–0 he acted as if he was doing me a favour.

During the warm-down the following morning I felt awful, but got through it. I even pushed myself through the manager's long week of sessions leading up to a Boxing Day game at Aston Villa. But things went pear-shaped again as we trained at White Hart Lane on Christmas Day before travelling up to our midlands base at the Belfry, the well-known golf venue. Almost forgetting my problem, I took a shot with my right foot and felt a sharp pain. I was in agony. I decided to go off and see Tony Lenaghan.

The next second, Christian Gross came storming into the physio's room and told me: 'Don't you ever walk off my training field.' I replied: 'I'm not training because I'm not fit. I've told you about my problem a hundred times.' It was a shouting match.

The doc and physio spoke to Christian, saying 'Darren's obviously not right, even though he played for you the other day against Barnsley.'

The manager seemed to accept this and said: 'OK, OK.' In hindsight, the physio should have said: 'He's not playing.'

I still travelled with the team and when we arrived at the hotel the manager said to me: 'Darren, you can be on the bench so you can start against Arsenal in two days time.' It was as if he thought he was doing me a favour – again. When I came on with about 15 minutes to go, we were losing 4–1. What was the point of me coming on? The game was over. I couldn't believe it. I had to run around but couldn't kick the ball with my right foot. On the journey home I was in agony.

The following day I went into training and saw the doctor. I told him I wanted to have a scan and if it didn't show up anything, then I'd play against Arsenal. If it did I wouldn't. I had the scan done and the doctor reported back to me within half an hour. He said: 'Darren, I'm sorry, but the news is not good. There's an immense amount of bleeding. So obviously you can't play against Arsenal.' He knew and the physio knew that what Christian Gross, albeit unintentionally, had put me through was scandalous.

That story shows why it still makes my blood boil every time I hear someone shout 'Sicknote' in the street. As I've stated, I always did everything in my power to be fit and yet was given bad advice which aggravated any problem I might have had.

I spent four months out of the game when it was finally proved I'd been playing with a torn groin for a manager who forced me, without appreciating the extent of the problem, to play on. People who said 'Oh he's bloody injured again,' implying I was some kind of wimp, should know the truth. And the truth was on the scan: it showed blood spattered everywhere. As I've said, I want people to know what really happened after keeping quiet at the time out of loyalty to the club that I played for.

Jürgen Klinsmann, who had just rejoined us on loan from Sampdoria, was there that morning after I had the scan, and I sat in the changing room telling him all about what had happened. He was appalled and told me he would send me to his doctor in Germany and would call Alan Sugar on my behalf to get his permission to get me over there. Jürgen was as good as his word and just after we drew 1–1 with Arsenal, he spoke to the chairman and said 'I've got a doctor in Germany I want to take Darren to see.'

Alan Sugar agreed to it and Jürgen set up an appointment for me straight away with Dr Hans-Wilhelm Mueller-Wohlfahrt at his clinic in Munich. It has since emerged just what a world leader this doctor is in treating sports injuries. Sometimes his methods are seen as controversial, as he injects honey, calves' blood and a substance called Hylart which is, apparently, extracted from the crest of a cockerel and acts as a lubricant and is nicknamed 'rooster-booster'.

Plenty of top sportsmen and women since have sworn by him. Besides Jürgen, I've read other footballers like Steven Gerrard, Michael Owen, Ronaldo and Jonathan Woodgate have been treated by him. Athletes Kelly Holmes, the double Olympic gold-winning runner, Paula Radcliffe and Maurice Greene, tennis player Andy Murray, cricketers Darren Gough and Michael Vaughan and golfer José Maria Olazabal have also been patients of the doctor, who looks after Bayern Munich and the German national team. Olazabal was almost crippled by rheumatoid arthritis when he saw the doctor and then won the US Masters for a second time after the treatment.

Anyway, the doctor sorted out the tear on my groin no problem. Two or three months later, however, after it had healed, I had to tell him I still felt an ache in the area. He had another look and said there was nothing wrong with the tear, but that the problem might be a hernia. Surely not! I explained I'd had two operations for a hernia already. He then recommended I visited a colleague of his in Munich called Dr Ulrike Muschaweck.

I arranged to see her and Christian Gross came back out with me and Dr Mark Curtin. Christian was very supportive. He wasn't a bad person in any way. He just had to be positive about everything and honestly thought he could get me playing. He genuinely felt bad about how it had turned out. Dr Muschaweck has also acquired legendary status in her field and famously helped Michael Owen return to the England squad after conducting a double hernia operation on him in later years. She confirmed I needed surgery on the hernia. Christian Gross asked me if I wanted to have it done, as he knew I was keen to play in the World Cup that summer and time was tight. I told him that after my previous troubles with hernia I'd just get it done as soon as possible. Christian Gross returned home and she operated on me.

Dr Muschaweck has been a bit of a pioneer in her field, like Dr Mueller-Wohlfahrt, and told me it was a new technique which, under normal circumstances, was supposed to get me back playing in 10 days. It would take more like three weeks for me to return to playing, though, because I'd already had two operations for the same problem. She was so good. I had it done half sedated then flew back home that night and was jogging within two or three days.

It was now mid-March 1998, with the World Cup Finals only a few months away and Spurs still in a relegation dog-fight. In my own time I again sought to speed up the recovery process. I liaised with Glenn again and began working with masseuse-cum-physio Terry Byrne, who had worked with Glenn when he was Chelsea manager before taking over England.

Terry was a great guy and good at what he did and went on to become personal manager to David Beckham. In a repeat of what I'd done with Terry Venables's England physio Dave Butler two years before, we ran around London parks building my fitness and stamina. He also treated my problems. Glenn had sorted all this out for me because he wanted to make sure I would be available for selection when the World Cup Finals arrived.

I also helped myself by moving from Hemel Hempstead to Chigwell, closer to the training ground. It enabled me to stop doing the round trips of an hour and back from Hemel every day, which were not doing my hamstrings any good at all. In fact, they were killing them.

I'd bought a penthouse apartment in the redeveloped St Katherine's Dock by the Thames in central London, but it wasn't going to be ready for a year so I rented a big old house in the well-heeled Essex town known by many for being the setting for the television comedy *Birds of a Feather*.

Kate lived there with me. But she had to put up with my brothers, who also moved in. The house had a snooker table and an indoor swimming pool, which helped with my rehab. Kate and I would always hear loud music blaring out of the TV by the pool every night from our bedroom.

Steffen Iversen, a Spurs teammate who lived close by, joined us. He was rattling around in this apartment in Chigwell on his own. He was only a young lad, about 20, over from Norway. I went round his place and all he had in it apart from the furniture was a bottle of Lucozade Gatorade, an energy drink, in the fridge, and a copy of *The Sun* newspaper lying on his coffee table. I don't think Tottenham were doing a good job of looking after him and so we invited him to come and stay with us. It was a fun house, with lots of visitors, and Kate was fine with it. She was a placid girl, in contrast to Kerry, who didn't really like having other people about.

I finally got myself fit with five or six games to go, but couldn't get back in the team. I was left on the bench while Colin Calderwood played central midfield, the position I now favoured. With all due respect to Colin, I thought I was the better player in that role. After all, I don't think he had played it before! I was absolutely livid.

I spoke to Glenn and he suggested I asked to go out on loan, saying that I needed games to get my match fitness. I needed to be fit in order for him to consider me for World Cup selection. He thought that Alan Sugar might not want me to go to the World Cup anyway, because he was paying me a lot of money to play for Tottenham, not England. I certainly felt that Alan Sugar didn't want me to go to the World Cup. He'd given me a great contract, but all he saw was me getting fit to play for England rather than Spurs, a thought that pissed him off. It wasn't true, of course, but whatever anyone thought I wasn't playing for the first team when I should have been.

Glenn had to send England goalkeeping coach Ray Clemence, who had managed Spurs with Dougie Livermore under Terry Venables during my first season at the club, to a couple of reserve games to monitor my progress.

I'd never really complained about anything before in the press, but this was ridiculous and something had to be done. So I verbally abused the manager for not playing me and said that I thought it was because he and the chairman didn't want me to go the World Cup. I stated the World Cup would be a bonus for me. All I wanted was to help Tottenham stay in the Premier League.

It all came out in the papers the following day and Christian Gross asked me about it. I told him someone had asked what I thought of what was happening to me. I had told them I wasn't happy about not playing.

I was still a substitute for the next game – a draw against fellow strugglers Barnsley. There were three games left and we were still in big, big trouble, seemingly destined for the drop into the second tier for the first time since 1978. And that is when I finally got my chance, by default. On the morning of our next game, which was against Newcastle at White Hart Lane, midfielder Allan Nielsen got injured running around that Cockfosters hotel car park where I'd detected my groin trouble at the end of the previous year. So Christian Gross had to pick me for the starting line-up. I played well and helped us win 2–0.

I kept my place for the penultimate fixture against Wimbledon at the Selhurst Park ground they were sharing with Crystal Palace. It was comfortable. We won 6–2 and Jürgen got four of them. Premier League safety had been assured. I like to think that me coming back was a big reason for us winning those two crucial games that saved the club from relegation. I played my third game in 15 days as we finished off the season with a 1–1 draw with Saints.

I'd got my match fitness back and felt like saying 'bollocks to you' to Christian Gross and Alan Sugar. I should have been playing from the moment I was fit. I was delighted, almost relieved, as at one time I had thought I might not get the chance to be in Glenn's pre-World Cup squad. But now I'd done enough. Glenn included me in his provisional squad of 30 for France.

What made the moment even more special was that I had been through hell and back to ensure my name was on his register. I thought the travails I'd gone through to make it for Euro '96 were bad enough. But the obstacles in my way for the 1998 World Cup had seemed so high as to be insurmountable.

I had begun to despair of ever finding a way to fix my hamstring. In many ways Eileen Drewery seemed the person least likely to discover it. Faith healers are, to this day, still viewed as charlatans by the general public and yet the unassuming woman living quietly in the Berkshire countryside, that Glenn had so much faith in, found the right answer for me, without question. The stubbornness of Christian Gross forced me to risk my career by playing on a bad injury, even though that is not what he intended. And I will forever be grateful to Jürgen Klinsmann for interceding to ensure I could find the path back to full fitness. I do not know where else I could have gone had he not found those German surgeons for me.

Alan Sugar's anger was hard to bear, especially as it was misjudged. There was never a time I was only concerned about England because I had a full appreciation of what the club had done for me. It was only through Spurs that I had gained international recognition. It was only through Spurs that I had achieved my goal of playing consistently at the top. I was always determined to try and repay them as much as I could for everything they had given me. My family and friends helped me through the trials and tribulations of the bumpiest of rides to my ultimate dream.

But even then I could not afford to count my chickens. Fulfilment was still a step away as Glenn prepared to trim his final squad to 22. With Jamie Redknapp and Ian Wright declaring themselves unfit from the original 30, six of us would miss the chance to perform on the world stage.

14
Global Stage

I had grown sufficiently confident in my ability to have fully convinced myself I deserved to be in the World Cup squad once I'd proved my fitness. I'd overcome mentally as well as physically draining injury worries I thought might never end in the run up to a second successive major tournament.

I hadn't thought my own club manager and chairman would plant what I viewed as potential landmines near the end of my road to winning a place; Alan Sugar, through what I considered was his anti-England stance towards me, and Christian Gross for leaving me out of Spurs' starting line-up. But I'd avoided having my hopes blown up, even if it was by default, when Allan Nielsen's injury gave me the opportunity to convince Glenn Hoddle I deserved my place while helping lead Spurs away from relegation. I was desperate not to be one of the six to be culled.

England were due to face Tunisia before Romania and Columbia in our group in the World Cup. So Glenn set up friendlies with Saudi Arabia, Morocco and Belgium. The Saudi and Moroccan games would give an idea of what it might be like to kick off our campaign against a team with a desert climate, like our African opponents in France.

With the squad still 30-strong, I was put straight into the starting line-up against Saudi at Wembley on 23 May 1998, in front of nearly 64,000 who wanted to give us a giant World Cup send off. It was, of course, the first time I'd played for Glenn. The first of many, I hoped! And I wanted to make as big an impression as possible on him as he held the key to whether I'd go to France the following month.

Glenn played me at wing-back, just like Terry Venables had done for Euro '96. I hardly gave the ball away and played well. But the crowd were on my back and I even got booed by some sections of it, which I felt was ludicrous. They might have been fans of David Beckham who saw me as a threat to their man's spot in the starting line-up for the World Cup opener against Tunisia. They might have resented me coming straight in and staying on for the whole 90 minutes of the goalless draw, while Becks was replaced around the hour mark by Gazza.

In the starting line-up, there were a few survivors of Terry Venables's squad when *Football's Coming Home* first rang out from the Wembley crowd, including David Seaman, Tony Adams, Gareth Southgate and Gary Neville and the SAS partnership of Alan Shearer and Teddy Sheringham up front.

Alan was now captain, in place of Tony. It was a decision that caused plenty of debate, especially as Tony was still in the team with Arsenal club-mate and fellow Terry old-boy David. Tony had always seemed to be the perfect skipper – a real leader – so it certainly came as a surprise to the lads when the armband was taken away from him and given to Alan Shearer. I've read that Tony was critical of the decision in his autobiography. It was the first time I'd played for England alongside Becks and Paul Scholes.

Overall it was a decent experience to be back in the England fold for the first time since that heart-breaking Euro '96 semi-final defeat under lights at the same stadium one month short of two years before as we drew 0–0. We flew out to the La Manga Club in Spain, which was to be our base in the final weeks leading up to the World Cup Finals. The Club's website states that it is 'one of Europe's finest holiday and leisure resorts in southern Spain, surrounded by beautiful hills and the intense blue of the Mediterranean Sea. Discover La Manga Club, the perfect resort destination for your Spanish holiday.'

We all knew this was no leisure break to soak up a few rays and sample some hot spots. Glenn knew La Manga provided exactly what he needed for us to put the final polish on our preparation for France. It seemed purpose-built, as its brochure proclaims: 'The excellent quality of the training facilities and the privileged climate of the area also attract high-calibre professional and amateur sports teams from across Europe, including football, rugby, cricket, golf and tennis.'

Four days later after our Wembley farewell we experienced the hot and dry temperatures in North Africa after flying in from our luxurious base. Myself and Gareth were the only two to start from the Saudi match as we defeated Morocco 1–0 in the friendly King Hussan II International Cup in Casablanca.

Glenn told me to run myself into the ground to see if I could get through a whole game again. I managed to do so and just hoped it was good enough to get me to France, as it meant he did not intend to play me in the final warm-up game against Belgium in the friendly competition a couple of days later; the last chance for all the players to clinch their spot for France. I didn't know one way or the other whether I would make it.

The Moroccan tussle announced the major arrival of Michael Owen on the international scene as he scored the only goal of the game after coming on as a sub for poor Ian Wright, who had suffered a hamstring injury which put him out of the World Cup. At 18 years 164 days, Owen had become the youngest player to score in a full international for England, a record he held until Wayne Rooney took it off him in 2003. I was impressed right away by his pace and, of course, his eye for a goal. I think the 80,000 watching at the stadium were quite taken with the crew-cutted Liverpool youngster too.

I was duly kept on the bench as we lost to Belgium 4–3 on penalties after a goalless draw following our return to Casablanca from La Manga 48 hours later. I watched my club-mates Sol Campbell, who became the youngest England captain since Bobby Moore 36 years earlier, and 'Sir Les' stake their claim for a spot, with Glenn scheduled to announce his final squad at our temporary home on the Costa Calida on the south-east coast of Spain two days later on 31 May.

La Manga might have been a superb facility, but no one among the players was enjoying the resort when we got back from our final warm-up game against Belgium. Tension was in the air as we settled back in our rooms. We knew Glenn was in his own room drawing up a list of the names of the 22 who would go to France and the six who had failed to make it. Decision time was looming for all of us.

We all had a few drinks in our resort's piano bar the evening after completing our commitments in the King Hussan II International Cup. Nothing crazy. Most were probably thinking ahead to D-Day.

When it arrived we were called into Glenn's room one at a time. I was either third or fourth in. This was it. Obviously I had missed a big chunk of the season, but I knew Glenn liked me as a player. While I was out injured, I remember him stating in the press that he hadn't had the opportunity to play the team he wanted. I hoped that meant I was the missing piece of his jigsaw.

I was shitting myself as I entered the room. It was bloody horrible. Glenn could see how I was feeling by my body language and said: 'All right, don't worry, you're going. There was never any doubt.' He added: 'You've been through hell with the injuries and rehab, but you've done everything asked of you. You've done great. We've got a couple of weeks training now which will make you fitter and fitter.'

The anxiety seeped away. I was so happy. Over the moon. I phoned Mum and Dad and they were buzzing. I told them all I wanted to do was perform for 10 minutes in the tournament so I could say I'd played in the World Cup, even though I'd started every full England game I'd been involved in apart from that one against Belgium.

My mind was racing. I thought back to the first World Cup I ever saw in 1982. I didn't know what the competition was all about back then, but my Dad appreciated I'd love watching it because I was so into football. He was right. I'd lapped up four weeks of continuous live football. I'd got totally involved in the competition. How Bryan Robson scored for England against France after just a few seconds that year in Spain. How our talismanic players, Trevor Brooking and Kevin Keegan, were included even though they had injuries, the sort of thing that has been repeated a few times since by us in the World Cup. And how manager Ron Greenwood, now sadly passed away, was criticised for not bringing Keegan on earlier in the second phase decider against hosts Spain at the Bernabeu. That had he done so Keegan might have been more into the game and not missed the header that would have given us the win we needed to take us into the semi-finals. I was only 10 but I agreed, having watched Keegan as a Saints season ticket holder. My knowledge was much improved from when I'd first started observing top level football.

I'd sat with my jaw open as I saw the incredible Brazilian team, with the likes of Zico, Socrates and Falcao and the way they battered Scotland. And when Argentina's Diego Maradona was sent off against them. It all gave me a sense of what the competition was all about; its history, importance and propensity to produce drama and skill in equal measure. My appetite for it was whetted. It was a big part of why the thumbs up from Glenn meant so much.

I went down to the swimming pool on the complex and saw Gareth Southgate, who had also got the same good news. We chatted, both obviously pleased, and were discussing who was and wasn't going – in our opinion. Then came the news Gazza wasn't in. It was a shock to everyone. Pure shock. He'd been the mainstay of the England team for years. Everyone's favourite player wasn't going. We thought 'What is going on here?' Everyone was quite worried for him because he wore his heart on his sleeve and football was his life. How would he cope with this? We were sure he didn't see it coming. And, of course, we heard that Gazza had gone berserk when told the news. He was obviously so upset. Glenn thought Gazza would be a disruptive influence if he wasn't in the starting line-up because he wouldn't be used to not being in the team with England.

Gazza and the five others – Ian Walker, Phil Neville, Nicky Butt, Dion Dublin and Andy Hinchcliffe – flew back on a private jet that night. They didn't want to hang around and we didn't see them. The rest of us flew home the following day. That's when I read the stories about Gazza. How he had kicked the room in when Glenn gave him the news. How Gazza had been pictured eating a late-night kebab on the street while Glenn had wanted his players to behave and look after themselves in the manner Arsene Wenger had taught him when he played under his management at Monaco. It had been a weird and crazy couple of days.

I felt sorry for Gazza. He had been so kind to me when I needed it and been so great to play with. I'd respected him so much because football was his priority. And he had battled through terrible injury to keep playing. If endorsements came along as a consequence of what he did on the field, fine, but never at the expense of his football. I guess, though, because he was so genuine, it made him vulnerable to attack and he did get stitched up all over the place in public and, I'm sure, in private with people who attached themselves to Gazza the Celebrity.

I've seen the lifestyle struggles he's had with drink, drugs and relationships through the media. It's been difficult to watch from afar. You do lose touch with teammates when your career takes you away from them, although when you do see them it seems like yesterday since you were last together. You slip straight back into the banter you had in the dressing room and on the training ground; the bond as strong as ever.

We got a few days off before heading off for France, during which we were under severe scrutiny from the media. I travelled down to Bournemouth and went out to dinner with family and friends, who included Ian Bird and David Fudge. Fudgey was big lad and gave the impression to onlookers that they should not to mess with me.

We had a lovely meal and decided to go to the bar across the road for a couple of drinks. A fight broke out in the bar which had nothing to do with us. Although Birdy was near the incident, he maintains it was nothing to do with him. Fudgey, with his ex-bouncer head on, ushered us out.

The following day there was a reporter and a photographer outside the house. Mike, my step-dad, spoke to them and said: 'What do you want?' They said 'Darren was given a black eye after getting into a fight in bar last night.' Mike said: 'Very funny. Come and have a look for yourself!' So they did and could see that was not the case. That morning, Teddy was on the front page of the papers with a cigarette hanging out of his mouth (not alight!) and it was reported that it had been taken at 7am in the morning in Portugal. The press jumped on this because Glenn had omitted Gazza partly because of his off-field activities.

The next day I turned up at the hotel and was on the front page with the story of my so-called bar brawl. Glenn asked me what had happened and he believed what I told him. But with Teddy he was more unhappy. Teddy had to apologise on national television. The squad all thought it was unnecessary and should have been dealt with in-house. I couldn't believe this article on me had come out. Some little tosser had made it all up. I found out who he was as a friend of my brother's went to the same university as the lad.

At first I wanted to have him done over, although I changed my mind in the end. Getting to the World Cup was something I'd worked my whole life to achieve and I had gone through such injury nightmares to do so and now some little idiot who maybe got £500 off the paper was trying to ruin it. I was livid and might have even been tempted to strangle him if I'd have come across him! I couldn't believe someone had done something like that.

Fair play to Glenn. He could have gone the other way with myself – and of course, Teddy – and booted us out. He'd helped me get fit, brought me into the squad and had been fantastic, so he might have felt let down when he saw the story. In the future, as I will outline later, there were things he did and said that I didn't like when he became my club manager at Tottenham and Wolverhampton Wanderers. But I would put all that to one side for the fact that he gave me my opportunity in the World Cup.

I had been struck down by injury in my prime and it would have been easy for him to discard me, to forget about me and concentrate on developing someone else to fill my role, but he didn't. He wanted me at the finals.

The final 22 was settled and I was pleased my Spurs teammates Sol Campbell and Les Ferdinand were among them. The squad was, excluding myself: goalkeepers David Seaman, Nigel Martyn, Tim Flowers; defenders Sol Campbell, Graeme Le Saux, Tony Adams, Gareth Southgate, Gary Neville, Martin Keown, Rio Ferdinand; midfielders Paul Ince, David Beckham, David Batty, Steve McManaman, Paul Merson, Paul Scholes, Rob Lee; strikers Alan Shearer, Teddy Sheringham, Les Ferdinand, Michael Owen.

We flew to France and went straight to a ground to play in a behind-closed-doors game against a local side. I was in the team with Becks inside me as a central-midfielder. I hoped this was the team Glenn was looking to start with in our first game.

We then went on to our base at Baule in western Brittany. It was a nice, out of the way place. The building we stayed in was a fortress with lovely grounds. Facilities included a swimming pool and golf course. We trained there in the morning and relaxed in the afternoons when we sometimes had a round of golf or watched other games on TV with Sheringham and Shearer our local bookmakers. Overall, though, they were long days.

We just wanted the tournament to start and, for us, it did so in Marseille on 15 June 1998, when we took on Tunisia. In the dressing room there were plenty of strong characters, just like there had been at Euro '96. After all, quite a few were still there, like Alan Shearer, Paul Ince and Tony Adams.

Glenn had a different approach to Terry. He was, like Terry, a fantastic coach, and, although he had less of his predecessor's man-management, skills, he more than made up for their absence in other areas. He was so tactically aware, good at working on technique and preparing thoroughly. He uncovered every stone. These are all qualities vital to being a good international manager. Perhaps that's why the England job suited him better than any he had at club level with its more day-to-day routine.

When we went out against Tunisia, and for our remaining World Cup games, the team was ready. One hundred per cent ready. Terry Byrne was there as one of the England masseurs and helped me do the hamstring stretch I'd worked out following the advice of Eileen Drewery before and after training and games. It certainly helped me to have a friendly face around, someone I could trust along with Gary Lewin, England's physio and a great one too.

As we walked into the changing rooms I looked over to see my shirt folded on the bench with 'ANDERTON 14' emblazoned on it. I had a wry smile. No one could take this away from me. I was about to play in the World Cup. It was a moment I had thought about a hundreds if not thousands of times playing in the garden at Oak Tree Road.

As you know by now, I am patriotic and the realisation that I was once more going to represent my nation in a major international competition made my chest swell and my nerves jangle. The excitement was mixed with the weight of responsibility.

I knew the Velodrome Stadium was packed with England fans, who'd taken over every bar in the port. I could hear those inside the ground from the dressing room, singing *Football's Coming Home*. It was Euro '96 at Wembley all over again.

But I also knew there were those among the 54,587 crowd who were ready to give me a hard time, for similar reasons to those voiced by a minority against Saudi Arabia not long before. I had been selected to play at right wing-back, the role Terry Venables had given me two year earlier. Wide right was where Becks played for Manchester United and his country. I had taken precedence over my dissenters' hero. Or so they thought.

Three days before Glenn had told us what the team would be. I was a little shocked to be starting even though I'd been in the team for the warm-ups against Saudi Arabia and Morocco. I'd presumed Becks would be in the team as well – in central midfield. But Glenn opted for Leeds' combative David Batty for tactical reasons; he wanted him to play alongside Paul Ince in a defensively-minded midfield to allow Paul Scholes the freedom to break from the centre of the field and play wherever he wanted to.

It was never going to be the case that I was going to keep Becks, who was an unused substitute, out of the team. Even so, it didn't stop people having the hump with me believing I had done. I got stick from when we kicked off. My family and friends were up in the stands having to listen to this faction who had taken against me and were casting a cloud over this sunshine experience in my career. I remember a cross later in the game, which I messed up, was greeted by excessive groans and boos from those supporters.

I thought I managed to play through it and do quite well – even going close to heading a goal in the first half – along with the rest of the team as we won 2–0 thanks to goals from Alan Shearer and Paul Scholes. It was the first time since 1982 that England had won their opening match in the World Cup Finals.

Scholesy, who was one of the best players I ever played with or against, had filled Gazza's boots with comfort and Michael Owen became one of the World Cup's youngest players when he came on as a late substitute for Teddy, I guess a passing of the baton from the old to the new generation in some people's eyes.

Unfortunately for me the press didn't agree with my assessment of my display. They said I had performed badly. That really pissed me off. That was when Dad – as I mentioned in the opening chapter – stepped in to save my World Cup by telling me to forget the knockers. And Graham Paddon, my Portsmouth youth manager, bolstered that support with a phone call to my hotel. Graham, who has since sadly passed away, said to me: 'I watched the game on television and wondered where's that smile of yours? You looked tense and wound up. Just ignore the critics. You played brilliantly at right wing-back. You don't want to play in that position but you did, you ran your socks off and did absolutely great. I bet you never thought when you joined me at Pompey running on that beach on your first day you'd be playing in the World Cup Finals for England. You are a top player. You've worked so hard to get there. Please enjoy the rest of the tournament, don't let it pass you by.'

His intentions were similar to Gazza's while pretending he wanted to borrow a shaving razor before my England debut against Denmark four years before. And just like Gazza's words, Paddo's stuck with me too. I spoke to him for about an hour and he really lifted my spirits.

After the rallying speeches I'd been given by Dad and Paddo, I played the rest of the tournament with every dark cloud lifted. Their attitude encouraged me to be more positive and worry more about getting forward in the second game in our group seven days later, which was against Romania, who included a former Tottenham teammate, Gica Popescu, in their side.

Again the ground, the Municipal de Toulouse, in a beautiful city in the Pyrenees, was rammed with England fans waving the white-and-red flag of St George. I had all of them on my side this time, even though Becks was still on the bench with Glenn keeping faith with David Batty. Maybe they'd realised I wasn't the bad guy after all, I'm not sure.

And I felt I put on a great performance. My confidence had been low after we had defeated Tunisia. This time it was high and I asked Gary Neville, who had come in for the injured Gareth Southgate, to cover me as I pushed forward. I drove just over from distance and showed some nice flashes of skill. I felt good and the team did too. And Becks showed his talent after replacing an injured Incey.

But Viorel Moldovan, the Coventry City forward, put Romania in front after being set up by their star player, Gheorghe Hagi, against the run of play. Glenn decided to replace Teddy with Michael Owen and, thankfully, Michael injected his pace and eye for goal to snatch a late equaliser.

Unfortunately, we were denied the point we deserved with a dodgy last-minute winner from Dan Petrescu, who I thought caught his old Chelsea teammate Graeme Le Saux high, with a boot in the face, before he scrambled the ball in. Our appeals fell on deaf ears.

Glenn was reflective too. He knew all about the player after he signed him when he was Chelsea boss! We were all mightily fed up with things as we sat in the dressing room. England were down – but not out.

15
World Cup Heaven and Hell

A draw against Columbia in our final group game at the World Cup Finals in France would be enough to see us reach the first knockout round, the last 16. Despite the result, my self-esteem was reasonably high as I'd had a good game against Romania. My confidence was back.

We trained hard for the game that was to decide our future in the competition against a team who had Carlos Valderrama, a world-class performer also famous for having the biggest blond Afro I'd ever seen.

What helped our fans was that Lens, where the game was to be staged, was only 50 odd miles south of Calais, the nearest port across the English Channel. It was a shame the Felix Bollaert Stadium was limited to 38,000, because I'm sure we could have filled it either two or three times over with the supporters who wanted to be there, although I did manage to get about 20 tickets for my family and mates, some of whom came from America. Dave and Joe Roy, for instance, flew in from Washington DC. Their flight into London was delayed, which meant they held up the plane carrying the official players' guests. They certainly weren't flavours of the month when they finally got on board two and a half hours after the scheduled take-off.

Temperatures were cooler compared to the two group games we'd played in the south of the country. Columbia, given their geography, were more used to an equatorial climate.

There had been loads of calls to put Becks and Michael Owen in the starting XI and their backers were rewarded against Columbia, with David Batty and Teddy losing their places. Glenn said it had always been his intention to bring in Becks and Michael for the third game and keep them in from there. He knew Becks and I were right-wingers who preferred to play centrally and, with the pair of us in the team, we could inter-change positions if needed. He had kept the plan under wraps because he wanted to keep us solid for the opening two games.

We were certainly on the front foot from the kick-off, rather than playing it safe for a draw. And halfway through the first half I experienced the highest of my footballing highs when I put England into the lead. I hadn't long provided a cross for Michael Owen, which he'd volleyed over, when our roles were reversed.

Michael crossed the ball from the right and Colombian defender Jorge Bermudez headed the ball straight to me at pace about 12 yards out on the angle. I really had a good touch, the ball sat up beautifully and I lashed it with the outside of my right foot and it went straight into the top corner. I couldn't believe it. I knew where my family and friends were sitting and tried to run like a lunatic towards where they were. All the players jumped on top of me. I was almost in tears.

A few minutes later Becks put us 2–0 up with the sort of free-kick that was to become his trademark and we continued to link up well together as the team finished off the job and put us through. Petrescu's late goal in our second group game ensured his Romanian side took top spot and we went into the last 16 as runners-up.

Had we finished first we'd have drawn Croatia, but second place meant we would have to get past the more formidable Argentina. The Argentinians were a top, top team with players of real quality like Hernan Crespo, Gabriel Batistuta, Juan Sebastian Veron, Claudio Lopez, Diego Simeone (more of him later!) and Javier Zanetti. They had won all three of their group games – against Japan, Jamaica and Croatia – without conceding a goal, while scoring seven.

We knew the match would be tough, but we had played well in qualifying and there was a real belief we'd go on and win the World Cup. There had been controversial history in the competition between us and Argentina. Diego Maradona scored his infamous Hand of God goal for the Argentinians to help them beat England in the 1986 quarter-finals, claiming at the time the goal was scored 'a little with the head of Maradona and a little with the hand of God'. And everyone had got hot under the collar 20 years before when England beat the South Americans on route to lifting the Jules Rimet Trophy in 1966.

I've seen those grainy black-and-white videos of the Argentinians riling home manager Alf Ramsey so much with their physical approach he labelled them 'animals'. And it was the moment when Argentinian midfielder Antonio Rattin was sent off during that game for 'violence of the tongue' which was to provide the closest parallel to the night the England side I was in took on the South Americans at the Geoffroy Guichard Stadium in St Etienne on 30 June 1998. On this occasion we were on the receiving end of a controversial decision against one of our midfielders – David Beckham – which turned the game on its head.

It was a fire-cracker of an atmosphere at AS Saint Etienne – a town famous for manufacturing firearms – before kick off. So intense. Our supporters had taken over the stadiums for our group games, but I couldn't believe how many Argentinian fans were there. They filled half the ground and were raucous and rowdy. And that was an hour and a half before kick-off. Lunatics! I'd never experienced supporters like it. There was a great buzz about the place, but it was so crazy. And, of course, the tension between the two countries over the Falkland Islands in the early 1980s might have been added to the mix.

We had a nightmare start when they went ahead with a penalty. The ref felt David Seaman had fouled Simeone, and Batistuta, who ended up joint second in the top scorers list at the tournament, drilled the kick past David. I thought 'we're going to get battered here', because we hadn't really had a touch up until then.

They had been playing well, but we took over and got a bit of passing going. Michael Owen was on fire and ran them ragged. They might have been able to live with the rest of us, but there was no way they could live with him and his pace, alertness and energy. We passed them off the pitch. Ripped them to shreds.

It was no surprise we equalised when Michael got fouled and Alan Shearer scored the penalty. Then came Michael's famous wonder goal. It's been replayed so many times! Becks slipped the ball to him from just inside our half and Michael took the ball in his stride inside the centre circle and sprinted by Jose Charnot, cut to the right, bamboozled Roberto Ayala to create space and thumped it home just inside the box. It was described as the goal of the tournament. I think it was the moment that clinched the BBC Sports Personality of the Year award for Michael at the end of that year. Sensational. We were totally dominant and could have had a couple more. We were flying.

Out of the blue, they got a free-kick right on half-time. The ref reckoned Sol Campbell and Tony Adams had fouled Claudio Lopez between them. I lined up in the wall, with Paul Scholes to my left and Becks, Alan Shearer and Paul Ince to my right – all clutching our privates – as Batistuta shaped to take the kick from just outside the area. But it was Juan Sebastian Veron who took it and craftily slid the ball low, down the left-hand side of us. Javier Zanetti, who had tried to disrupt our wall while the kick was being taken, sneaked out behind myself and Scholesy to receive the ball in space and stick it in. It felt like a killer blow. A goal changes everything. We were gutted, especially after going 2–1 up and playing so well.

In the dressing room, everyone was down, but Glenn reminded us it was all still to play for.

After a quiet opening to the second half came an explosion: Becks was sent off for a so-called 'moment of madness'. Thirty-two years before, with the score at 0–0, Rattin had been so incensed at German referee Rudolf Kreitlein's decision that he refused to leave the pitch and sulked on the red carpet laid down for the Queen before the police 'moved him on'. Then Geoff Hurst got a late winner against the departed skipper's 10 men.

Becks looked equally stunned when our ref, Dane Kim Milton Nielsen, held up the red card in front of him after he had clashed with Simeone, although he didn't delay his exit like Rattin. It was 2–2 at the time and meant we had to hold out for almost the entire second half and, as it turned out, for 30 minutes of extra-time.

I was one of the closest players to the incident. Becks was about to cushion a header back to me when the guy went straight into the back of him and knocked him flat on the floor and then leaned all over him as he got up. It was a foul and a booking for Simeone.

I turned away for a second, before I heard a big roar and turned back wondering what was going on. I thought someone had thrown a punch. Becks was being spoken to by the referee, Batistuta was bending the official's ear and being pushed away by Alan Shearer.

Suddenly, Nielsen was raising a red card and Becks was spinning round and walking off. I shook my head in disbelief. How? Why? Did he do anything? I discovered he had flicked his right boot out as he lay face down with his legs raised and it lightly caught the back of Simeone's leg on the calf. Simeone fell backwards as if he had been shot. It was a million miles from a sending off. Disgraceful. Simeone, I felt, had 'conned' the referee. And Simeone's teammates who crowded round the official in the middle to try to convince him to punish our man with the ultimate sanction were just as guilty as Simeone.

When I came off halfway through extra-time I saw Becks standing in the tunnel. I went over to him and told him 'Don't worry about it. The referee's an arsehole.' But I couldn't console him. He still couldn't speak. He'd left the field close to tears. I know it ripped his heart out because, as we know, he has been one of the most proud Englishman ever to pull on the shirt emblazoned with the Three Lions.

Everything seemed to be going against us and now we just had the 10 men against one of the tournament favourites at full strength. But we defended well. I moved to a more central position to cover for Becks's absence – a role I preferred as I felt more involved – while Alan Shearer moved out wide and played a double role: right-wing and right-back.

The whole team mucked in and battled. It was a great defensive performance. They kept us on the back foot; showing how technically gifted and comfortable on the ball they were. But they didn't look like breaking us down.

Extra-time was looming when I thought I had laid on the goal which would put us into the quarter-finals. We had forced a corner on the left,

I swung the ball in and Sol Campbell headed home. It was a brilliant goal! Sol ran to the other corner flag where six or seven of the others followed to celebrate.

I could see the referee blow his whistle and award a free-kick for a foul against Alan Shearer on their goalkeeper Carlos Roa, which wasn't one (a similar fate befell Sol when what would have been a last-minute winner against Portugal in the 2004 European Championships was ruled out when John Terry was supposed to have committed a foul in the air).

Argentina took the kick and quickly got it forward. I could see the players hadn't heard the whistle and were still celebrating. As much as I screamed and shouted, there was no way they could hear from the other side of the pitch in this incredible atmosphere.

We had just one man back when I reacted and had to run the length of the pitch across to the far side to get in a tackle on Hernan Crespo, who was inside our box and about to pull the trigger. It was so surreal, One second I was in heaven celebrating Sol's goal, the next I was thinking 'Shit, they're going to score! I was so relieved when I made the tackle. And, to be honest, I was shattered after it and didn't last much longer after that.

Halfway through the first period of extra-time, in which a 'golden' goal would decide the result for the first time in this competition, David Batty came on in my place. It meant, as against Spain two years before, I would have to watch helplessly as the tie went to penalties. We might have gone out in shoot-outs at the 1990 World Cup and Euro '96, but I was convinced there would be no unwelcome hat-trick.

Alan Shearer banged his penalty into the roof of the net, just like he had done during the game, to level Argentina's opener from Sergio Berti, and when David saved from Crespo hopes rose. Incey stepped up, but Carlos Roa saved. Paul Merson and Michael Owen replied to successful kicks from Veron and Marcelo Gallardo. But when David Batty had his effort saved it was all over.

Again, when we had been put on the spot, we were unable to make it count. Nobody blamed either Incey or David, of course. The reaction would have been the same if David had stayed on the bench and I'd had my kick saved. But we were all devastated. We were going home.

Although it had been a tough game, I felt we'd deserved to beat Argentina. It was a bitter pill to swallow. The sting in the tail came as we waited to board our coach, which was taking us back to our hotel. Our families were there with us. Everyone was one down in the dumps. I was almost in tears as I said to my Dad: 'I thought we'd win the World Cup.' He soothed me by saying how the team had done brilliantly, but what happened was just one of those things. All part of football.

Argentina's coach was parked next to ours and their players and staff boarded it. They were jumping up and down with music blaring and banging on the windows to attract our attention and then giving it all sorts with gestures to goad us – right in front of our faces. Batitusta was giving plenty of those. It was the most disgusting display I'd ever seen. They behaved like absolute animals. You expect that sort of thing from fans, but not fellow professionals. I thought: 'Where is your respect?' Maybe Alf Ramsey had a point when he called the Argentinian team he faced 'animals'. This current version were acting like a bunch of monkeys! My Dad was so worked up he replied with a 'wanker' sign. Until that night I'd never had a problem with Argentina. I do now.

There was nothing more I wanted at that moment than to see them stuffed in the last eight by Holland. The Dutch obliged me by beating them with a last-minute winner from Dennis Bergkamp; one of the best goals I've ever seen. It certainly gave Michael's a run for its money!

Back at the hotel, we chatted over a few beers before going to our rooms. I couldn't sleep. It was awful. After breakfast, we packed our bags and headed for the airport – where Concorde had been sent to pick us up. The fans were great. They welcomed us back like heroes, almost, because we had battled and played so well with 10 men. The whole country was proud of the team. Apart from Becks. My heart went out to him over the coming months because he got pilloried as being responsible for our World Cup demise. He seemed to become Public Enemy No.1 He was totally vilified. The *Mirror* newspaper ran the headline '10 heroic lions, one stupid boy'. That paper also published a Beckham-faced dartboard within its pages for fans to 'take their fury out on'. I also understand an effigy of him was burned outside a London pub.

And, inevitably given all the furore, he went on to be booed by opposition fans across the country throughout the following season. We hadn't known what was going on back home when we returned. How he'd been slaughtered in the media, the pubs, everywhere. I saw the incident which had formed so many viewpoints, as did the rest of the players, as an appalling decision by the referee. Simple.

Maybe he shouldn't have even offered that light flick – which was in no way vicious – in a game of such importance. You have to keep calm. I experienced the sort of 'conning' the Argentinians acted out that night in other matches for England. It is part and parcel of what happened when I played in international football, along with the spitting and pulling. It used to wind me up like you wouldn't believe. But I appreciated I needed to keep calm otherwise the opposition would take advantage of the situation.

Glenn Hoddle had told Becks a year before, when he got a silly booking for petulance which put him out of the next game in the Tournoi tournament, that he had to learn from the experience. He said that if he showed the same response the following summer it could be more costly. And when Becks did that tiny flick, which the whole world has seen, I guess he was proved right.

But that doesn't take away from the fact that the last thing the ill-advised action deserved was a sending off. It was a disgusting decision by Mr Nielsen for which Becks paid big-time. It was sad to see it happen to a quiet lad who kept himself to himself and just wanted to play football.

Becks let his feet do the talking. That's why I was surprised when he became captain in Peter Taylor's only game in charge of England against Italy and I came off the bench. He doesn't shout or holler, but proved himself effective in the end by leading by example as England captain in future games. He carried on growing as a player, turning things round with Manchester United and England despite the criticism. He showed how talented he was with his crosses, free-kicks and all-round play. He worked hard and did everything right.

I read not long ago that the United States international Landon Donovan – definitely no relation to Mike, who has helped me write this autobiography – had slaughtered Becks for not giving his all for LA Galaxy by also playing for AC Milan in order to bid for a place in the England squad for the 2010 World Cup. It is one thing you should never aim at Becks. He always works his socks off and plays for the team.

He showed amazing strength of character through the dark days that followed the 1998 World Cup, helped, I'm sure, by the upbringing he got from Fergie that kept his feet on the ground. The following year, he helped United win the Treble, the Premier League, the FA Cup and the Champions League. In 2000, he became England captain. Then he helped England complete a successful 2002 World Cup qualifying campaign against Greece, by producing an injury-time free-kick equaliser and an all-action performance which turned him into a national hero. And he went on to become a national treasure.

The way he is now thought of around the world as an ambassador for our country, while appearing to have earned more from his image than his football, has been incredible. Mixed in has been getting married to Victoria Adams with her high profile as Posh in the Spice Girls, who have sold millions of records. Now they've got their own perfume. It is all light years away from the Becks I knew in France, but he essentially remains the same bloke I knew from then. He has a good way about him, never big-headed. He's grateful for the career he's had and the lifestyle he leads and is a great family man; someone you never see falling out of night clubs. He's such a good role model.

I felt the Euro '96 squad was better than the one at the 1998 World Cup because it had more leaders, but Glenn's squad ran them close. It was great combining with Teddy on the field and socially as always, but it was the partnership between his SAS partner Alan Shearer and Michael Owen that caught the public imagination in France.

Alan was the same as he had been two years earlier: the leader, the goalscorer. Our Roy Race. His sarcastic, dry sense of humour would keep the dressing room amused, but he shunned the glitz of being seen at film premieres and such. He was a regular guy, serious about his football.

And he was clearly someone Michael viewed as a hero. Remember, Michael was only 18, and despite the outward confidence of youth it was important he should have a figure to look up to, someone who would be his protector if things got rough. He naturally shared Alan's down-to-earth approach as far as his career was concerned. Football came first. But he came across altogether different in his style of game and general personality. His game was about phenomenal pace, directness and finishing, which gave the world-class defenders in front of him during the tournament nightmares.

It is difficult to compare Glenn Hoddle with Terry Venables as England manager because no one could match up to Terry for me. He was the best of all my managers because of the way he handled me as a footballer and person. Glenn proved he was the nearest in the game to Terry as far as tactics were concerned, however, and we played very good football under him that summer in France.

As I've said, he wanted things his way, and felt he was always right. It is the way things have to be when you are the manager. But there were times he didn't get the best out of players because of his presence.

I remember one morning at training before the Columbia game when we were practising free-kicks. Becks was supposed to flick the ball up for me to volley. After two or three goes he hadn't got it right. Glenn was standing behind him tutting and saying: 'Can you not do that or what?'

Becks was intimidated. Glenn then showed him how to do it and did it perfectly. Terry would have laughed and said 'it'll be all right on the night.' That was an indication of where Terry's management style would shine through.

But as I said earlier, Glenn made my dream come true and proved Becks and I, although generally viewed as right-wingers, could play in the same team.

Apart from my first couple of games under Glenn, the fans were brilliant to me. It is hard to say whether I enjoyed either Euro '96 or the 1998 World Cup more. In a way they both felt like home tournaments because all the stadiums, apart from the one at Saint Etienne, reverberated with the sound of our adopted anthem *Football's Coming Home*, as well as *God Save The Queen*, as they were packed solid with English fans.

Despite the bitter disappointments at the end, I wouldn't swap what I experienced in both for the world. The memories will there forever – something to tell my children or grandchildren.

After the tournament I headed off to Boston in the States where I was best man for Dave Roy as he was getting married to Kristen on 12 July – World Cup Final day. That role had given me two reasons for playing in the Final: one to win it, of course, and the other to get out of doing the best man's speech!

Although the Final experience didn't happen, I managed to get through the speech and everyone had a wonderful day.

16
Glittering Prize

Three weeks after the World Cup finished I was back for pre-season with Tottenham following a break with my friends in Boston for Dave Roy's wedding and in Washington DC. Christian Gross was still in charge when many thought he might lose his job over the summer because he hadn't taken the world by storm at White Hart Lane.

We went on a training camp in Holland where the well-meaning Christian was still cutting a figure that was prone to light-hearted ridicule. The trip was a nightmare, which involved 7am forest runs, followed by training at 11am and 4pm. It was tough and went down like a lead balloon with the lads.

One morning, after the forest run, I was sat having breakfast with Ian Walker, Chris Armstrong and Steffen Iversen when Christian came over and said: 'What is this?!' as he pointed at our plates, which were full of eggs, bacon and sausages. He said: 'Are you lorry drivers or professional footballers?' We laughed and stopped eating our fry-up and went and grabbed a piece of toast instead.

We upset the manager again out there. It was after a game, which we won about 8–0. He saw a few of us, including Les Ferdinand, Nicola Berti, Steffen and Chris, sat outside the our opponents' club bar having a beer. Christian didn't mention it until the following morning when we had a team meeting.

Then he said: 'Darren and Les, do you drink beer after you play for England at Wembley?'

To which Les replied: 'Yes, that's exactly what we do.'

Christian had a different mentality. A mentality that you now see a lot of in the Premier League.

I felt pretty good and my confidence was sky high after my performances in the World Cup. Unfortunately, we had a disastrous start to the 1998–99 season and the manager was sacked three games into it. We were useless in our opener at Wimbledon, losing 3–1, and shocking in our first home game, with Sheffield Wednesday thumping us 3–0. And, although we managed to stick our finger in the dyke and seal a 1–0 win against at Everton with a goal by Les, the writing was already on the wall for Christian Gross.

I reported for England duty. It was the start of my country's 2000 European Championship qualifying campaign against Sweden in Stockholm on 5 September. Glenn Hoddle was hoping we could build on the positives from our World Cup campaign and go all the way in this latest adventure.

We were all full of confidence from the way we had played in France and that was evident as we made a good start when Alan Shearer put us ahead. But the Swedes came back at us with a couple of goals in that half, which proved enough to give them the win.

But what I remember most was going over on my knee in the first 45 minutes. I went to twist one way and then the other and got my studs caught in the ground and I felt my knee going. I thought I was in trouble. But I just managed to whip my studs out in time before too much damage was done. I dread to think what I might have done otherwise. I could have injured every part of my knee.

It looked a bit like the incident involving Michael Owen during the 2–2 draw with Sweden in the 2006 World Cup, except Michael wasn't so lucky and was out for 10 months after rupturing his anterior cruciate knee ligament. I tried to carry on but had to come off a few minutes later, just before the interval. As it was, I still felt I'd done something quite serious because the knee had popped out and left me in agony. I sat on the plane home alongside Alan Shearer. He'd had knee injuries and asked if the knee felt insecure. I told him I didn't know, but it certainly didn't feel good. He added that hopefully I'd be OK because I'd been able to carry on for five or 10 minutes. I might have just strained the ligaments. I still thought it might be worse.

Unbeknown to me and the other Tottenham lads in the squad, Les and Sol Campbell, Christian Gross had been sacked earlier that day, which was a bit of a surprise after our success at Everton. The FA kept it from us until after we'd boarded the bus following the game to go back to the hotel and head off to the airport. Perhaps they thought it might put us off our game! Paul Merson, who was at Arsenal, said to me: 'George Graham will be your next manager.' An ex-Gunners boss in charge of their arch-rivals in north London?! And he was already in a job at Leeds United. Mers had got the information because he had the same agent as George. I thought 'Surely not?'

When I got back I went to see Dr King at the Independent Hospital in London right away to assess the extent of my knee problems. He revealed I'd just strained my ligaments, as Alan had thought. I was lucky. It meant I was out for about three weeks, but it could have been 100 times worse. I was relieved.

David Pleat had been put in caretaker charge of Spurs while a permanent successor to Christian Gross was found. Just under three weeks later I was fit and back in training and, after finishing my first day, Pleaty asked if I wanted to go on the bench the following night for our first-round second-leg League Cup tie against Brentford at White Hart Lane. I said: 'No problem.' When I arrived at the stadium for the game he pulled me into his office and said: 'I want you to start. You might as well play an hour from the start as opposed to half an hour at the end.' I agreed.

I strolled through the game and we won it to go through. My knee felt good. Finally, I'd come back in the expected time frame for an injury. Little did I realise just how significant that competition would be for myself and the club that season.

That weekend, George brought his Leeds side down to play us in a 3–3 League draw, and it was pretty much known then that he was coming to us. A few days later it was confirmed. George came in to see the players and introduce himself just before our next game, at Derby, with Pleaty still in charge of the team.

I had to go away with England before I had a proper chat with our new boss. England had a couple more European Championship qualifiers within the space of four days that October. The first one was against Bulgaria, who included the world-class performer Hristo Stoichkov, at Wembley. It was a pretty dour game which ended up goalless. I managed to provide a cross which Sol headed wide, but it was pretty thin gruel for the 73,000 spectators, that's for sure.

Fortunately, we managed our first victory in the competition in the second game in Luxembourg, with Becks back from a two-match suspension following his sending-off against Argentina in the World Cup. Although we beat our hosts 3–0, it didn't start too well. We'd been slaughtered in the press for the way we'd played against Bulgaria. And they were waiting to batter us again. So what was the first thing we did? Give away a penalty! Luckily they missed it and I set up a couple of goals as we won 3–0, although I remember getting absolutely butchered by one of their players. My leg felt like it was in pieces after the crunching it got from him in what turned out to be my final competitive game for England.

The press got stuck into us anyway because they wanted Glenn Hoddle out, reporting that the manager had had a huge row with Alan Shearer in the dressing room, which never happened. I guess they were just trying to cause trouble to succeed in their aim of getting Glenn the sack.

Glenn hadn't done too badly, but the fact he then came out with the remark that we should have taken Eileen Drewery to the World Cup was a bit silly, because it gave the press an excuse to go for him. Eileen had helped me, but the reason we had gone out was we'd got beaten by Argentina and one or two things didn't go our way.

A week later I was playing my first Tottenham game with George as our manager: a 2–1 defeat at Leicester City. I had a good chat with

George in the build-up. He told me he rated me as a player and wanted to get me super-fit, as I had been before my injuries started in 1995. I was pleased with George's appointment and had no problem with his wishes for all his teams to be super-fit. I thought if you can get good players, which we had aplenty, to work hard, get fit and play for the team it would be a recipe for success.

Training was hard and he did a bit extra with me because he knew, through Terry Venables, a good friend of his, how fit I had been. I'd missed a lot of football in the previous couple of seasons, but with George's tough new regime I was able to get back to my peak fitness and ended up playing well over 40 games that season.

George preached that although we had to play as a team, we also had to play good football. He had a reputation at Highbury for producing defensive-minded teams, happy for it to be '1–0 to the Arsenal' as he led them to the League (twice), the FA Cup, the League Cup (twice) and the European Cup-Winners' Cup in nine years, helped along the way with some great signings like Ian Wright and David Seaman. He nevertheless had plenty of flair players, such as Mers, the late David Rocastle and Anders Limpar.

When George took over at Chelsea, he had to adopt a safety-first approach to avoid relegation. Then he introduced exciting players like Jimmy Floyd Hasselbaink, who went on to do so well at Chelsea and guided them to fifth in the Premier and a UEFA Cup place by doubling their goals tally on the previous season.

He had a record for creating good players and good characters down the years for any team he managed – his Arsenal and England captain Tony Adams comes to mind. So when he came to us, it was good news.

George was old school in his approach to training, believing in hard work, but he wanted us to go out and play football, which has always been the Tottenham way. That was music to our ears after Christian Gross, who wanted us to play direct all the time. That just did not work and was never going to be accepted by the Tottenham fans. George didn't mind going long if it was needed, but he got the balance right, while also getting the defence playing as a solid unit. We scored loads of goals and were exciting to watch. It certainly wasn't a case of '1–0 to the Tottenham' that season. It was hugely enjoyable.

We had Ian Walker in goal, Sol, John Scales, Stephen Carr, and Justin Edinburgh, with Ramon Vega in reserve, at the back. As strikers there were Chris Armstrong, Steffen Iversen and Les Ferdinand as well as myself, and Steffen Freund, Tim Sherwood and David Ginola as midfielders.

David was the one who caught the public imagination. He was a great talent, a real individual. But he wouldn't help defensively. He didn't think it was his job. And when we were struggling he could be frustrating. For those reasons, we thought he'd be the first to go when George came in, but George got the best out of him. He knew about David's attitude towards tracking back, but he also knew that if he produced every week he would be a huge asset. That season he certainly produced. He would rip his full-back to shreds. He was unplayable at times. David was great in the dressing room and training ground and on social occasions. He was a very nice guy and an absolute gentleman. He always had a smile on his face, apart from when I screamed at him to track back!

George was a great character. Although training was hard, he made it good fun. He had a good sense of humour and took the mickey out of a few of the lads. He knew I was friendly with Chris Armstrong and Steffen Iversen and he'd go to me 'C'mon Darren, sort out the "Dum-dums"!' when they screwed up in training.

The banter was good and he man-managed us well. He was a good coach and an inspiration from the sidelines when we played. If something was wrong, he'd be up screaming and shouting and verbally abusing the referee. I liked that. He wanted to kick a few balls himself. It showed how passionate he was.

We all wanted to play for George and, although we had an average League season, finishing 11th, we proved to be a good Cup team. Especially in the League Cup, which was sponsored that year by Worthington.

After beating the Bees in September 1997, we slipped past more lower League opposition, beating Northampton Town, with Chris Armstrong proving himself not so dumb, with a couple of goals to land us a last-16 date with Liverpool at Anfield where historically we had always struggled to get a result.

The Reds had a great record in the competition and the odds were against us but we put in a superb performance as we raced to a 3–0 lead, playing brilliantly, before they pegged us back with one goal. As of the end of the 2009–10 season, it remained Spurs' last victory over Liverpool at Anfield in any competition.

Our League Cup campaign didn't get easier – Manchester United were next in line. United were on their way to the Quartet. Besides the Worthington Cup, they wanted the Premier League, FA Cup and Champions League. That's what I call ambition. But because of us they had to settle for just the Treble. Their side included Teddy, as I've said. They had rested a few players, yet it was still a strong line-up. But Chris Armstrong bagged his second double of the competition in a 3–1 win on a memorable night at White Hart Lane.

Now in the semi-final, we had to beat Wimbledon over two legs. As everyone in football knows, the Dons, as they were before evolving into MK Dons, were never a pushover. The Crazy Gang could live up to their name under Joe Kinnear, with their ferocious team spirit.

The first leg at White Hart Lane wasn't much to write home about, although I hit the post. A goalless draw made for an uphill task in the second leg at Selhurst Park. A fantastic Steffen Iversen goal, when he lobbed Neil Sullivan from the edge of the box, was enough to get us through after we had survived the Dons' up-and-at-'em approach. I couldn't believe it. I'd finally won a semi-final – at the fourth attempt. I was beginning to think I was jinxed. A Final experience was ahead. I couldn't wait for it.

After we beat Wimbledon, George displayed his man-management skills superbly. We were in our tracksuits on the coach travelling back to Tottenham. The lads were all drinking beers as they celebrated. George piped up: 'Do you boys want dropping off in town?' I knew a West End club in London that would be good fun and wouldn't mind us going into it in our tracksuits because the owner was a Tottenham fan. I made the call and the coach driver dropped us off and we had a great night out. George might have had a dour image, but it was – and is – a misconception.

We faced Leicester City for the last League Cup Final at the old Wembley Stadium on Sunday 21 March 1999. Spurs had had their moments in the shadow of its Twin Towers in the FA Cup in the 1960s, 1980s and at the beginning of the 1990s. Now it was the current team's opportunity to seize the moment. We'd lifted the League Cup twice, but it had been 26 years since the last success and we were aiming to make up for lost time to secure the hat-trick.

George had turned us into a good team, which included Sol, Steffen Iversen, Les, David Ginola and myself. I felt we had the better players overall. Also, George had been there and done it twice in the League Cup with Arsenal. He was a winner.

But Leicester, who had beaten Sunderland in the semi-finals, were no mugs. Martin O'Neill helped build his respected reputation as a manager during his five years as the Foxes' boss and would go on to lead his side to a place and two points above us in the Premiership that season. His Leicester side on that wet Sunday afternoon in north-west London wasn't bad on paper, with the likes of Emile Heskey, Robbie Savage, Muzzy Izzet and Neil Lennon in their starting line-up.

George geed us up in the dressing room while myself, now a senior player, with Sol, Les Ferdinand and David Ginola, were on hand to give encouragement and settle the nerves of others. I'd played in so many big games for England at Wembley in which it was pressure, pressure. But I was glad to be there with my own club because I felt I could almost enjoy it more. The big reason I came to Spurs in the first place was to be successful and involved in Cup Finals. Now, after seven years of trying, I was in one. I was excited at the prospect of winning my first piece of silverware as a professional footballer.

It was a great occasion, but like so many, the match itself was a let-down. It was awful, shocking. The worst ever. The pitch was heavy due to the rain and Leicester just tried to shut us down, man-marking all over the pitch. They were good at what they did because they got about you. We were playing OK, not great and then Robbie Savage got Justin Edinburgh sent off with about half an hour left by diving on the floor and rolling around when Justin seemed to retaliate to a challenge by brushing against him. I was furious at Robbie's antics. I certainly didn't think I'd end up being good mates with him a few years down the line at Birmingham.

You'd have thought, with them having the extra man, that they might have played a more expansive game, to go on and try to win it. But they didn't. It looked like they were playing for extra-time and penalties. I found that strange.

But then the moment arrived for us to seal victory. It came in the last minute. Les passed the ball to Steffen Iversen who shot. Leicester 'keeper Kasey Keller, who joined me at Spurs a couple of years later, merely parried it out and Allan Nielsen dived to head the ball into the net.

We were in ecstasy. The fans were even chanting 'There's only one George Graham', forgetting on this afternoon of glory about his Arsenal past. I walked up the 39 steps to the Royal Box to receive my medal and watch as captain Sol lifted the Cup to our fans. We did our lap of honour, deliriously happy. The celebrations continued in the changing rooms with endless bottles of champagne.

George had arranged a big celebration party at the Sopwell House hotel, which was once the Georgian country house of the late Lord Mountbatten, the Queen's cousin, at St Albans. It was a beautiful place and great venue. All the club staff were there. It was all done properly and we had a great time.

I wished we could have provided a more entertaining match for the 78,000 crowd at Wembley, but Leicester made it difficult to provide a spectacle. From what I have heard, the 1961 FA Cup Final between us and Leicester wasn't much of a game either, but it provided an historic moment in football because it sealed the double of League and Cup for Spurs, who were the first team to do it in the 20th century.

But the bottom line is that players from both of these Tottenham teams were able to collect the medal they wanted – the one inscribed 'winners'. And for me personally, it is particularly treasured as it is the only one in my collection of mementoes after 18 years of blood, sweat and tears.

For the record, the line-ups that day were:

Tottenham: Ian Walker, Stephen Carr, Sol Campbell, Ramon Vega, Justin Edinburgh, myself, Steffen Freund, Allan Nielsen, David Ginola, Les Ferdinand, Steffen Iversen, Substitutes: Espen Baardsen, Luke Young, Jose Dominguez, Andy Sinton, Chris Armstrong.

Leicester: Kasey Keller, Robert Ullathorne, Steve Guppy, Matty Elliott, Steve Walsh, Gerry Taggart, Neil Lennon, Muzzy Izzet, Robbie Savage, Tony Cottee, Emile Heskey. Substitutes: Pegguy Arphexad, Stuart Campbell, Theodoros Zagorakis, Ian Marshall.

It also looked as though I might make an FA Cup Final appearance after three losses in the semis. I managed a goal as we beat Watford 5–2, with Steffen Iversen bagging a couple in the third round.

We needed a replay to get by Wimbledon. The same happened in the fifth round against Leeds. Both goals in the replay were pretty memorable in the 2–0 win under the lights at White Hart Lane. I faded one into the top corner from fully 35 yards with the outside of my right foot past Nigel Martyn. It was without doubt my best goal for Tottenham. David Ginola scored the second with a fantastic volley. Victory was sweet for George Graham too, of course, after he had to return and face the Elland Road faithful in the first game.

David put us in the semi-finals by taking on the Barnsley defence single-handed on a run past about half-a-dozen of their players after picking up the ball way over on the left-hand touchline to score the only goal.

It typified the form he showed that season, which won him the Football Writers' and the Professional Footballers' Association Player of the Year, outstripping Jürgen Klinsmann, who could 'only' win the PFA trophy four years before. It certainly put him in an exclusive club. Clive Allen (1987) is the only other Lilywhite to do both, although plenty of Tottenham legends have managed one or the other, including Pat Jennings, the late Danny Blanchflower and Gary Lineker.

Unfortunately we fell again in the last-four, this time to Newcastle. We were the better team that day at Old Trafford on 11 April 1998, but they edged through 2–0 in extra-time. What added to my disappointment was the fact that I had to go off after about 20 minutes when Nobby Solano, the former Peruvian captain who was a popular figure with the Magpies, caught me with an unintentional elbow in the hip – and I couldn't move.

17
Bittersweet Sugar

I'd had a couple of memorable England appearances during Tottenham's Cup runs in the 1998–99 season. Eight days after we'd won our League Cup tie at Anfield and four days after a goalless League draw against George's Arsenal old boys at Highbury, I had Three Lions on my shirt once more. It was for an international against the Czech Republic in a friendly at Wembley on 18 November 1998. It turned out to be the last one I played under Glenn Hoddle.

The Czechs were formidable opponents that night. They were in the middle of a successful qualifying campaign for the 2000 European Championships and included Premier League performers like Karel Poborsky, Vladimir Smicer and Patrik Berger.

We played well and I managed to score midway through the opening half with a low drive at the far post from an Ian Wright cross off a Becks ball. Mers bagged a second and Rio Ferdinand, who has gone on to captain his country, impressed as we ran out 2–0 winners. It was a decent result, even though there was nothing riding on the outcome except pride.

Glenn went a week before I lined up in the next friendly, against world champions France on 10 February 1999, at Wembley. Howard Wilkinson was put in caretaker charge. A couple of weeks before, Glenn had given an interview to Matt Dickinson in the *Times,* talking about Eileen Drewery and his faith. He was quoted as saying:

'My beliefs have evolved in the last eight or nine years, that the spirit has to come back again, that is nothing new, that has been around for thousands of years. You have to come back to learn and face some of the things you have done, good and bad. There are too many injustices around.

You and I have been physically given two hands and two legs and half-decent brains. Some people have not been born like that for a reason. The karma is working from another lifetime. I have nothing to hide about that. It is not only people with disabilities. What you sow, you have to reap.

You have to look at things that happened in your life and ask why. It comes around.'

This was interpreted in the article as the fact that he had 'a controversial belief that the disabled and others are being punished for sins in a former life'. The issue immediately became political, with Prime Minister Tony Blair and the Sports Minister, the late Tony Banks, giving Glenn stick. I suppose the outcome was inevitable.

FA executive David Davies told the press on 2 February:

'The FA and Glenn Hoddle have agreed to terminate Glenn's contract.

After more than 24 hours of meetings and discussions it became apparent to all those concerned that this was the right decision for England football.

The position had become increasingly untenable for both the FA and Glenn Hoddle, who accepts he made a serious error of judgement and of course he has apologised.

The past few days have been painful for everyone involved but that is as nothing compared to any offence caused to disabled people in our community and our country.

This was not what Glenn intended.'

Glenn stated:

'I accept I made a serious error of judgement in an interview which caused misunderstanding and pain to a number of people.

This was never my intention and for this I apologise.

My sincere thanks for the support goes to loved ones, family, friends and media colleagues who have worked with me over the past few days to try and establish the truth.

My personal thanks go to my staff, colleagues and in particular the players with whom I have worked over the past two years as England coach.

I thank them deeply.'

I appreciated his recognition of his players' efforts, and it was a shame Glenn went for non-footballing reasons, but he didn't help himself with his comments.

Anyway, as a player you just have to get on with it. And that's what I did against France. They had some fantastic players, not surprisingly considering they'd won the World Cup we'd wanted so badly the previous summer in their own country. All you need to do is list their line-up and it tells you all about the strength of their side: Barthez, Thuram, Blanc, Desailly, Lizarazu, Deschamps, Petit, Zidane,

Djorkaeff, Pires, Anelka, with substitutes such as Leboeuf, Vieira, Dugarry and Wiltord. Wow!

The name that stood out among them for me was Zinedine Zidane. He was probably the best player I've played against. He made everything look so incredibly easy with his control. He collected the ball and moved with it as if it was glued to his boots. I tried to kick him a few times, but he knew how to bounce off challenges because he was so strong. He was the footballing equivalent of Roger Federer at tennis. Federer makes everything look so easy. What he does seems effortless to him. Sometimes you wonder whether he's even got a sweat on. It was the same that night against Zidane, my first of two experiences playing against him.

We had a decent enough side on paper – with guys like Seaman, Dixon, Le Saux, Ince, Adams, Keown, Beckham, Redknapp, Shearer, Owen and myself – but two Nicolas Anelka goals did for us.

My post-World Cup season brought changes in my private life. My lovely penthouse apartment at St Katherine's Dock in central London was ready to move into in the first week of January 1999. It was time to leave the Chigwell house I'd been renting. On the day we moved out, I took delivery of my Ferrari. I'd had a Mercedes sports car – which had been my favourite car as a kid. But I had developed back problems driving it, so it was time for a change.

I hadn't let on it was coming. Suddenly, a big truck turned up outside and a gleaming red car rolled off the back of it. My brother Ben turned to me and said: 'You tosser', implying I was a flash so-and-so. It was all part of the banter we had together, of course. I wanted to drive Ben to the new place in my new pride and joy. When it was time to go, I drove out of the drive. I turned right and put my foot down on the accelerator. As I did, I lost the whole back end in the wet conditions and nearly ended up off the road. I thought: 'Oh my God, I'm not going to be able to drive this thing. It's too powerful for me.'

Despite what had happened, I managed to get us to the apartment in it. But my car trouble wasn't over. I had to park the Ferrari down in the basement of my new apartment block and the kerbs leading down were so high and narrow that I clonked the body just below the passenger door and caused £2,000 worth of damage. What a nice first drive! I phoned Les Ferdinand, who is mad about cars and also had a Ferrari, and told him what had occurred and he warned me: 'You've got to be careful with Ferraris when it is raining!'

Scott and Parker were staying with us at the apartment with Kate, although Kate and I split amicably a few months after moving in. Generally, life was good. I enjoyed living in London. It was a great city – and I was in the heart of it. We used to go out to fantastic restaurants about three or four times a week and it was only 20 minutes drive to the training ground.

I hadn't been involved as England began the second half of their European Championship qualifying campaign with a 3–1 win over Poland in March 1999, which marked the first game in charge of the national team for Kevin Keegan, my boyhood hero, who had taken over from Howard Wilkinson following the friendly against France.

And it was the same again as England drew with Sweden (0–0) at Wembley and Bulgaria (1–1) in Sofia in the summer. I'd missed out on the summer games against Sweden and Bulgaria after I tweaked my groin on the last day of the 1998–99 season at Manchester United. I decided not to risk making myself available for them after consulting Dr King, who advised me to completely rest throughout the close season. I thought this was a good idea because I wanted to come back firing on all cylinders for Tottenham the next season.

I went off straight off to America for a few weeks, and when I came back I took my Dad, brothers and friends Parker, Birdy, Sailsy and Fudgey on a golfing trip to Puerto Banus in Spain, which I'd remembered from the trip with Tottenham a few years earlier. It was a wonderful trip with Dad and he loved it there. The standard of golf, however, was horrific after the many late nights we had. Birdy was left constantly searching for his ball in people's gardens.

Everything looked good for 1999–2000. Tottenham's League Cup win had earned us a place in the UEFA Cup and we made a fantastic start to our Premier League campaign. I started the season at the top of my game, along with the rest of the team, as we won three of our first four League games.

My contract was up at the end of the season and the Bosman ruling had come in, which allowed players to leave at the end of their deal for free. Spurs had offered me a new contract, one George thought was a good one, but I hadn't signed it. And, of course, I did have the option to run my current contract down. George joked with me: 'You are on a Bosman, no wonder you are flying.' He was always all right, George.

Yet I wanted to stay. I was happy at the club, although obviously I wanted what I thought was right. But injury began to be thrown into the equation. It started in the warm-up to our third game, a 3–2 against Everton at home. I felt pain in what I thought was either my right Achilles or calf. I went in and saw the physio, who by now was Ali Beattie. He asked if I thought I could play in the next game at Sheffield Wednesday. I said: 'It should be OK, so I'll give it a go.'

I struggled through training that week but was able to start at Sheffield Wednesday on the Saturday, a match we won to go top of the table, but there was a price to pay as my Achilles felt awful. I laboured through the next week in preparation for the visit of Leeds. On the day before I said to George 'Gaffer, I'm really struggling with my Achilles'.

He said: 'You're not moving well, go and see the physio. Make sure you walk around the back because the press are at the front. You've had enough shit from them.'

I saw the physio and we decided I wasn't to play and I would see Dr King on Monday. The doctor told me I had degeneration in my Achilles, the build-up of a lot of micro tears over the years. He said I needed an operation to scrape away scar tissue and it would keep me out for 10 to 12 weeks. I was close to tears. The last season had gone so well. And I had started this one like a house on fire. This was a big year for me. I was 27 and in my prime. Then this.

What didn't help was that Tottenham had laid a new type of training pitch, which was sand-based. I guessed, judging from the fact we had three or four Achilles injuries to players six months after it was installed, including myself and Les Ferdinand, who ended up having the same operation as me, that the new pitch was the cause. It is the sort which is commonplace for stadiums these days. It means the pitches are immaculate and wonderful to play on in comparison to the mud heaps back in the day. But the problem is that they are like concrete to run on. It is OK to play on once a week, but not to train on every day.

The following morning it was all over the back page of the *Daily Mirror*. I was slaughtered for being injured again. The article listed my injury record and stated that surely no one would touch me if my contract ran out. I was devastated. It was hard enough knowing that I had to have another operation. To see all this highlighted in a tabloid was the last thing I needed, especially as I'd only been told about the extent of my latest problem the day before. I wondered who could have given the paper this information. I knew Dr King and Ali wouldn't have done. Nor George. My thoughts then turned to Alan Sugar. I knew, when he'd had his bust-up with Terry, that a lot of what he had to say on the matter had appeared in the *Mirror*. It made me strongly suspect it was him. And if he had done it, I wondered how my own chairman could be so insensitive. So I called him from home and said: 'Please don't tell me you fed them that story in the *Mirror* this morning.'

He started ranting: 'Well you and Teddy are always f***ing slaughtering me in the press.'

I'd remembered they had had a slagging match when Teddy had moved to Manchester United, and replied: 'I've never done that. Your arguments with Teddy via the press are nothing to do with me. You're a disgrace! I've just been told that I'm not able to play football for three months. I'm absolutely devastated. I didn't play for England this summer in order to be spot on to play for your club. How f***ing dare you feed the press a story like that on me. I turned down Manchester United to sign for you when you were begging me to stay!'

He replied: 'You're f***ing injured again and you won't sign a new contract.'

I said: 'I've never said I won't sign a new contract. I'm just not happy with the one that is on the table. It's called negotiating!!! You're an absolute joke! I still can't believe what you've done to me with that shitty article.'

The conversation mellowed as he admitted that he shouldn't have done it and hoped I would have a speedy recovery from the operation.

I had, and have, no problem with Alan Sugar. He always said what he thought. And I was able to do the same with him. We were always honest with each other. But when I put the phone down I was still seething inside.

My new girlfriend Katie, whom I'd just started seeing, turned to me and said: 'Who was that?!'

I said: 'The chairman, Alan Sugar.'

She said: 'Oh my God! You speak to your boss like that!'

I'd met Katie Rata-McMahon while on a night out in Southampton with my mates in a club called Rhino's. I remember noticing her across the bar, and gesturing for her to come over. She declined and tells me now her thoughts were 'What an arrogant muppet'.

Luckily for me, she was standing close to our group later in the evening and I ordered Parker, who I used wind up about him being my butler, chef and gardener, to get her a drink. Then I started chatting to her. And the rest, as they say, is history.

With the injury, instead of having an operation straight away, I was advised to try and have complete rest for a week or two to see if it would solve the problem. So I had put a boot on to protect the Achilles, and me and Katie went to Spain for five days to stay at her parents Mike &

Jane's apartment. Then I tried to run. It was no good so I flew out to Dr Mueller-Wohlfahrt in Munich to seek his opinion and he told me I would have to have an operation. I could have had it done out there and wanted to do just that. But George wasn't happy about me doing it abroad for some reason and said I should let Dr King do it.

I replied: 'Dr King seems to do every operation for us. I've seen Dr King plenty of times for other injuries. Shouldn't I let an Achilles expert do it?' I had no problem with Dr King, but at this point I swore by Dr Mueller-Wohlfahrt.

But George was insistent. So I called England physio Gary Lewin, who had worked with George at Arsenal, about this surgeon. Gary told me Dr King was the guy he sent his Arsenal players to for that type of injury. He had even operated on Gary's own Achilles after someone had rammed it accidentally with a shopping trolley in a supermarket. He advised I should get it done as quickly as possible otherwise the Achilles could rupture and I would be in trouble as far as my career was concerned. He told me not to worry, and that he'd take me through exactly what I needed to do in the rehab. And he also told me that Gunners manager Arsene Wenger would be happy with the arrangement because he was very interested in signing me that summer. So I had the surgery. I was off for a couple of weeks to rest it before starting the rehab, which was good.

Things were very different under George as far as the treatment side was concerned. When he came in Spurs had a terrible injury record and he wanted to make sure everyone got the full treatment they needed by coming in at 10am and staying until 4.30 each day. That regime scared players who might have been exaggerating problems to return to training. It suited me, although it was very boring. It involved a lot of sitting around doing nothing. It seemed like punishment having to stay there all day, as there was only so much treatment you could get.

One day me, Chris Armstrong and Ben Thatcher went for lunch near the training ground. I drove myself and Chris drove Thatch. Thatch decided to order himself a beer and a double vodka and orange and went on to have seven or eight more double vodkas, while Chris and I drank water. Thatch was steaming as we headed back to the training ground. Unfortunately for Chris he had to drive Thatch back, which involved him continuously pulling his handbrake.

When we got back to the training ground I said to Ali: 'You've got to send Thatch home. If George sees him, he'll sack him.'

Ali said: 'No problem.' He then turned to Thatch said: 'F**k off home, you muppet!'

Thatch said: 'No chance. I'm staying here. I'm going to see the gaffer.'

World Cup dream maker: with my England, Tottenham and Wolves manager Glenn Hoddle.
(Action Images)

Reasons to be cheerful: clutching the League Cup after the 1999 Final. (Action Images)

Look what we've got: myself with Les Ferdinand, David Ginola, Chris Hughton and Ruel Fox after the 1999 League Cup Final. (Action Images)

Getting one over Frank Lampard, the Chelsea and England midfielder, (Action Images)

FOOTBALL & ATHLETIC CO. LTD

Members of The Football Association and FA Premier League

Darren Anderton
71 Swan Court
Star Place
St Katherines Dock
London E1 9AS

12th May 2004

Dear Darren,

I am writing to inform you that Tottenham Hotspur Football Club will not be offering you terms of re-engagement upon the expiry of your current contract on 30 June 2004.

Can I thank you for all your efforts on behalf of the Club and wish you good luck for the future.

Best wishes,

Yours sincerely,

John Alexander
Club Secretary

Dear Darren: Tottenham Hotspur's way of saying goodbye after 12 years service, but I will always be grateful to the club for helping me realise my footballing dreams.

My biggest top-flight influence: Terry Venables. (Action Images)

With Gazza after we had combined for his goal against Scotland in Euro '96.
(Ben Radford/Allsport UK)

With Alan Shearer after his goal against Switzerland in Euro '96. (Action Images)

Cool Britannia: with David Platt, Gareth Southgate, Teddy, Terry and Tony Adams at Euro '96. (Action Images)

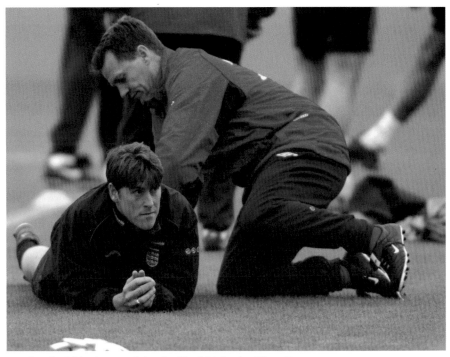

Keeping the faith: the stretch inpsired by faith healer Eileen Drewery. (Action Images)

Greatest moment: savouring my World Cup goal against Columbia with David Beckham.
(Ross Kinnaird /Allsport)

My boyhood hero: I played once for England with Kevin Keegan as manager. (Action Images)

Substitute: replacing Robbie Savage for Birmingham City. (Action Images)

Look behind you: at Wolves with Paul Ince. (Action Images)

Happy days: enjoying my final goal with AFC Bournmouth. (Action Images)

The last goodbye: thanks for the memories. (Action Images)

The American clan: I'm welcomed to the United States.

On the Strip: with the Bournmouth boys in Las Vagas.

Dining out with family and friends.

With family and friends in Spain.

Dad, Katie and me.

Grown up 'monsters': Scott, Ben, Kelly and me.

The happy couple: with my Katie.

Me with my god children Jake and Carter.

My rock: cheers, Dad.

He then proceeded to go into the gym and started doing weights. Reserve coach Chris Hughton was in there and started speaking to him and obviously noticed the smell of booze and said: 'Thatch, have you been on the sauce?'

Thatch replied, giggling to himself, as he pumped out these weights: 'You wouldn't think so, would you?'.

The idiot still decided to go and see George and ask him why he wasn't in his team. George fined him £15,000.

The following day Chris Armstrong and I had to take him to the bank to get the money out in cash! It was a funny couple of days. Thatch was a great lad. A real character.

At first I couldn't do much and went around the training pitch on my crutches to get some sort of exercise. I even played head tennis on them. When I got going, the treatment was great. I worked with Ali Beattie, who had replaced Tony Lenaghan as physio. I was constantly stretching the Achilles. The scar tissue from the operation was so thick it had to be broken up. Ali managed to do just that. It got to the point after about five or six weeks that I could start jogging. It had been a lot of hard graft, but it seemed to be paying off.

George was pleased with the effort I'd put in and said I should have a break before I stepped it up and started running. I was surprised he gave me such advice but his thinking was that I'd worked hard and a week off would put me in the right frame of mind to push on. I took Katie to Barbados for a week, travelling by Concorde. We had a lovely time, and returned refreshed. I was ready to start running and get fully fit. George's plan had worked a treat.

Not long after, I was back training with the lads. After four or five days, George told me he was thinking of naming me on the bench against Liverpool in our next match on 3 January 2000. I hadn't even had a warm-up game. It seemed appropriate. The start of a new Millennium and the restart of my career. It had been four months since my last involvement on match day.

It had come out in the paper that day that I still hadn't signed the new contract and the fans, who had always been so good to me, were, for once, giving me grief as I warmed up. They weren't happy I hadn't signed. I had to laugh inwardly. I could have left the club but stayed loyal and now I was getting verbally abused.

I stayed on the bench for the whole game as Chris Armstrong secured us three points with the only strike of the game. I would have to wait. My return came nine days later against Chelsea at Stamford Bridge. George put me in the team. Brilliant! I wore studded boots as I warmed up but felt pressure on the Achilles on the hard ground, so switched to boots with softer moulded studs. This eased it and I came through the whole game feeling good and the fans were back on my side.

I finished off the rest of the season reasonably well until the final game as Spurs finished 10th, while the contract issue was resolved when I signed in March.

While I was sidelined, early on the lads' League Cup defence was ended against Fulham, while our European adventure was scuppered in the second round by German side Kaiserslautern.

In the meantime, my Achilles problems had put paid to any involvement in the remaining 2000 European Championship qualifiers under Kevin Keegan. We'd got to the Finals after a two-legged play-off with Scotland in November 1999 after thumping Luxembourg 6–0, with Alan Shearer still banging in the goals, getting three that night at Wembley, and drawing 0–0 with Poland in Warsaw.

I'd still hoped that I could figure in Belgium and the Netherlands for my country in the Finals. I was in Kevin Keegan's thoughts because he'd mentioned he had wanted to play me in the qualifiers. But it was not to be. That fateful last match of the season I mentioned earlier – which was at home to Sunderland – ended the dream. Late in the game I whipped the ball into the box and ended up in a heap. I knew I'd torn a groin. After all, I'd done it so many times I knew what to do: rest it for two weeks and get in the gym to rebuild it.

Instead of the 2000 European Championship Finals I hired a villa in Marbella for family and friends to have a week away. I couldn't grumble as I'd had a reasonable season considering I'd missed so much of it. As it turned out, the Finals were good ones to miss from England's point of view. We needed a draw from our final group game against Romania to seal a quarter-final against Italy after beating Germany and losing to Portugal. Unfortunately the Romanians, who included my old Spurs mate Gica Popescu, got a last-minute winner.

18

Club Hoddle

We were never short of a drama or two during my whole time with Tottenham, and the 2000–01 season was no exception. The campaign started well. I got myself on the scoresheet and Sergei Rebrov, who had cost a club record £11 million, debuted in the opening-day 3–1 win over George Burley's newly-promoted Ipswich Town after coming from a goal down. We followed it up with a midweek draw at Middlesbrough, a match we should have secured three points in. We carried on winning a few, losing a few and struggling to score.

The FA Cup looked like our best chance of winning silverware. In our opening round, the third, Leyton Orient stood in our way, just like they had all those years ago when I made the last four with Portsmouth. And, just as in 1992, the result went the way of my side. I managed a goal as we eased into the fifth round thanks to a 4–2 victory at Charlton.

Unfortunately my other Achilles – my right – felt sore and there was more aggravation at Manchester City in the League three days later. I had to come off during our win because I felt as if someone was stabbing that Achilles. I didn't know it yet, but my season was over.

I spoke to Dr Mark Curtin and Ali. They sent me to numerous specialists to try and diagnose the problem. But no one seemed to be able to get to the bottom of the injury. My foot was put in a boot for a week to rest it, but that didn't work. So the Achilles was put in plaster, which went up to just below the knee, for a couple of weeks to see if that made a positive difference. But when it came off it was still no good.

I called my American friend Dave and explained the problems I was having. He said he knew a surgeon who dealt with the semi-pro soccer team his brother Joe was with. The same guy worked for all the professional sports teams in Philadelphia and was highly regarded in his field. He had been performing a new procedure relating to Achilles tendon injuries. Dave said he could set up an appointment with him, no problem, and that I should fly over to see him. I had another word with Mark and he encouraged me to go and see this Dr McShane.

Funnily enough, when I got to the airport to fly out to see him the Achilles didn't feel too bad, but my plane was taking off from the furthest terminal and by the time I got there it was aching and I was thinking 'Thank God I'm going out there to get it sorted'.

The surgeon did a scan using ultrasound while moving my Achilles, and it showed up a small tear. He explained that his procedure involved pricking the Achilles area to reinjure it so that it would rebleed and heal faster. The doctor asked if I was prepared to go ahead, and said that he could do it there and then if I got Spurs' permission. He called Dr Mark Curtin and they had a conversation. I took over the receiver and spoke to Mark and he said to me I should get it done. I told him I wanted to, but that I also wanted to do the rehab in the States with Dr McShane's physio department so that the doctor could monitor my recovery. Mark said to let him just clear it with the new Spurs manager, who OK'd it.

Back home, you see, it had been all change, with Glenn Hoddle coming in for George Graham and Alan Sugar stepping down. At the end of February, the chairman sold his majority stake in the club to ENIC and was replaced as chairman by Daniel Levy after 10 years in the job. When he got rid of the remainder of his shares to the company Daniel worked for in 2007 he was quoted as saying his spell with the club has been a 'waste of my life'.

Alan Sugar also had a parting shot for me in the press, saying I was away in America sorting out another injury and that my body parts wouldn't be good to anyone, not even a museum. His outburst, I believe, was a reaction to me saying that Tottenham should give Sol Campbell whatever he wanted in his contract to ensure he stayed at Spurs because I considered he was the best defender in the world.

I'd watched Sol from that moment he came off the bench we'd shared when he was an 18-year-old making that scoring debut against Chelsea back in December 1992. Ossie Ardiles had switched him from striker to defender and he'd gone from strength to strength to play for England and did not give Brazil's Ronaldo (then considered the best player in the world) a kick when they came up against each other. People spoke in glowing terms of Marcel Desailly, the French defender, but Sol was the better player.

Sol had the choice of going to any club he wanted should he leave Tottenham: even Real Madrid or Barcelona. He was a nice, laid-back guy who largely kept himself to himself, but what a player! I really did want Spurs to make every effort to hang on to him (although, of course, as we now know, he moved to Arsenal that summer). However I don't think the departing chairman appreciated my input on the matter!

As I've said, I liked Alan Sugar, but he was good and bad during his time at Tottenham. He wanted to do well for Tottenham Hotspur. He was prepared to take a risk to achieve it. He paid me ridiculously good wages compared to players at other clubs to keep me and brought in the likes of Jürgen Klinsmann for, I'm sure, big money. And he wasn't shy in splashing out all that money for Rebrov to Dynamo Kiev. And he kept the club afloat through difficult financial periods. But overall success didn't happen.

I still think he made a huge mistake in forcing Terry Venables out. Who knows what Spurs would have achieved if Terry had remained? And when times were bad, his way of reacting to it was by screaming and shouting. He was fair – to a point – but was easily riled. I think it pissed him off that Leon had got the better of him a couple of times in my opinion, such as with the clauses he negotiated for me, which included having to be the best paid Spurs player by £5,000 a week.

I have watched him on *The Apprentice* – which I think is an entertaining television programme – and it makes me smile to think of those occasions. I'm sure he might have felt like uttering his famous catchphrase – 'You're fired' – to me sometimes! He was obviously a great businessman, and has served the government and been knighted and made a lord, but he didn't have a clue about football. What chairman does? Niall Quinn at Sunderland has been the only exception in recent years.

Alan Sugar's replacement, Daniel Levy, didn't waste much time in making his presence felt and sacked George Graham just a few days after George had got the team into the last four of the FA Cup with a 3–2 win over West Ham at Upton Park. Director of football David Pleat was put in temporary charge prior to Glenn being announced as our manager at the start of April. The timing of George's dismissal was a huge shock because he was doing well, especially as he'd got us to the FA Cup semis again.

Daniel Levy seemed to want his own man in the job and, possibly, to make a statement of intent. Bringing in a Tottenham playing legend covered both bases. I thought working with Glenn again was exciting. I knew first-hand how he wanted his football teams to play, his attention to detail and tactical know-how.

I also appreciated that gesture of giving me the green light to get all my Achilles treatment done in the States. He knew I wouldn't be overly comfortable getting the operation done in this country for reasons I've already gone into. His support meant I was able to stay with Joe in Philly for four days a week while I had my treatment, close to Dr McShane's surgery, and go down to Washington DC with him at the weekends to see my other mates.

I watched us lose the FA Cup semi-final to Arsenal in a dingy Irish pub in Georgetown, a district of DC, at eight in the morning. I sat there with my foot in a huge boot wishing I was out there playing. It was really depressing in a season in which we ended up a disappointing 12th in the Premiership.

It was Glenn's first match in charge. Sol Campbell and a couple of others had just come back from injury for us. We took the lead through Gary Doherty, but they overran us to win 2–1 and Sol got injured again.

I took a break from the rehab to go back to have a chat with Glenn about everything. He wanted me to stay, and said that it was just a matter of negotiations in terms of giving me a new contract, with my current deal expiring in the summer. I was more than happy with that. It was great to know he still rated me as a player. And he wanted to play me centrally, which appealed hugely to me. I also knew that Glenn was trying to get Teddy to come back to Tottenham from Manchester United. I'd obviously been chatting to Teddy and we both wanted to know what the other was doing. He didn't want to re-sign for Tottenham if I was moving on. But he did not have to worry because I'd agreed the new contract with Daniel Levy for another three years.

It was now just a question of getting myself fit. Glenn was concerned the rehab was taking longer than was at first thought. I explained to him that I'd had it in a boot and plaster for three and a half weeks and hadn't walked on it for eight. I had no real strength in my calf, it was so weak. The rehab was great out there and the physio Joe Rule and his team were superb. Joe and Co. proved my faith in them was justified because they got me fit for the 2001–02 season.

I ended up being out in America for three months. It was perfect. I had no media to deal with. I could just concentrate of getting myself fit and enjoy being in the States, going to watch Philadelphia 76ers play basketball as they made their way though to the NBA Final to play Los Angeles Lakers. We went to all the games, which kept my mind off the injury.

I didn't figure in the 2002 World Cup qualifiers through 2000–01. England lost to Germany in what was the last-ever international at the old Wembley, with Kevin Keegan resigning afterwards before a goalless draw in Finland four days later under Howard Wilkinson. My injury ensured I missed three qualifying wins against Finland, at

Anfield and in Albania and Greece with new national boss Sven Goran-Eriksson from March through to June.

But I had managed to earn another cap in February, before being struck down my Achilles. It was against France in a friendly on 2 September 2000, at the Stade de France. The country was looking for a pick-me-up after the disappointment of Euro 2000.

Significantly for me it meant, with Keegan still at the helm, I was playing for my third England manager in as many games following matches for Glenn Hoddle and Howard Wilkinson. It was a dream considering what he had meant to me as a kid. He was a good guy, who cared passionately about England and was good with the players. I was particularly chuffed because he said that England had missed me in the Euro Finals. He thought he would have had a better passing team had I been playing.

It was the first time I'd played for my country since taking on the same nation a year and a half before. We'd faced the French as World Cup-winners on that previous occasion. Now Zidane, Emmanuel Petit, Marcel Desailly and their teammates were European champions with, largely, the side that won them the Jules Rimet Trophy. But we got a creditable 1–1 draw thanks to a late equaliser by Michael Owen.

On 15 November 2000, I got my fourth England manager in as many games. Peter Taylor, who was managing Leicester, was put in charge for this one night, with Sven Goran-Eriksson to take over as full-time boss.

We took on Italy at the Stadio Delle Alpi in Turin for the friendly after Peter had decided to use the opportunity to see what our younger players could do. As I mentioned earlier, Peter, surprisingly to my mind at the time as he was such a quiet lad, made Becks captain of his country for the first time and used quite a few young players, including Gareth Barry, Rio Ferdinand, Jamie Carragher, Emile Heskey, Kieron Dyer and Seth Johnson. Sven was there to cast his eye over the players he was about to inherit.

Peter stuck me, as one of the old guard, on the bench, but I got a few minutes towards the end in place of Ray Parlour, whom people had touted ahead of me for inclusion in Glenn's England World Cup squad. We had to face up to a strong Italy line-up, some of whom went on to help their country lift the World Cup six years later like Gianluigi Buffon, Fabio Cannavaro and Gennaro Gattuso, who all performed in the 2010 Finals in South Africa.

But we did OK. I thought Peter's experiment worked well and gave encouragement to Sven, although I remember there wasn't much of a crowd in a stadium which held 70,000. It was about two-thirds empty. I enjoyed it, though, despite my limited role, and was pleased to see Peter, who had done so well with the England Under-21s under Glenn, encourage us to get the ball down and play.

I got a shock when I returned from America after completing my rehab a week before pre-season training for 2001–02. Spurs insisted I had a medical before signing the three-year deal I'd agreed. I thought it was a cheek. I'd been there 10 years! I spent about six or seven hours having a scan. My back was in pieces! All was fine and I signed my new contract. I was really looking forward to the season.

Teddy had come back and Glenn had also signed Gus Poyet from Chelsea and Christian Ziege from Liverpool. I'd played against Poyet when he was with Real Zaragova, of course, but my experience against Christian was much more memorable as he was in that German side which beat us that night in the semi-finals of Euro '96. Ledley King emerged from the shadow of Sol Campbell, who had just moved to Arsenal, a decision, as we know, he has been criticised by Spurs fans for ever since.

Everything was looking good. I felt great in my first full game since February as we played Reading in a friendly. And the team was performing well, playing one-touch football. It was a pleasure.

Near the start of the season itself I picked up a small calf problem which stopped me playing in a couple of friendlies. But was I OK to go on the bench for the opener against Aston Villa. I was pleased to be involved on the opening day. I came on for about 30 minutes as Villa held us to a goalless draw at White Hart Lane. Two days later, I started at Everton and got our first goal of the campaign in a 1–1 draw in front of the Sky television cameras. It was quite a match as we finished it with nine men.

Everything I'd gone through in America was proving worthwhile. I was so positive about everything. Then we went to Ewood Park at the weekend. We played Blackburn off the park even though we ended up losing by the odd goal in three, with Christian, although a defender, getting our goal.

I played well but my Achilles was sore in the second half, and I ended up hobbling around on the right wing. Straight away it was panic. I wanted it looked at and, as we had a week off from fixtures with England off to play Germany (and beat them 5–1!) in a World Cup qualifier, I thought it would be a good time. I told Glenn: 'I'm worried about the Achilles. We've got a couple of weeks off because it is international week, can I got back over to the States?'

'Sure,' he said. 'Not a problem.'

I flew over for a few days to see Dr McShane again. He said: 'You've had a terrible injury and you've got to come back slowly. You've played two 90 minutes of soccer. You've got to reduce it to about 30 minutes and build it up. You'll be fine if you don't overdo it.' He also advised me to put my foot in a bucket of ice after every training session and game because my Achilles was inflamed and I needed to calm it down each time.

I went back and told Glenn all this and he said: 'That's no good to me. I want you starting games.' I said I wanted to play and would do so, but only if he brought me off when I was beginning to feel it. He said that was fair enough.

Against Chelsea at home a couple of weeks later, he seemed to just ignore me when I indicated the Achilles was feeling sore about 20 minutes from time. I'd been feeling great taking part in a great game, which they won in the last minute, but needed to come off. I told Glenn afterwards that he couldn't do that and he insisted he hadn't realised I was struggling. I wryly thought to myself: 'Good one, Glenn!'

He was desperate for me to play and suggested I limited my training. I'd play on Saturdays, rest Sunday and Monday, train Tuesday, rest Wednesday and then train Thursday and Friday. Again I had reason to be grateful to Glenn because it worked out really well and I only missed a couple of games for the rest of season.

We managed to make the League Cup Final. I took part in what I considered Spurs' finest performance in my time there in the second leg of our semi-final against Chelsea on 23 January 2002. The first thing was to overcome the 2–1 deficit from the first leg at Stamford Bridge. My old housemate Steffen Iversen did that within a couple of minutes. I helped lay on one for Teddy with a left-wing cross that Gus Poyet knocked back to him. We ended up winning the match 5–1. It was breathtaking. From start to finish we were superb and the bonus was, of course, that we hadn't enjoyed the best of records against Chelsea.

Hopes were high when we travelled to the Millennium Stadium for the Final on 24 February. Our opponents, Graeme Souness's Blackburn Rovers, had some decent players in Mark Hughes, Andrew Cole and Brad Friedel. But we had a strong team out there that day. We were big favourites to lift the trophy. I'd waited so long to appear in a Final as a professional footballer and now I was playing in my second in three years. I couldn't wait to get started.

Unfortunately, it didn't go to plan. Christian levelled for us after Matt Jansen put Blackburn in front. But Andrew Cole, the former Newcastle and Manchester United striker, proved he'd lost none of his instinct in front of goal by netting their winner. Gus hit the bar and Teddy had a penalty claim turned down by referee Graham Poll. It was a huge disappointment.

For the record, the line-ups were:

Tottenham: Neil Sullivan, Ben Thatcher, Chris Perry, Ledley King, Mauricio Tarcicco, myself, Tim Sherwood, Gus Poyet, Christian Ziege, Teddy Sheringham and Les Ferdinand. Substitutes: Kasey Keller, Anthony Gardner, Simon Davies, Sergei Rebrov, Steffen Iversen.

Blackburn Rovers: Brad Friedel, Nils-Eric Johansson, Martin Taylor, Henning Berg, Stig Inge Bjornebye, Keith Gillespie, David Dunn, Mark Hughes, Damien Duff, Matt Jansen and Andrew Cole. Substitutes: Alan Miller, John Curtis, Craig Hignett, Alan Mahon, Yordi.

Chelsea got their revenge for their League Cup defeat. They returned to White Hart Lane and beat us 4–0 in the sixth round of the FA Cup.

We improved our League position on the previous season by three places, finishing ninth. The season had promised more for the team and the manager, but as I had been able to take part in almost every game it proved a personal triumph for me. I enjoyed it so much because we played some great football and I was back to my best.

19
Engl-end

Glenn Hoddle's first full season in charge at Tottenham also saw an end to any hopes I had of making the 2002 World Cup squad and, as it turned out, my England career. After Glenn and I had worked out a way to deal with the Achilles problem and, of course, by carrying on with the hamstring stretch Eileen Drewery had inspired, I'd been playing consistently and well for Spurs.

I'd not been involved in the remaining three qualifiers in September and October 2001. That 5–1 win over Germany, which was in Munich, where Dr Mueller-Wohlfarht was based, had been followed by a 2–0 victory over Albania at St James' Park, Newcastle, and the dramatic 2–2 draw with Greece at Old Trafford in which Becks got a last-minute equaliser to secure our place in the Finals.

My form had been good and I'd been recalled to the squad for the friendly against Sweden at Old Trafford on 10 November 2001. The fact that Sven became my fifth different England manager in as many matches must put me in the history books somewhere.

I earned my 30th cap as a substitute for Trevor Sinclair. It seems appropriate, as I look back on what was to prove my England swansong, that Teddy Sheringham came on with me. I replaced Kevin Phillips in the last half hour at Old Trafford that day after Trevor had forced a penalty and given one away in a 1–1 draw.

I was chosen for the next squad in February 2002, against Holland in Amsterdam. By this point, I was struggling with an injury. When I arrived at the squad get-together, Gary Lewin assessed the injury and confirmed I'd been playing with a hamstring strain, so I withdrew from the squad.

I then played in our Cup Final against Blackburn nearly two weeks later, something that I believe may have upset Sven, as I never figured in his plans from that point on. By the time the announcement for the World Cup squad was made, I'd lost a bit of form and was shattered anyway after playing nearly 50 games that season.

When I look back I should have gone to the World Cup. Trevor Sinclair went instead, which reflected the fact that Sven's team were all about pace and power, with passing ability of secondary importance.

The way England played under Sven was never particularly pleasing to the eye. It was very direct. We used the long ball, with either Becks or Steven Gerrard trying to put Michael Owen through every time they got the ball. We gave the ball away for fun, as opposed to trying to keep it and pass it, which I believed was the way international football should be played.

I guess the style suited the players he had chosen, with Emile Heskey a real handful in the air up front and Michael Owen picking up the bits. Unfortunately, if you keep playing that way you keep giving the ball away. That means you spend most of the game chasing it – and end up exhausted. That is what happened in the end when we got knocked out in the quarter-finals by Brazil at Shizuoka in Japan, even though their opponents finished with 10 men after Ronaldinho had got sent off.

Sven seemed fine in the few days I spent with him for the friendly against his native country, although I didn't have a lot to do with him. He was quite quiet and just told his players what he wanted before games. He has been relatively successful in his career overall, but I think England went backwards under him.

I loved playing for my country, despite all the pressure, with the press ready to slaughter you. I can't describe how proud I felt from the moment Terry Venables gave me my opportunity. I am so grateful to him and Glenn Hoddle for giving me the stage on which to realise my dreams. The fans were great to me and I felt as if I was representing each one of them every time I crossed the white line.

For the record, the England line-up for my final England appearance against Sweden was:

Nigel Martyn, Gary Neville (Danny Mills 58 mins), Gareth Southgate, Rio Ferdinand, Jamie Carragher (Phil Neville 86 mins), Nicky Butt (Danny Murphy 58 mins), David Beckham, Paul Scholes (Frank Lampard 86 mins), Trevor Sinclair (Robbie Fowler 58 mins), Emile Heskey (Teddy Sheringham 58 mins), Kevin Phillips (myself 58 mins). Substitutes not used: Ian Wright, Chris Powell, Martin Keown, Ugo Ehiogu, Alan Smith, Ian Walker.

Glenn liked to have a 'pre' pre-season while he was manager at Tottenham. It was a nightmare! People always complain our season is too long and say that maybe we should have a Christmas break, but we don't and yet one of our top managers wanted to make the season even longer for us. It completely baffled me.

It meant we'd come back in the middle of June and spend about nine or 10 days in La Manga. Glenn, I guess, must have got some good rates there because that's where we went for the 1998 World Cup, if you remember! He used to take us on these 7am runs over the La Manga golf course. The lads hated it. We were bored out of our brains. We'd get ourselves fit and then go back on holiday for another two and a half weeks. It was a complete waste of time.

The first season with Glenn had gone well, but after a hard campaign we should have been able to go away for seven weeks and not even think about the game, in order to return refreshed and eager to get back in to football mode. Still, we got on with it, and during the second lot of pre-season in 2002–03 we took on Celtic in a friendly on the Monday before the season started. I did a block tackle and felt my knee ligaments but played on. Next morning I woke up and couldn't walk around the corner because the ligaments on the inside of my knee felt that bad.

The physios treated the injury and had me back running in a couple of days, hoping I'd be fit for the season's opener at Everton. Unfortunately that wasn't the case as I could only run in a straight line. I asked if I could go and see Dr Mueller-Wohlfahrt and it was agreed. He did lots of tests and told me my knee was unstable and I needed it in a brace for four weeks and that it wasn't good. He felt I was lucky not to have ruptured the knee ligaments when running on it the previous few days. I was gutted. It meant I was out for a couple of months. I thought that bullshit 'pre' pre-season had not exactly done me the world of good.

When I mentioned it to Glenn on my return, he didn't agree with the diagnosis. He wondered how it could be that bad, pointing to the fact I'd carried on playing almost the whole game against Celtic. But the fact I had done so was merely an indication of my tendency to stay on and play with injuries when I shouldn't have.

I understood Glenn's position. There was a lot of pressure on him as the Tottenham manager because it was a new season following on from one in which we didn't finish very well. So he wanted his better players playing when he needed them.

During pre-season it also came up that Leeds United wanted to sign me. Terry Venables had gone to the Elland Road club as manager. Glenn spoke to me about his desire to bring in another striker and that it was Robbie Keane. He had to get rid of players before bringing any in and I was one of the only saleable assets. He knew of Leeds' interest and how Terry valued me as a player. So he asked me whether I wanted to go. I didn't really say either way.

It was on my way back from Germany that Leon called me to say a swap deal had been done between myself and Robbie Keane. I told him: 'I'm not going anywhere at the moment. The knee is a lot worse than we originally thought. I'm out for two months.'

Robbie Keane ended up coming in anyway, to join another newcomer, Jamie Redknapp, my England colleague who had signed from Liverpool. But there were then discussions that I'd go to Leeds at Christmas, with Daniel Levy wanting to reduce the Spurs wage bill. I understood he wanted to bring in youngsters, which I thought was a useless idea.

The Leeds switch faded away, even though Tottenham might have agreed to letting me go up there if I had wanted the move. Terry had by this point realised that there were so many underlying financial problems at Leeds he would have to sell everyone of any value. This was reflected in Rio Ferdinand moving to Manchester United as well as Robbie coming to us. In hindsight, it was good I didn't end up there.

I made my first appearance of the season when I came on as a substitute for Tottenham against Burnley in the League Cup at Turf Moor on 6 November 2002. It was only our second tie in the competition, but there was going to be no run to the Final – we got beaten 2–1. I started the next game, a League fixture at Sunderland, which we lost 2–0. It was great to be back playing, but it wasn't the best start to my season in terms of results. The campaign further unravelled when we lost 4–0 in our third-round FA Cup tie at Southampton, which was particularly embarrassing for me, of course. The season wasn't going well.

It had been fantastic under Glenn for much of the previous season. Everything was rosy. But now it had changed and people were unhappy. There were lots of video nasties to watch of erratic performances and uncomfortable team meetings with the side being chopped and changed. It became a disjointed season.

I damaged my knee as we lost 2–0 to Manchester City on 18 April. There were four games left but that was me done for the season. We finished 10th, one spot below the previous term with the same number of points, 50. It was not as good as Glenn, Mr Levy or anyone at the club had been expecting.

At the end of the season, we went to America to play a friendly against Washington DC, which I was buzzing about because it meant I could start my summer holidays from there. Teddy had been told he wasn't going to get another deal, but he came on the trip and I showed the boys around DC with my American mates. We had a few great nights out in Georgetown and had a couple of games of golf at my friend Vic Roy's country club.

History was close to repeating itself for me as I prepared for what would be my last season at Tottenham, 2003–04. 'Pre' pre-season was this time at Five Lakes Resort in Essex. We were at La Manga for the second part of our pre-season when Harry Redknapp called Leon to see if I wanted to join Portsmouth. I believed Daniel Levy was keen for me to go in order to reduce the wage bill.

I had a year left on my contract, which Pompey could nowhere near match. Daniel felt they should pay the difference directly to me as there was no transfer fee involved. It dragged on. I felt Tottenham should have paid the difference if they wanted me to go. By the time Daniel agreed to my way of thinking on the matter, Milan Mandaric, the Portsmouth chairman, had decided not to sign me. He had pulled the plug because he felt things had gone on too long.

I discovered how impatient the Portsmouth chairman had become when my Dad phoned me while we were at La Manga and said: 'You are still in La Manga aren't you? Well, you need to get back here quickly if you want to sign for Pompey, because Mandaric has just been on the radio and said you need to sign by 5pm or the deal is off.' It was, of course, a deadline I physically couldn't meet because of where I was.

I wasn't happy, as by this point I was considering a move back to Fratton Park because my Dad's emphysema had got worse and I wanted to be closer to him so I could spend more time with him. Another couple of reasons were that Spurs were happy for the deal to happen and also Teddy had just signed for Pompey.

Glenn's ideas on bringing the lads back for training halfway through the summer break backfired again for me when I damaged my hamstring in the final friendly, versus PSV Eindhoven, prior to our Premier League opener against Birmingham, who were to later play a part in my story.

I was furious and pledged to myself I'd never do this start-stop-start pre-season again and I told Glenn's assistant John Gorman, a good bloke, just why I felt that way. I'd been injured two years on the spin doing it. It was crazy. That pre-season was hard work and to have it wasted was devastating.

I missed the visit to St Andrews, which saw us lose 1–0, and a 2–1 home win against Leeds, who had sacked Terry, putting Peter Reid in charge. I came off the bench for a decent goalless draw at Liverpool and a 3–0 loss at home to Fulham. Glenn gave me my first start against Chelsea at Stamford Bridge and we got beaten 4–2. But he didn't think I was fit enough to start in the next game on 20 September against Southampton, the club he had managed before returning to us, and put me on the bench. I was fuming.

Going into the game, Glenn was under the cosh with talk flying around that he would lose his job if we lost to the team he'd walked out on to fulfil his dream of becoming Tottenham boss. The fact he had come from Saints gave them an extra incentive and my home city club turned us over 3–1 in front of our own fans. It meant we only had four points from six games. That was it. Glenn was fired the following day.

Daniel Levy outlined the reasons in a statement on the club website:

'Following two seasons of disappointing results, there was a significant investment in the team during the summer, in order to give us the best possible chance of success this season.

Unfortunately, the start to this season has been our worst since the Premiership was formed.

Coupled with the extremely poor second half to last season, the current lack of progress and any visible sign of improvement are unacceptable.

It is critical that I, and the board, have absolute confidence in the manager to deliver success to the club.

Regrettably we do not. It is not a decision we have taken lightly. However, we are determined to see this Club succeed and we must now move forward.

Glenn occupies a special place at this club. Today's decision in no way detracts from the fact that he was one of our greatest players.

He will always be welcome at White Hart Lane. I should like to personally thank him for his determination and commitment and wish him well.

We shall be thorough in our search for a new manager. It is a crucial appointment and we shall take the time necessary to make the best choice.'

Glenn's dismissal left me with mixed feelings. When things were good with Glenn they were very good, and yet when they were bad they were pretty awful, really. I wasn't completely satisfied with how things were going overall. I certainly didn't agree with Glenn's recent decision to drop me to the bench because he felt I wasn't fit. I thought: 'You are the manager, you can put on the right training sessions to get me fit. Or not take us on stupid training camps midway through the summer, rather than the normal pre-season training which had got me fit for the previous 14 years.' My belief was he was always trying to do something different and prove himself ahead of his time. He didn't try to get rid of me in the two years he was in charge, but he didn't seem to be attempting to stop the club from selling me.

Yes, Glenn had 'lost' the dressing room when it came to the parting of the ways, although what was the alternative? You couldn't help but feel a little uncertain about how a different manager would go about things. Glenn had been superb for Spurs preparation-wise and tactically, just like he had been with England. But maybe the real problem – as that incident with Becks and I at a national team training session had shown a few years before – was that he expected everyone to be as good as he was as a footballer.

He had been highly thought of as a player, but with that comes a bit of arrogance. You know what's best. Screw everyone else. Look at when he queried the medical opinion of Dr Mueller-Wohlfahrt over my knee injury the previous season. The Spurs lads used to smile and say he was an expert in ALL fields. Yet, when all is said and done, no one likes to see the manager lose his job.

Harry Redknapp, Martin O'Neill, then at Celtic, and Alex McLeish, who was soon to feature in my tale and Glasgow Rangers manager at the time, were linked with replacing Glenn. The board put David Pleat, our director of football, in caretaker charge assisted by Chris Hughton, who went on to do a great job for Newcastle in getting them promoted back to the Premier League at the first attempt in 2009–10. We were back in training the day after Glenn had gone. There was a League Cup tie at Coventry City two days later.

20
Thank You, Tottenham

Daniel Levy talked about having David Pleat in charge for the rest of the season. It surprised me and the rest of the players that a big name was not lined up to take over from Glenn Hoddle. It seemed the Spurs board had just not liked what they were seeing from Glenn's team and dismissed him, quite happy for their director of football to be in charge. I found David Pleat a little strange and his coaching methods were definitely old school. We didn't really warm up before training, which was weird, although his knowledge of the game was very good. He encouraged you to get in crosses and shots, pass the ball into your front men as soon as possible. He was always thinking about football. He loved the game.

He restored me to the starting line-up for the trip to Coventry and we won 3–0, with Fredi Kanoute, one of three big summer signings by Glenn along with Bobby Zamora and Helder Postiga, among the goalscorers. It was the first of three wins in four games, with the other drawn. An instant turnaround of results is often the case when there is a managerial change. And I was delighted to be part of it.

Pleaty, who had managed a great Tottenham team in the late 1980s, which included Glenn, Ossie Ardiles, Chris Waddle and Clive Allen and got to the FA Cup Final, went back to a more rigid 4–4–2, whereas Glenn played with different systems.

We extended the unbeaten run to five with a goalless draw at home to Middlesbrough, but it was always going to be a difficult season following the start and results began to go against us, including one at Arsenal after I'd put us 1–0 up and Postiga missed two one-on-ones with the 'keeper in the first half. The Gunners, who remained unbeaten in the League for the whole season, scored two late goals, one a deflected effort. It was extra disappointing that we lost in the end because we deserved to win that one.

My run of games was interrupted when I tweaked my calf in the warm-up at home to Manchester United on 21 December. I knew I'd done something but started the game, although I had to come off after 20 minutes in a game we eventually lost. I then flew to Munich in the morning for treatment on what proved to be a torn calf, which healed in 10 days. The real problem was that my Achilles, which had been operated on in America, felt very painful.

I missed the games over Christmas and the lads struggled with a couple more defeats which put us back in the bottom three, a position we had occupied under Glenn. Pleaty came to me before our next League game, at home to Birmingham on 7 January, and asked me whether I could play because the team needed me badly. I wasn't sure and told him the problems didn't feel great but that I'd train over the next couple of days and see how it went. It proved sore but just about manageable and, with the team desperate and in the drop zone, I played and we beat Birmingham 4–1. The Achilles held up for an hour and a half, but I was in agony afterwards.

I then played through the pain as I helped us win 1–0 at Leeds, with Robbie Keane scoring the winner, and 2–1 at home to a Liverpool side which had been going well. I'd come back and we'd won three on the bounce, which ended up helping us to avoid relegation. But I'd done myself again. Sacrificed myself. In the next match, a fourth-round FA Cup tie at Manchester City which we drew 1–1, I found that every time I ran it was like a knife going through my Achilles and I had to come off at half-time. There was no way I could continue.

After missing three League games and the Cup replay with City, which we lost 4–3 after being 3–0 up, I managed to get myself back with the help of a cortisone injection. I came off the bench in a 4–4 home draw with Leicester City, with Jermain Defoe grabbing a couple shortly after joining from West Ham.

I started the following game against Middlesbrough at the Riverside on 9 March 2004, six days after my 32nd birthday. We lost it 1–0. My Achilles became inflamed yet again. I was struggling and it proved to be my final game for Spurs after 12 years service.

In the meantime, over the New Year, discussions started over a new contract. We went back and forth. They offered me a deal but asked me to take a big pay cut, which would slash my earnings in half. I had been convinced it would be a bad offer because I was one of the top earners and knew all along that the chairman wanted to reduce the wage bill and bring in the kids, as I've mentioned. Some of the elder statesmen would be let go, which is how it turned out for Gus Poyet and Christian Ziege, who were not given new deals.

Spurs' offer might have been poor, but I was still happy at the club and told Pleaty I would accept it and sign. Myself and Leon then had a meeting with Daniel Levy and Pleaty, at which they told me the club was going to hold out until the end of the season before handing any new contracts. I was furious and said: 'So you are reneging on the contract you've offered me and I said I would sign? Surely you can't treat a player who has been here for 12 years like that, especially after the last month or so in which I played three matches which we won – and another we drew – and further messed up my Achilles for you. Matches you personally asked me to play in, Pleaty!'

Daniel Levy said: 'This doesn't mean you are not getting a contract. We are just going to leave it until the end of the season.'

I thought to myself: 'Yeah, good one.' But that's how they wanted to go about it. It was ludicrous. I was disgusted. David Pleat had to take part of the blame for it. It was naughty. If you offer a contract, you honour that offer, I thought.

I knew they were only going to keep one of the more experienced/big-earners on. I also knew my Achilles was in a very bad way. I saw a couple of specialists in London, but they couldn't diagnose what the problem was. So I flew to Philly to see Dr McShane. He found the problem, saying I had a small tear in my Achilles. I was furious as I'd been playing games on it a couple of months earlier when Pleaty had asked me to turn out for the sake of the team. Dr McShane told me I needed to have the same procedure that he had performed a couple of years earlier. By this point it was April and I was apprehensive as I steeled myself for becoming clubless and knowing I'd be unfit for three months.

My fears were justified when Leon got the call from Daniel Levy to confirm I would not be offered a new deal. Written confirmation came in the form of a short letter from club secretary John Alexander, on headed Tottenham Hotspur Football Club paper.

This is what it said:

Dear Darren,

I am writing to inform you that Tottenham Hotspur Football Club will not be offering you terms of re-engagement upon the expiry of your current contract on 30 June 2004.

Can I thank you for all your efforts on behalf of the Club and wish you good luck for the future.

Best wishes,
Yours sincerely,

John Alexander
Club Secretary

What Spurs did was wrong. No question about it. I always try and reason out and think why people do things and try and think the best of them. But I couldn't this time. It was scandalous. I was on the other side of the world. I'd just been told I wouldn't be fit for three months. Any specific thanks I was due for performing with injury when the club had needed me had been forgotten. I'd been discarded. It was one of the hardest things I've ever had to deal with.

A couple of days later, I phoned Daniel Levy to ask him why, after offering a contract and saying that he would leave it till the summer, nothing was happening. He said they had decided to give a contract to Jamie Redknapp instead, who, after missing most of the season with injury, had come back to figure in the last few games. I asked him why they had come to that decision. He told me Jamie was very settled in the area with Louise who had recently become pregnant.

I replied: 'I've been here 12 years. Do you not think I'm settled?'

He said: 'You don't seem happy here anymore.'

I said: 'I'm very happy, but obviously not happy that you withdrew a contract offer. Why would I be happy with that?!'

I just put the phone down. I didn't want to listen to any more. He had let me down more than anyone has ever done in my life. In my opinion when you go back on a such a promise, it is unforgivable. I had no problem with Jamie Redknapp getting a contract instead of me. He was a fantastic player and a top, top lad, who had also suffered with injury a few times during his career. It was Daniel using the excuse of him 'being settled' that really infuriated me. That, and, of course, going back on the contract offered to me. I much preferred Alan Sugar. You knew where you stood with him. You could have a conversation with him. He was an arsehole at times, but on other occasions he was all right.

When people asked me about a player who jumps ship for big money, I'd have always said it was wrong and the player should stay loyal. After what I went through I don't blame them, although I still don't condone it. Football is very much a business these days and the players are part of it. The player is just a commodity, an asset, 'a piece of meat' as my Dad used to put it. When it is going great, a player is wanted. When it is not, he's out the door. That's how it was for me. It was a case of 'see you later'.

That's why it makes me laugh when I see a player kiss the badge. I remember that was something we picked up from the foreign players coming into our game, I never did it, but when I see players do it now I find that very odd. All these players are pledging undying loyalty when all they are doing, often, is waiting for the next big offer to come along and they are off.

That wasn't my way. In hindsight maybe it is one of my regrets that I was too loyal. But you are what you are. To me, it was more important to do the right thing. I like to think the Tottenham supporters appreciated that. They always come up to me and say 'Thank you for what you did for us' and 'You were a great player for us'. That's all that matters, really. I enjoyed playing for Spurs and believed I was one of the better players in the Premier League with them while they gave me the platform. I hadn't left on my terms and didn't want to go back to White Hart Lane because of the way it ended. In fact, apart from sitting in the stands soon after I'd signed for Birmingham in the wake of what happened to me at the finish with Spurs, I hadn't – until the 2009–10 season.

The memory of how it all ended is starting to fade and I've enjoyed going back recently to watch them play. I did some live commentary for ITV when Spurs beat Fulham in their FA Cup replay at White Hart Lane that term, giving my thoughts before, during the interval and after as Tottenham got through. It was a new experience I thoroughly enjoyed, and I would like to do a lot more of it.

On 3 December 2009, I was honoured to be inducted into the Tottenham Hotspur Hall of Fame in front of my family, including my Mum and brothers, and friends who go way back to my childhood. Spurs manager Harry Redknapp and David Ginola (loved the flat cap, David) said some lovely things about me as a person and a player in front of a packed room which also included Spurs legends such as Pat Jennings and, of course, fans, who as ever, gave me a great reception.

When you think of the names already inducted it was humbling. I was very proud and wished my Dad had been there to witness it. It was a strange to think that the room next door was where I'd met up with Terry and Alan Sugar for the first time that European night when Feyenoord came to White Hart Lane. It put me on the list with David, Pat, Glenn Hoddle, Ossie Ardiles, Chrissie Waddle, Gary Lineker, Dave Mackay, Cliff Jones, the late Danny Blanchflower and others known to most of football as well as Spurs supporters. It's company I'm so proud to keep.

I can tell everyone who was there that night, anyone who saw me pull on a Spurs shirt or others, that I will always feel privileged to have served such a great club despite all that happened. The good far outweighed the bad. Tottenham were very good to me overall.

As I've mentioned, I owe my England career to Spurs, which gave me such a thrill, especially in the two major international tournaments I took part in. I could have gone off and signed for one of the biggest and most famous clubs in the world, Manchester United. But I didn't think it right that as soon as things were going well, thanks to Spurs, that I should just jump ship. Spurs had taken a chance and spent a lot of money on me when I'd only played one full season in the second tier. They'd stuck by me when I was struggling.

It was so up and down over the years, but I absolutely loved it. Tottenham were a massive club for me as a kid and not far from Southampton for this home-town boy. There was something about them. Not flashy, just a club with a charisma and class, one with a tradition for winning Cup Finals with skilful players who reflected that image, like Glenn Hoddle. Playing football the way it should be played. It is what their fans expected and, in the main, what they got while I was there. And still get.

I also got to play football in one of the best old-style English stadiums. White Hart Lane certainly created a white-hot atmosphere on a lot of occasions for me. I got the chance to play with so many quality players, such as Jürgen Klinsmann, Sol Campbell, Les Ferdinand, Gus Poyet, Ledley King, David Ginola and Robbie Keane. It would take up too much space to list them all.

Jürgen was an incredible front runner and, of course, someone who looked after me when I needed it during that nightmare time when Christian Gross thought I'd imagined I was injured. And I was proud to be alongside some underrated performers like David Howells and Paul Allen, who did so much donkey work holding the midfield together while others caught the headlines. There were also the eccentric players such as Ramon Vega, whom Teddy Sheringham advised Gerry Francis against buying, who proved themselves and were good guys. But I'd have to put Teddy Sheringham at the top of my list as far as my favourite player to play with is concerned – for my club as well as country. I've read that Jürgen Klinsmann agrees with a lot of what I've said about Teddy, saying he was the most intelligent strike partner he ever had. And look at the players Jürgen had as teammates in his glittering career!

I served a host of bosses who all, to a man, believed in me as a player. Terry Venables, ostensibly my manager although he put Dougie Livermore and Ray Clemence in to coach the team, Ossie Ardiles, Gerry Francis, George Graham, Glenn Hoddle and David Pleat certainly did. Even Christian Gross, whom I would name as my most off-the-wall manager, did that in between compiling stats, criticising our 'greasy spoon' diet and implying I should be running into empty penalty areas with the ball down the other end of the pitch.

I was lucky to have a relationship with someone like Alan Sugar in that he thought very highly of me as a player and a person despite the lively debates we had. As I've said, he paid me ridiculously high wages to ensure I stayed. He cared about me – and showed it when getting frustrated if I had an injury. He had the same reaction when the team played and didn't win things.

And you know about how things went between Daniel Levy and myself. He'd wanted a low-pay structure, but he's now having to pay big money with the way football has gone. Yet I wish him well in charge of the club that has the biggest place in my heart of all the ones I served.

I finally got to win a trophy, the League Cup, my only success, unfortunately.

My choice of Spurs instead of a club like either Manchester United, Liverpool or whoever clearly did not affect my England career adversely. They were, and still are, one of the top clubs in the country. I was fortunate to move into the top flight with them at the start of a football revolution, with the Premier League kicking off and Sky television giving it wall-to-wall coverage.

As a youngster, I wanted to play in Cup Finals, play at Wembley, play in front of the television cameras and play for England. Tottenham gave me all that, and I will be forever grateful.

Off-the-field there were ups and downs to being a 'face' with a famous London football club. The majority of the time it was fine. People treated you well. They'd come up and say 'Hi, Darren. How are you?' Then they'd ask for an autograph. It's all part of it. I never ignored people who approached me like that. You should never think you are above anything and not sign autographs in that situation. I've never refused one.

But sometimes being well known in London, particularly in North London and surrounding areas, gave me problems if I happened to be in either a bar or a night spot. I'd get verbally abused and have to walk away from it, remembering what my Dad had told me, although once in a while I might tell people where to go.

One New Year's Eve my American friends were over. There were about 10 of us in the party and we went out to we went to a place in Watford. Some of my friends noticed while we were in there that there was spit all over the back of my jacket. It's the sort of thing that riles you, winds you up. How cowardly! But it is something you had to deal with in a town with so many rival football clubs.

Regrets? Maybe I should have gone on to Manchester United when I had the opportunity because they went on to win things, like the Premier League, FA Cup and Champions League in 1999. After all I was ambitious. As it panned out at Tottenham, I had frustrations in not winning as many games or trophies as I would have liked and with injuries and the treatment of them. But I certainly enjoyed my time there, despite the rollercoaster ride. I might have been too loyal, but I wouldn't swap it.

My years at Tottenham allowed me to live out the biggest dreams I ever had growing up.

21
Banging the Brum

I'd been left without a club – and lumbered with a reputation for being injured – after playing with an inflamed Achilles tendon to help my team steer clear of relegation from the Premier League. No matter how angry I was with Spurs about the way they had treated me in the circumstances – by not renewing my contract and leaving me high and dry – I was determined to keep my career at the top alive. I still felt I had plenty to offer.

However, I wasn't physically fit enough to take a medical should I find a new club and I worried about whether I'd be able to play professional football again. I feared it could be over. As I said, I went to America to see Dr McShane, and fortunately he was able to diagnose the problem, finding that small tear in my Achilles, which hadn't been spotted before.

The doctor said I would need to come back to him and have the procedure. An operation would end my hopes of being fixed up for the start of the 2004–05 season with the three-month recovery. But I wanted to do what was right. I flew back to England not sure what to do. How can you try and join another team if you don't know whether or not you are going to have an operation? Deep down I knew I probably needed to get it done.

I was making plans to fly back over to the States when one morning my Achilles started to feel better. It was strange. I was playing snooker at home and noticed, when testing it by standing on tip-toes, something that would normally bring on the pain, that I felt no discomfort. I phoned the doctor in America to tell him what I thought was good news. He told me to hold fire on coming over and to see how it was for the next few days as it was possible the Achilles was healing itself.

In the second half of the 2003–04 season, I'd started seeing my own private physio, Kevin Lidlow, which turned out to be handy when Spurs sacked Ali Beattie in May. The club doctor said it would be OK to see Kevin and that Spurs would pay the bills, although I ended up paying them out of my own pocket. Kevin was giving me lots of treatment and exercises in liaison with Dr McShane. Things continued to improve, with Kevin doing a fantastic job in getting me back to a fitness level where I could run at 100 per cent and the Achilles would stand up to a medical.

It was a difficult situation because whenever a club showed interest I had to hold them off, knowing I wasn't fit and that a bad medical would frighten them off completely. Or perhaps they would be put off because I'd been sidelined for so long? Or they might take a dim view of my injury record? Or they might not want to sign me for both reasons! But there was interest.

Harry Redknapp got on the phone to ask me to come down to Pompey. I also spoke to Steve Bruce at Birmingham and Alex McLeish at Glasgow Rangers.

I went up to see Rangers and told Alex my Achilles was medically OK and I was able to run at 100 per cent. I hadn't done any real fitness work since that Middlesbrough game, so I was still a month away from full match fitness. I told Alex I would come and have a medical to assess the Achilles and if they were happy with it I would sign. They wouldn't have to pay me until I played my first game for the first team.

I thought I was being incredibly fair. The physios were happy with the Achilles. However, they then asked me to do some fitness work with the club's fitness coach. They ran me into the ground – it was a joke! I even had to borrow someone's boots as I hadn't expected to need a pair as I had told them I wasn't physically fit. Their doctor said I was a month away from match fitness, which is what I had told them before I came. He told Alex they shouldn't risk signing me, even though the Achilles was OK. I was fuming. They'd wasted my time after I had been honest about my level of fitness.

I don't blame Alex, I blame the doctor, who was obviously worried that if he gave me the green light his decision would rebound back on him if I got injured. Alex McLeish was cool, a nice guy, but he went along with what his doctor told him.

I wouldn't have minded joining Rangers with my Dad being Scottish, remembering those trips up there as a kid when he was running his removal firm and making up those stories of him playing at Ibrox.

The option of going to either Portsmouth or Birmingham was still there. A few weeks earlier, Steve Bruce had wanted me to go up to St Andrews to see how my injury/fitness was. I thought that was basically a trial, something I was not willing to do.

Now I made the same suggestion to Birmingham that I had put to Alex McLeish – that I would not need to be paid until my first appearance and that wasn't likely to be for another four weeks. I was willing to go to and work for nothing until then. They agreed, and I told Steve Bruce I would be coming up to sign.

Birmingham had just had a successful season in the Premier League, finishing 10th after being in the top six for most of it, and were bringing in a few new players like Emile Heskey, Dwight Yorke, Mario Melchiot and Muzzy Izzet. It showed their ambition, while Pompey had just got rid of Teddy Sheringham, which made me less inclined to go back to Fratton Park.

Just before I went up to St Andrews to complete the deal with Birmingham, I had second thoughts. I was driving around Southampton with Katie and thinking to myself: 'Do I really want to be going up to Birmingham when I can be back here on the South Coast?'

Harry Redknapp spoke to Leon that day. He wanted to sign me and turn up at their training ground the following morning to do so. I decided that was what I was going to do. I felt a need to be on the South Coast as my Dad's emphysema was getting worse and I was fed up with how it had gone at Spurs in the end. I wanted to be home.

Leon phoned Steve Bruce on my behalf to tell him I was going to Pompey. Steve turned round and told Leon that he didn't think I was like that. That he thought I would want to join a team with more ambition. Not one which was close to my 'beach' house, in reference to my main home in Bournemouth. I thought Steve had a point and did another U-turn and went off to Birmingham.

Leon tried to contact Harry but had no luck. In hindsight, it was a great decision because Harry didn't call back to tell me what time to go to their training ground. I'm glad I made the decision to join Birmingham, as it seemed Harry had changed his mind.

I was happy to sign a pay-as-you-play deal with Birmingham, which would be renegotiated to a normal contract once I'd proved my fitness after eight appearances. I remember driving up on the evening before I was due to sign with Katie and feeling edgy. I'd spent my entire adult life as a Spurs player, living in and around London, with Katie also living her whole life in Richmond, apart from her university years at Southampton.

The city of Birmingham, we thought, might not be so wonderful. But we were pleasantly surprised. After staying in a hotel for the first month, we moved into a rented house in the lovely village of Knowle, on the outskirts of Birmingham. We absolutely adored it. The people up there were so friendly.

My first day at training left me with that awful feeling of starting over again. But I ended up loving it up there, on and off the field. I immediately settled in. The lads were great. I knew Stephen Clemence, son of Ray, and Jamie Clapham, from Tottenham and the rest from playing against them. Guys like Robbie Savage, along with Matty Upson who, with Emile, played for England in the 2010 World Cup, were there. Kenny Cunningham, a Republic of Ireland defender, was a great captain and also great at organising bonding sessions which involved going out for a drink after a game – even though he was teetotal. There were golf days aplenty and we had membership at the Forest of Arden championship course.

Steve Bruce encouraged our get-togethers because he was big on developing team spirit. He didn't want to see the lads getting pissed, but he believed in us spending time together, being a team. If you are out with your mates and looking out for each other, then you would do the same thing on the pitch. That was what Steve Bruce believed. The great camaraderie among the players was something maybe we had got away from at Tottenham, where they were able to sign some better foreign players later on in my time there, and the newcomers didn't necessarily create the sort of team spirit we'd once had.

Katie and I were enjoying the area so much we decided to buy a house when I signed the proper contract after making my eighth appearance. It was close to a few of the players, Maik Taylor and Martin Taylor, who made us feel at home.

I was impressed with the medical set-up in comparison to what I'd been used to at Tottenham during much of my time at White Hart Lane. The guy in charge, Neil McDiarmid, was incredible. He drove round in a Porsche so I presumed Birmingham were paying him what he was worth. They knew the value of having your best players on the pitch as opposed to the treatment table. At Tottenham, the players had their Ferraris and Bentleys, but, as I said earlier, the medical team looking after them were paid peanuts in comparison and would have struggled to find the money for equivalent cars.

I had a problem with my Achilles a couple of times because of the new boots I was wearing and Neil sorted it out – just like that – by massaging the area. He did the same to get my blood going when I had a bit of groin trouble. Whenever I had any injury problems he would join me on the runs to ensure I was ready to go back into training. He was a marathon runner and appreciated exactly how far to push you because he was right there doing it with you. He was in a different class.

I arrived at Birmingham only a week before the start of the season, and my priority was to get match fit. I hadn't played for five months when I started my pre-season with my new club. But I had built up plenty of core fitness working with Kevin.

It had been expected for me to take two weeks before being able to join in training with the first team, but after one, the club's fitness guy,

John Briley, told Steve I was ready to join in training with the team. I'd got my fitness back at a high enough level to get involved.

I made my Birmingham debut against Lincoln City in the League Cup at St Andrews on 21 September 2004. We won 3–1, I did well and was named man of the match. It was nice. The fans were good to me right from the off and proved brilliant in all my time with the club. I think they appreciated that, although I was a flair player, I would always work my socks off.

My initial League game for City was as a substitute in a goalless draw at home to Manchester United the following month. That was followed up by full League debut, as it had been for Spurs, away to Southampton with the same result as 12 years earlier: a 0–0 deadlock.

My first Birmingham goal came against Liverpool at Anfield a few weeks later after coming on as a sub. It was from a yard out and proved to be the only goal of the game. Everything was working out quite well, and I scored again two weeks later in a 3–3 draw at Blackburn.

We started to struggle and lost 3–0 to Arsenal at Highbury, our fourth match without a win since my goal on Merseyside. When we went in to training the following Monday Steve told us: 'Don't bother bringing your cars in tomorrow. I'm taking you down my local pub for the afternoon!' This brought an instant result in our next match – a 2–1 win over Aston Villa at Villa Park. It was great man-management.

Unfortunately, that victory was a flash in the pan. Steve had decided by this point to go back to basics, which involved playing two defensively-minded midfielders, and our pattern of play involved going from back to front in a direct style. Steve might have been a good manager, but that was definitely not the way I liked to play the game. I started to find myself being used as a substitute a fair amount because of this change in tactics, often playing three or four games on the wing and sitting on the bench for four or five.

Steve's way showed me how football was changing. A lot of clubs were coming in to the Premiership just wanting to survive and setting up their teams on a Saturday not to get beaten, and maybe sneak a win. If you play long and direct you are not likely to make as many mistakes and, if you do, they are almost certain to be in the opposition's half.

The fear factor with those sort of teams is huge now. That includes everyone bar the top six, pretty much. That philosophy produces football that is not good to watch and is not good for the game in general. I hadn't been used to that at Spurs. Whenever we went out we played to win. Our fans expected it. But Steve – who got Birmingham back into the Premier League for first time – was good at setting his teams up as difficult to beat.

That was exactly how we were at Anfield. I remember thinking we could grind out a 0–0 there and, when a couple of friends asked how I thought the game would go, that is what I told them. Imagine their faces, after they'd decided to have a bet on a goalless draw on the strength of what I'd said, when I popped up with that winner. One of them, Marc Sails, called me on the team bus on our return to say: 'Thanks for that, you twat.'

I laughed and said: 'Don't worry. I'll give you the £20 to cover what you'd have won.'

The rest of the season was a bit of a struggle for the team, but we managed to steer clear of relegation. I thoroughly enjoyed the season with my new 'Brummie' mates, who even asked me to organise the Christmas party in Bournemouth, because they knew I had a home there. It all went to plan and we all had a great weekend.

I was declared fit for our last game of the season at home to Arsenal after my Achilles had been treated all through the week leading up to it. But Steve said: 'Don't worry about it. It's not worth risking you for a game in which nothing is at stake. Go off and enjoy your summer holidays.'

Katie and I went off to Miami and the Bahamas for a great break. We absolutely loved Miami to the point of buying an apartment there on South Beach. Miami is like either London or New York with its hotels, bars, restaurant and shops, except it's by the sea. And its beaches remind us of the Caribbean. It was perfect for me because I can't sit on the beach all day. It's a place you can never get bored in.

When we came back for the 2005–06 pre-season, we were surprised to see that Steve and his assistant Eric Black, a fantastic coach and great guy, had decided to bring in a fitness coach from France. Spurs had had good one with Kunle Odetoyinbo. It had become all the rage to add these kind of specialists to the backroom staffs at clubs across the country.

Everything City's new boy did was based on heart monitor readings. He wouldn't allow our heart rates to go over a certain figure. If it did we had to slow down. There were a few hard bits to his routine, but it was all about being sensible. It was nice. The lads loved it. Normally the pre-season is a real killer, but what we were doing with this guy was bearable.

On the Saturday morning after the first week's training, Steve gave the fitness coach the weekend off so he could run the bollocks off us. We didn't love doing that, that's for sure! It was back to the old school ways.

I did OK in the pre-season friendlies but realised in one of them where I stood in the pecking order with Steve Bruce. It was our last one before the Premier League season started at Fulham and in Spain against Deportivo La Coruna. I sat on the bench with Damien Johnson.

Damien had been sent off at the end of the previous season and was banned for the first two or three weeks of the season. Someone came off with about half an hour to go. I thought: 'Right, I'm going on.' But I was wrong, Steve put Damien on instead. I was baffled. I was eligible to play when our campaign proper kicked off at Craven Cottage. Damien, of course, wouldn't be. Straight away I felt, 'I can't do this. This is a joke!'

The game had been arranged as part of the deal which had brought Uruguayan international striker Walter Pandiani to Birmingham from Deportivo La Coruna. After it, the staff and players all went to his restaurant in the city where we were treated to plenty of drinks and food.

Before heading back to the hotel, Kenny Cunningham asked the gaffer if the boys could continue the night out. He decided for once not to allow it. The boys weren't happy about that. We decided to sneak out of the hotel, but unfortunately Steve and his staff were milling around in the lobby. We looked for another way out and found one via the basement and enjoyed our night out after all.

The following morning, rumours were in the air that the gaffer knew we'd been out as we'd apparently, been spotted on the hotel's CCTV cameras. When we got back to Birmingham, Steve called a meeting and told us we'd taken the piss and he would fine the whole squad £30,000. We had to sort out who paid what among ourselves. It was fair play, he could have been a lot worse about it. A few days later I was gone – so I didn't have to pay a penny!

I knew the forthcoming season was going to be the same as it was in the second half of the previous campaign when Steve started to use me as a substitute. I'd been used to starting with Tottenham over 12 years and with England as well. There was no way I was going to be happy continuing my sub role for Birmingham. I thought: 'I don't want to do this for a second season.' I was really wound up about it. Totally pissed off.

The truth of the matter was simple – I wanted to play. I'd missed enough football, and the people being selected in front of me weren't as good footballers as me. It didn't matter that I was 32. If I had been at a top-six Premier League club and those players were with me I'd have played in front of them. No question.

I loved the training and being with the Birmingham lads, but I'd always felt you shouldn't settle for being a substitute. You should always want to start. Then the opportunity came along to join Wolverhampton Wanderers in August 2005. And it was to reacquaint me with a certain manager for the third time.

22
Fool's Old Gold

Glenn Hoddle had heard I was unsettled at Birmingham. He was now manager at Wolverhampton Wanderers and phoned Steve Bruce inquiring about whether Steve would consider an offer to take me to Molineux on a free transfer. Steve said he possibly would and called me into his office and said: 'We've had an inquiry from Glenn. I know you've worked with him before and possibly his style of play would suit your game more, but if you don't want to go I'm more than happy for you to stay here. You know everyone here – the players and the staff – thinks the world of you as a player and a person. I would think you'll have the same sort of role as you had here last year, probably starting half the games and being on the bench for the other half.'

My initial reaction was that I didn't want to take a step down with Wolves in the Championship for 2005–06. I'd been grateful to get my League start in the second tier, but all I had known for 13 years in club football was the Premier League.

Yet I'd seen how Glenn had done OK with Wolves the previous season – with one defeat in the final 25 games – and thought they'd walk through their League with the players they had, like Paul Ince, my old England mate, and Jolean Lescott, and make the top flight by the end of that season.

Harry Redknapp, who had made the switch to boss Southampton by now, expressed an interest in bringing me to Saints. I was on the phone to Harry and Glenn. It was a similar story at the beginning of the previous season, although it was with Steve and Harry then.

I decided on Wolves because of my belief they were destined for the Premiership at the end of the 2005–06 season. I had no problem playing for Glenn again either, even though in his last game in charge at Spurs he had put me on the bench, which had left a bad taste in my mouth. And at times his man-management wasn't ideal. I knew his style, of course, from my time serving him for England and Tottenham, and his way of playing football suited me.

The evening before I was due to sign I had a medical and, on the way home from it, I spoke to Harry, who said he wanted me to come to Southampton but his chairman Rupert Lowe, who had upset many

Saints fans over the years for the way he ran the club, was against it. So I decided to go ahead and join Wolves in the morning, although I wasn't sure if I was making the right decision.

In hindsight, I should have pulled out if I wasn't 100 per cent convinced, but I wanted to play regular football and I'd presumed if I went to Wolves I would be. Glenn was very keen for me to sign and in the end I thought: 'Why not sign for a year?'

On the very first morning, I half-regretted it. As I drove home, I thought 'Shit, what have I done?' Maybe I should have waited until Christmas. Birmingham had only played one game of the season and things can change very quickly in football.

The following day I made my debut in Wolves' Old Gold against Chester City in the League Cup at Molineux on 23 August 2005. I managed to score from a free-kick as we defeated our lower League opponents 5–1. I enjoyed it. And we played some good football, something I hadn't witnessed much of at Birmingham for the second half of the previous term. That made me feel a little better about having signed.

We secured a decent point at Cardiff on my first League appearance and three days later enjoyed a 3–1 home win over QPR in front of the Sky television cameras. I thought that if the team were doing well, which I expected, then everything would be fine.

The training was good, although it could be long-winded. On a Monday we would train, have lunch, and then watch a video of our previous game. Mondays were long, long days. But Glenn was just being thorough, applying the attention to detail I remembered when I played for him on our two previous occasions together. He hadn't changed on that score. He went over things in even more detail if anything.

So far so good. The football was going well. A 1–1 draw at Luton extended our unbeaten run. But things started to go wrong for me in the very next game when Millwall came to Molineux on 13 September. The Lions had been struggling near the bottom, and it was a game we should have cruised through. It was going to plan. We were 1–0 up. All of a sudden a Millwall player accidently careered into me. He started a run to latch on to a pass his full-back was trying to put into a channel for him. He had his eyes on the ball and didn't notice I'd stepped in to cut it out. Bang! My knee took the full force and I went down in agony. It felt like a dead leg. I tried to carry on – as usual! – but the knee felt so unstable. I had to come off just before half-time. I was in a lot of pain, but didn't know the extent of the problem when I left the ground on crutches. And on top of that, we lost 2–1.

I saw the physios and had a scan which revealed a hairline stress fracture just below the knee. There was no real treatment for it apart from putting my injured leg in a boot. I was told it should heal reasonably quickly. Even so, I was devastated after making a good start. Then the reality of the daily routine I would have to undertake kicked in. It meant me arriving at the treatment room every day at 9.15am, which necessitated my leaving the Solihull house I shared with Katie at around 7.45am and driving an hour and a half through the rush-hour traffic to go on either the bike or the non-weight bearing cross-trainer in the gym.

I found the drive to and from training really pissed me off. I'd had enough of Wolves there and then.

The physios, who included Steve Kember, and fitness trainer Kunle, who had worked with Glenn at Tottenham, were very good and got me back in a month after plenty of treatment and rehab. There I was, dreading the worst, and it hadn't been so bad after all. I returned to the team against Sheffield United at Bramall Lane on 15 October. We lost 1–0.

Glenn started picking me for about three in a row and resting me for three. He told me he wanted to save my energy, that as I was getting older it was the right way to get the best out of me. I said: 'You know that's no good for me. I need three or four to get going and then another three or four to get myself up to a level where I'm at the top of my game.' I was pissed off. I might as well have stayed with Birmingham in the Premier League if I'd known that would happen.

We were drawing lots of games, but I felt I did well whenever I played. Yet the season was going nowhere and it appeared we were destined for mid-table.

I sustained a hamstring problem in a goalless draw with Stoke City at Molineux on 7 March 2006, just four days after my 33rd birthday. It proved to be my last match for Wolves. I was fed up and thought: 'Here we go again, 7.45am in the car and off to treatment. Great!'

I returned to fitness quickly after seeing Dr Mueller-Wohlfahrt in Munich. Unfortunately, after my first two-hour training session, Glenn decided to get the squad to do sprints. 'Just what I don't need', I thought. On the second sprint I felt my hamstring go. I knew it was a bad one. My season was over.

I flew back to see the German doctor and when I explained what we did in training, he said: 'No, not again, Darren. It is suicide for your hamstring to train that long – and then do sprints when only just returning from a hamstring strain. It's crazy. Why did he [Glenn] do this?'

I made up my mind then that I did not want to stay. I really wanted to go back to the South Coast this time. Even if I had got an offer from a club in the north of England to play in the Championship I wouldn't have been interested. The ambition that was fired up by Steve Bruce two years before had gone. To be honest, quitting the game did cross my mind because I'd had enough of what had happened to me at Wolves. Unless something came up that totally suited me and was going to be enjoyable, that was it for me. Another iron I had in the fire was playing in America.

Wolves ended up eight points off a Play-off place, 19 draws from 46 fixtures, while scoring only 50 goals. Glenn had ordered the players in for a week of running and fitness work at the end of the season because of the failure. I told him I didn't want to do it and was heading off to the States, possibly to speak to some teams out there. One thing was for sure, I wasn't going to stay at Wolves. They hadn't said whether they were going to offer me a new contract or not. I was sure they weren't going to offer one anyway.

Without any involvement in the 2006 World Cup Finals, I enjoyed the time through the tournament with Joe, Dave, Vic and Bert on the other side of the Atlantic. It was a big summer for Bert, in particular, as he was getting married. And, ironically, I attended his wedding to Bonnie in San Diego on the day England were knocked out of the game's global event. He had three best men – myself, Joe and Dave.

But, of course, there was my career to sort out. And it was clear things were rapidly coming to a head. About a week after I'd arrived in the States, I received a voice message from Glenn that had been left at about 6am US time. He must have known I'd be asleep at that time. I presumed from that that he'd rather leave a message, which stated that the club had decided not to offer me a new contract. When I heard it, I spoke to my friends and played the message on loudspeaker for them to hear. I said: 'Listen to this for a nice way to be treated.'

'Holy shit, that's scandalous,' Joe replied when the message finished. We all laughed and agreed it was not quite like the glory years! When Leon spoke to Glenn about it he told him he didn't realise the time difference and that he thought I'd be up. Leon added that Glenn wanted to speak to me but, by that stage, I didn't want to talk to him.

I've got no problem with Glenn. As I've said, I will always be grateful for the opportunity he gave me in the 1998 World Cup Finals and the support he gave me in the lead up to it. He put me in touch with a faith healer who kept my career going with her advice and ensured I'd be fit for France 1998. But my time at Wolverhampton Wanderers proved a nightmare. I wanted to do well for Glenn with the history we'd had together, and the team seemed good enough to comfortably ensure a Play-off spot. But it was clear the side wasn't as good as everyone thought it was, including myself. Glenn was turning me into a player who went in and out of the side – just like Steve Bruce had done – and led me to be disillusioned with the game at that level.

Ironically, Glenn himself was in far from an ideal situation himself. The Molineux crowd had got on his back as dreams of promotion were not realised. Not long after he left that voice message to me he resigned, insisting he and the club had different expectations. As this book went to print, the Wolves post remained Glenn's last job in management. He seems happily occupied by his football academy in Spain and popping up on Sky TV as a pundit. But I wouldn't be surprised if he took over a hot seat again. Perhaps as an international manager for England again. I feel that arena suits his style, and recent World Cup performances have shown just how well he could get his England teams to play in comparison.

In the meantime, I instigated a move to a club close to what Steve Bruce had described as my 'beach house'.

23
Cherries on the Cake

I was without a club and, I have to admit, out of love with the game in the summer of 2006. But I made a decision that was, looking back, one of my better ones. My experience at Wolves had soured everything that had gone before in my playing career. It would have been so sad to leave the game that had been my passion for as long as I could remember with such a negative feeling. There is no doubt in my mind I'd have felt that way until my last breath – because you always remember how something ends – without the move I made next: to approach AFC Bournemouth. It was that important.

My disillusion dissolved into delight and I can now look back fondly on the sport which enabled me to live the dreams of my childhood. Colchester United had just come up to the Championship and I spoke to their manager Geraint Williams, who was very interested in me joining his promoted club. By that point, however, I didn't want to travel to Essex, London or anywhere from the south coast. Southampton might have been an option but they showed no interest. They seemed happy with the players they had under George Burley.

But Bournemouth also made perfect sense. I'd always seen myself finishing back on the south coast, liking the idea of going off from training knowing I was returning to my home in the area. Indeed, I'd bought a house in Bournemouth in 1996 and in 2000 had moved to a new one in the town. So joining the Cherries would very much make that happen.

I started the ball rolling by asking Leon Angel to find out how they felt about me playing for them. Manager Sean O'driscoll then called me and set up a meeting. We had a chat, and I was quite keen to join. There were a few things that needed to be sorted out and it dragged on for a few weeks. In the meantime, I saw a couple of their players out socially, Neil Young, who was a youngster at Tottenham when I first went there, and Warren Cummings, and asked them how their players would react to someone like me joining them. They said they would love it and I should come.

A friend of mine, Matt Ford, who ran the Poole speedway team, knew outgoing Cherries chairman Peter Phillips and soon-to-be new chairman Abdul Jaffer and I went to see them. They told me they would really like to do it, but needed to find sponsorship for my wages. I wasn't asking big money. It was peanuts compared to what I had been on, but Bournemouth was a club in financial difficulty. Also there was a takeover imminent. It was going to be difficult to make a deal work.

After a couple of weeks, everything was ironed out and I signed on the pitch at half-time as the Cherries beat Crewe on 9 September 2006. The very same day manager Sean O'driscoll, who had been keen for me to come, left with his assistant Richard O'Kelly. Sean had got an offer to boss Doncaster Rovers, which he took up, wanting Richard with him. That was a shame. Sean ran the club pretty much from top to bottom, and I liked what he had to say when we met up. Also, I'd heard he'd got his teams to play good football.

I was happy and ready to enjoy my football once more and my first experience of the third tier (League One). People connected with the club seemed to be pleased I was there. Coach Stuart Murdoch, who had managed Wimbledon, and Joe Roach, promoted from youth manager, took over while the club searched for a permanent successor to Sean. The chairman, now Abdul, asked me whether I would be interested in becoming manager here in the future or even a coach. I told him firmly: 'Not a chance. I didn't come here to do that. I've made it clear all I want to do is play.'

He then asked me if I knew anyone who might want to and wondered about the possibility of getting a big name there. I mentioned Les Ferdinand, my old Tottenham and England teammate. When I spoke to Les, who had just retired as a player and was doing his coaching badges, he said he was interested and would come down for an interview – which he did. But in the end he decided against it. He mentioned the distance might be a problem from where he lived in London, but, knowing he had one, I joked: 'It can't be that far in your helicopter.'

I got into the training and found the lads, mostly young, a down-to-earth, regular bunch. They took to me and we used to do a lot socially together, with me getting them into clubs on Saturday nights where I knew the owners. They could see I was a normal lad. I might have been able to enjoy the trappings of being a top player for over a decade, but they knew I wasn't a Big-time Charlie and was just one of the lads.

On the field, I earned the respect of the other players by proving my attitude was the same as when I played for England and in the Premiership. I moaned like hell, tried my nuts off and made every effort to show I was a complete team player. I'd always been like that and I wasn't about to change just because I was playing League One football.

It was perfect for me. I loved living and working in Bournemouth, where I had started coming down on days off from Tottenham in the summer. It now felt like I was on permanent holiday. I walked around with a smile on my face. It felt so right. Obviously, things were different to what I'd been used to. We even had to take our training kit and boots home to wash and clean. I joked to the kitman Bernie: 'No one told me that before I signed!'

I played my first game a week after signing. I went to watch the team draw against Brentford at Griffin Park and the following Tuesday I had a run out – and scored in a 1–0 win – in the reserves against Salisbury, a non-League club managed by Nick Holmes, a member of Saints' 1976 FA Cup-winning team. I loved it. It was great to be playing for the first time in six months.

Four days later, on 23 September 2006, I made my first-team debut – perhaps a bit too early considering my lack of match fitness – against Scunthorpe United at Dean Court. I got a lovely reception from the fans, which meant a lot. But I was nervous and I wondered if my match fitness was up to it. It was baking hot, we were 1–0 down and I was shattered. Thankfully, after about 30 minutes I equalised with a 30-yard free-kick into the top corner. I was buzzing. It was a great feeling because I felt a bit under pressure to perform. That certainly got the fans on my side from day one.

I'd played about 70 minutes against the Iron and lasted a few minutes longer in my second League game for Cherries at home to Bristol City three days later. We lost but I felt I played well before getting a 'dead leg'. I figured for about 70 minutes in a draw at Huddersfield that Saturday. I'd been involved in three games in a week after not having played for half a year and a fortnight's training! I was having a ball.

Kevin Bond, who I'd watched as a Saints player and joined Tottenham as Harry Redknapp's assistant at Tottenham in October 2008, became Bournemouth manager after we drew the next game at Northampton and extended the unbeaten run to four games.

He had been assistant to Harry at Portsmouth where I had met him a few times. I'd heard good things about him and he was a nice fellow. And of course I respected him from when I watched him play as a kid. The training was good, but strangely we lost our first six League games under him.

I played in all but a couple of matches that season and, although we struggled, was able to help the team keep their status with a draw against Gillingham in our last home game. And I was voted Player of the Year. I had not had that honour since my first year at Spurs. I even managed to hit the first hat-trick of my career that season – in a 5–0 home win against Leyton Orient on 10 February 2007.

It had been a very successful first season for me. With a new set of teammates I hit it off with from the first day, enjoying nights out after games and barbecues around mine on a Sunday, with them bringing their families. Among them were Steve Fletcher, Neil Young, Warren Cummings, Shaun Cooper, Danny Hollands, Brett Pittman and Stephen Purchase. A few – mainly Wally, Brett and Coops and Danny – would turn up at my place unannounced after training during the week to play snooker and sit by the pool. Good times. Everything confirmed my decision to join Bournemouth was the right one. I had no hesitation in accepting the offer of a new one-year deal when Jeff Mostyn, yet another new chairman, offered it to me a couple of weeks before the end of the campaign.

It was a difficult summer before we kicked off the 2007–08 season. Players were released like Steve Fletcher, who had been at the club a long time and was real fans' favourite. Fletch was devastated. He was such a good lad. Fletch saw himself as the King of Bournemouth – until I arrived (ha ha, Steve!). He wasn't the only one out the door. A few more were also released the day after our end-of-season party.

Kevin had his own ideas, but did things in the wrong way as he got rid of players before securing others, so it became a bit of a panic because we weren't left with many players. I believe there were nine of us contracted – with two of them goalkeepers. It got to be a bit of a muddle. We had trialist in all the time. We signed Lee Bradbury, the former Pompey, Crystal Palace and Manchester City striker, from Southend and a few young lads from Reading on loan.

I did OK pre-season and in one friendly against Pompey their manager, Harry Redknapp, spoke highly of me when he told the *Bournemouth Echo*: 'In the right team and with the right players around him, I honestly think he could still be playing in the Premiership.' That was a nice thing to read. Flattering.

I had another reason to feel the same emotion when Kevin made me club captain. I'd skippered Spurs once or twice, but this was the first time I'd been given the job full-time, although it was taken away from Neil Young, which I felt bad about because he was a good mate.

We kicked off with a decent enough result, a goalless draw at Nottingham Forest, and lost against West Bromwich Albion (in the League Cup) and Huddersfield before everything was hunky-dory once more thanks to an outstanding victory at Doncaster. But a run of bad results – despite the fact we should have won many of them – saw us nosedive down the table. When we faced Leeds United at Dean Court on 6 November 2007, it was our 18th match of the season – and I was making my 18th appearance.

Out of the blue, I felt my hamstring. Not that it had completely gone, but that I'd tweaked it. I played on for half an hour like an idiot and felt it go a little more and came off. A scan revealed a small tear. It started to feel better before I began to get these terrible aches and pains in the hamstring and my back, and I did not play for another five months, during which I had my 36th birthday.

I didn't know what was wrong. I thought I might not have a choice this time and that the injury would force me to end my career. While I contemplated whether I had a future, the team was deducted 10 points after going into administration. It was reported that the Cherries were £4 million in debt.

But on the field we revived. The guys got a home win double against Tranmere and Millwall. I then returned for a 2–1 win at Swansea.

It was two days after a press conference in which the administrators warned the club might fold before the end of the season unless sufficient funding was found, as they revealed a bid they had originally accepted from a consortium headed by chairman Jeff Mostyn was no longer acceptable due a 'breach of the agreement'.

At least the players were doing their bit and we went on to win our next three games. We went into our final fixture at Carlisle knowing that either victory or Sean O'driscoll's promotion-pushing Doncaster beating or drawing against our relegation rivals Cheltenham would maintain our status.

Harry Redknapp, who began his managerial career at Bournemouth, was quoted as saying that staying up for his old team 'would be more than a Great Escape, it would be a miracle. If Kevin doesn't get manager of the month then something is wrong'.

Unfortunately we could only manage a draw and Donny missed an automatic promotion spot by losing to the Robins. Sean O'Driscoll, who eventually guided his team up via the Play-offs, had inadvertently done us again. It was a horrible feeling, especially as I'd never experienced relegation before. And what made it more difficult for me and the rest of the boys to take was the fact that as a team over the course of the season we would have achieved a mid-table finish but for the points deduction due to what was going on behind the scenes.

24
Fairytale Finish

I wanted to carry on playing. The run-in to the previous season had revitalised me despite the despair of relegation. I was mindful of being paid during my long absence through injury in 2007–08. I spoke to Kevin and said I would do a pay-as-you-play deal so that if I did pick up another problem the club wouldn't have to pick up the tab, which would be tough for them to do given the financial state they were in. I said I would retire if necessary, but otherwise I'd just continue. He agreed with that. We then spoke to the chairman and it was sorted out. I could then look forward to the new season in the fourth and bottom tier of English professional football in my 37th year.

Things looked as though they were looking up off-the-field when the chief executive, Alistair Saverimutto, announced the 'biggest sponsorship in the club's history' in July. That respite was short-lived. Just before we kicked off the 2008–09 campaign, the League were reported to be considering putting the block on our participation in League Two for the season because of all the background troubles. It was said the club had to prove it could complete the fixtures and get out of administration. The day after, on 7 August, they decided we could take part but deducted 17 points for breaking the rules. What had I let myself in for?

The punishment left us feeling that our opening fixture for the 2008–09 season against Gillingham at Dean Court on 9 August was a 'must-win' game. I put us ahead, but Gills grabbed a point with an injury-time equaliser. We followed it up with a draw at Aldershot and defeats against Exeter City and Port Vale, with a League Cup loss at Cardiff. And after a 3–1 defeat at Port Vale, Kevin Bond lost his job with us earning only two out of 12 points in our opening games.

I was disappointed because we had a good working relationship and he had helped me enjoy my football as I wound down my career. I was pleased to see him become Harry's assistant at Tottenham.

There had been rumours that Jimmy Quinn, the former Northern Ireland international and Bournemouth striker, was to be the new

manager, but Joe Roach took charge in our next game as we battered
Bristol Rovers from the division above us in the Football League Trophy.
It was our best performance since I'd arrived and, sadly, too late to save
Kevin.

Jimmy was in the stands and would be in place for our next League
game at Notts County. He immediately talked about the need for us to
close down better and said that we weren't fit enough, even though we
had played Bristol Rovers off the park. We'd heard conflicting stories on
how he liked his teams to play. Some said he liked his teams to play, but
mostly it seemed that he wanted to play direct.

Training was quite good at first. Jimmy wanted us to get the ball
down and pass. That was music to my ears, and we went out and did
that at Meadow Lane on 6 September. We earned a 1–1 draw. We played
well and I enjoyed it.

Jimmy's first home game against Macclesfield saw us concede an
early goal and, at the interval, Jimmy told us we had gone too direct
after they'd scored, and that we should pass it more. We passed them off
the pitch, but they held on. He introduced a sweeper system, with Shaun
Cooper, who was so comfortable on the ball and read the game
brilliantly, behind the centre-backs. This enabled us to pass the ball
more easily and we went up to Bradford City and won 3–1. The lads
were overjoyed with the style of performance. So was I, in my role in
front of the back four, receiving the ball and spraying the ball around.

Jimmy the manager stuck with the way we were playing and we
overcame Darlington, who were top, in our next game. We were doing
well and continued to produce respectable performances. Alarm bells
started ringing in my head after we'd defeated Dagenham and
Redbridge, who had employed a long-ball game, on 21 October. I'd just
come off the Dean Court pitch thinking that the way our opponents
had played was precisely the reason why I never wanted to play in
League Two in the past, although it was the first time I'd seen it since the
start of the season. It was crash, bang, wallop. They launched the ball
into the corners looking for long throw-ins, corners and free-kicks.

We were due to entertain Lincoln City four days later and, while
practising our team shape in training on the Friday before the game,
Jimmy stressed how we should put the ball into the corners and go more
direct, like Dagenham had done against us. I thought 'Oh shit, this could
be shocking'. Bournemouth had always tried to play football over the
years and had a reputation for doing so under Sean O'driscoll. That's part
of why I went there in the first place. So this was not music to my ears.

We lost the game and then drew against Chesterfield before losing to
Colchester in the League Trophy. It wasn't the best of outcomes for three

home games in a row. Things got worse for the boys as Jimmy decided to take us the following morning to an Army camp to prepare for our home FA Cup tie with Bristol Rovers.

When Jimmy mentioned this to me I thought it was the most ridiculous idea I'd ever heard of. Jimmy thought it was for team bonding. I said to him: 'If that's the case, why don't we go off to Marbella?' He insisted it would be good. I replied, less than sincerely: 'Sounds great!' We were to spend Wednesday through to Friday at the Army camp, then we'd return for the match the following day.

On the day of the Colchester defeat, my Mum had phoned to say my step-dad Mike had been taken into hospital with a heart murmur over in Spain where they lived. I guess I should have flown out the next day. But I was the captain and felt obliged to go with the team as Mum didn't seem too concerned.

We got to the camp around lunchtime on the first day and straight away I was given the hump when I was asked by Jason Tindall, Jimmy's assistant, whether I would collect all the players' mobiles so our 'bonding' sessions wouldn't be disturbed while we were there. I told him 'f***ing good one!' and explained I was waiting for a call from my Mum about Mike's condition.

Our first task involved a drill sergeant barking out instructions. As we marched 'left-right-left-right' around the courtyard with big rucksacks on our backs and kitted out in Army gear, I thought to myself: 'What the hell am I doing here?' I'd been in the game for 20 years and had never seen anything quite like it.

Afterwards, I had a message from my Mum and called her. She was in tears and told me Mike had been moved from the local hospital to the one in Seville. Mike wasn't doing so well. He had had a massive heart attack. I spoke to Jimmy and explained the situation and said that I was going home to fly out to Spain in the morning.

Thankfully, Mike was fine and I flew back to London late on Friday night and drove down to Bournemouth the following morning for the Cup game against Rovers. We won it 1–0, with the boys saying how the camp had turned out to be three days in hell. They told me about how they had to do all sorts of tasks, like putting up tents and starting bonfires before sitting around them and then standing up one at a time to tell stories about their careers. I thought: 'How ludicrous, what a shambles.' I understand Jimmy Quinn stood up for about half-an-hour telling everyone about every winning goal he had scored. Thank goodness I'd gone to see how my step-dad was by then! After the win, Jimmy was going on about how wonderful the camp had been and saying that our victory was down to it.

In our next League game at Accrington Stanley, we earned a massive bollocking off Jimmy when we outplayed our hosts but found ourselves 3–0 down after about 20 minutes, missing three chances of our own. He wanted more long ball and that's what our entire game turned into.

There were also some more bizarre ideas introduced. The team did some boxing training and the boxing trainer came into the dressing room up at Grimsby to do our team talk. He told us: 'You ARE winners. You BELIEVE you are winners. Your teammates ARE winners.' It was shocking, absolute craziness. Again, something I'd NEVER experienced before. Mind-blowing!

It was clear I didn't want to get involved in these odd methods involving boot camps and motivational speeches from boxing trainers. Jimmy needed his captain onside with what he was trying to do. So he told me he wanted someone else to take over as skipper. I said: 'That'll do me.' Shaun Cooper, a good lad and a player with the ability to play at a much higher level, took over.

A goalless draw at Dean Court to Morecambe was followed up by a home FA Cup tie which produced the same scoreline and huge embarrassment as far as I was concerned. Blyth Spartans were known as a team that had produced some sterling exploits in the Cup over the years.

And what got me about their performance that evening was they played the better football. And they were a non-League team! The game, which kicked off at 5.30, was televised and you could see my disgust when I threw my boots down on the ground as I sat in the changing room afterwards as if to say 'Sod this, I've had enough.' The way we played that night and the previous few weeks was horrific.

We were due to play in the League at Luton three days later. It was a Tuesday night. The day before, I went into the ground. I always worked with the physio rather than train on a Monday. If we had a midweek game I'd go up and see the team working on their shape.

This morning I watched with Lee Bradbury and realised from the manager's conversation with the team that I would not be playing the following night. Bradders turned to me and said: 'Has the gaffer said anything to you?' I said: 'No.'

He said: 'That's got to be the final straw, hasn't it?' He knew how I was feeling.

I replied: 'You could be right.'

I was furious – and not because I wasn't playing. Terry Venables, Glenn Hoddle and George Graham – all top managers – had always told me if I wasn't playing and explained why they were leaving me out. Bradders was right. It really was the final straw and showed a complete lack of respect towards me.

Things had been building up for a month or so. I'd promised myself if I wasn't enjoying it I would stop. As I sat there watching the team play well for a 3–3 draw at Luton I was thinking: 'These are the two bottom teams in the Football League and I'm sat here on the bench. And the manager didn't even bother to tell me I was out of the starting line-up.' I knew there were players in the team more suited to Jimmy's way of playing football than me. I thought: 'That's it for me.'

The following day I went and had dinner with my Dad. That was when I told him: 'I've had enough. I'm not doing this for the money, I'm supposed to be doing this for the enjoyment. I'm fed up with the whole way the team is run so I might as well stop now. There's no point going to the end of the season with something you are not 100 per cent happy with.'

He agreed, saying: 'If you've had enough, you've had enough. You know what you want and don't want and you're old enough to make the decision. If it is going to make you hate going in every morning stop.'

That's when I did just that. I called Jimmy after mulling it over and told him: 'Saturday against Chester is going to be my last game.'

He said: 'All right then.'

Jimmy didn't try to talk me out of it, and I was happy he didn't.

There was a sponsors' dinner that evening. Jimmy and I both attended. As I was leaving, he came up to me said: 'Just a quick one. I've had a think about it.'

I thought: 'Oh, no'.

He carried on: 'Coops and Danny Hollands are on four bookings and if either pick up another booking they're going to have a suspension. Is there anyway you can stay around if one or both are suspended?'

I said: 'No, I've made my decision. It's not something I did lightly.'

At training in the morning he asked me again. I said him: 'I've made my decision, although you don't have to rip up my contract. I'm not going anywhere so if anything were to happen before the January window I'm not going away, you can pick up the phone. I'm not going to lose my fitness in two or three weeks.'

I was being nice about it, but I was thinking: 'You cheeky f**k.'

That week I enjoyed training with everything out in the open and sorted out. The news I was quitting was in the media the following day and the TV cameras were there for my final training session as a professional footballer that Friday. It was nice there was interest in the end of my career, especially as I was now playing in the fourth tier. I tried to enjoy it.

Personally, there was a lot to sort out. I'd told my friends in America a couple of weeks before I might stop. When I confirmed it, they said

'It's such short notice, can't you wait a couple of weeks?' I said: 'Not a chance. I've had enough.' So Joe Roy was the only one who made it over.

Then came match day: Saturday 6 December 2008. Opponents: Chester City. Kick-off: 3pm. I didn't have time for a pre-match meal because I was picking up people from the station, arranging tickets and so on. All I had to eat in the lead up was ham, egg and chips. Not very suitable for a professional footballer! I also spoke to my Dad in the morning, who woke up not feeling well and told me he wouldn't be able to make it, which, as I said at the beginning, upset me and pissed me right off.

I knew I'd be on the bench again. The morning paper said Jimmy had wanted to start me, but the team had done well at Luton. Yet he said I would definitely get on. Jimmy also said it was a shame I was quitting, that I'd always have a job at Bournemouth and that the club were not going to get rid of my registration and that if I ever changed my mind I could return.

Wally (Warren Cummings) – my chauffeur for the day! – picked me up from my home. Sky wanted to follow me around. They filmed me arriving at the stadium and interviewed me before the game and then filmed me getting ready for my last game. I was presented with a silver platter from Bournemouth, which was a fantastic gesture. I remembered how I'd left Tottenham after 12 years of service with nothing.

It was all a bit surreal. Then the game started. It was pretty uneventful for the most part. A shocker. Jason Tindall came over to me at half-time and told me to make sure I was ready. He said: 'This game is made for you.' I came on with about half an hour to go and received a great reception from the crowd.

The first time I got the ball I gave it away and they nearly scored. Then I started to play pretty well. I created a few chances and played with a smile on my face. A weight had been lifted. I smashed a 30-yard free kick about six inches wide with five minutes to go.

Into the last couple of minutes, the ball went up in the air and bounced around the edge of their box. Brett Pitman was able to get a head on it and knock it back in my direction. I just ran onto it and hit it on the full volley and it went in like a rocket. I couldn't believe how well I'd hit it. I remember trying to run off. I don't know where I was trying to run and just got mobbed by the boys. That was it, the game was over. My goal was the only one of the match. I'd won the match. It was a fairytale ending.

I didn't know what to do next. Sky interviewed me on the pitch again, but my mind was all over the place, although I tried to make sure I thanked everybody: the fans, the club, my family and friends. It was weird walking off knowing that was it. I was thinking 'Oh my God, I can't believe it's over. Wow! What a great way to go. Should I be stopping?'

In the changing room, Jimmy was happy and enjoying the *craic*. Laughing, he joked to me: 'You can have Monday off!' All the players were in there. It was just nice. They all came up to me and asked me to sign their programmes.

Later that night, we players had our Christmas party, which had officially been BANNED. A few of us had gone off to watch an NFL game between San Diego Chargers and the New Orleans Saints at Wembley a couple of months before. One of the players had posted pictures on Facebook of another player on the floor looking like he was drunk. A few of the fans had written in to complain and Jimmy Quinn issued the ban. So we had the party in Southampton. The next morning, it hit home that it was all over. I was actually quite cut up about it. Football had been the only thing I'd known and it was all over. I went to America on the Monday to see my friends and just get away.

In my absence, Blyth knocked Bournemouth out of the FA Cup and the Cherries' League survival chances remained dodgy. When I got back, I went along to Dean Court to see them play Barnet. They lost 2–0. It was awful. If it carried on like that they were down and out. This turned out to be Jimmy's last game in charge and he was sacked on New Year's Eve. If I'd known that was coming my decision might have been different!

Eddie Howe, who was a player-coach under Kevin Bond, took over. At 31, he was the youngest manager in the League, and managed to help ensure the club's Football League status against massive odds that season. And then, unbelievably, he led the Cherries to promotion in 2009–10 with a lot of the guys I'd played with – while their off-field problems eased.

Seeing that success doesn't give me any twinge of regret. It is corny, but I'm just pleased for the lads. They are top, top guys.

I'd only been pissed off at the Cherries for a couple of months before finishing, but knew the time was right because my enjoyment of the game had finally gone. I like to think I'd been in the game long enough to know when things weren't being done right. A lot of people make the decision and then give six months notice. I don't think you know how you will feel that far ahead of time. Also, overall, I had had such a great couple of years at Bournemouth I didn't want to spoil my memory of the good times.

I didn't find the difference between the third and fourth tiers massive. I believe the standards in the bottom two divisions have improved because the influx of foreign players into our game at the top level has pushed homegrown talent down the levels. I feel enriched by being part of such a club in the lower divisions.

And I was pleased to be at Dean Court to share the moment they made sure of surviving by beating Grimsby in their final home game of that 2008–09 season. People at the club remain good friends, including my ex-teammate Eddie and all the boys, and I will always feel fortunate that I was able to play down there. I couldn't have wished to have spent my final years as a professional footballer anywhere else.

25
Outlook Positive

I was always more suited to playing at a high level with top players who were on the same wavelength. That's probably why it went so well with England. But I really welcomed the respect and friendships I built up with Bournemouth. It might have been because I hadn't enjoyed my time at Wolves. It felt good to get the recognition for the career I'd had.

Yet the moment the final whistle blew against Chester City, I was looking forward to the best year of my life. Retired as a professional footballer, I had the freedom to do what I wanted and enjoy the rewards of what I'd done for 20 years.

However, 2009 turned into the worst year of my life by a million miles due to the passing of my Dad in the February. I'd planned to spend so much more time with him. When he died I felt as if I might as well have carried on playing to help keep my mind off the most tragic thing to have happened to me in my life.

Katie and I had planned a round-the-world trip, but that was abandoned. Everything was abandoned. I didn't know what to do. I struggled as my world had been turned upside down. In the space of two months, the two main pillars of my life had been knocked away: my football and my Dad.

I was a kid in a man's world when I made my breakthrough in the game and had to grow up quickly, to be disciplined, not late for anything and work for someone. There was a firm structure, and it was a case of sink or swim. Now things were completely different. I could do what I wanted when I wanted. It sounded nice, but it made things 10 times worse when it came to deciding what to do. And I was searching for what I wanted to do for the rest of my life in the wake of my loss.

Katie and I had a few holidays which were good fun, and distracted me from what had gone on. But each time we came back home the reality of my Dad not being around became harder and harder to take. It was such a tough time. I was more than fortunate to have her alongside me, with my Mum, brothers and sister, as we rallied together.

Katie was a rock for me in those dark days, so caring and supportive as every person who has ever met her would testify. She gets on with everyone, always seeing the best in people, while also being so down to earth. She is full of life. She really is a world away from the typical WAG, a phenomenon which has had an awful fascination for our country's media since the 2006 World Cup. We've had our ups and downs, like all relationships, but considering the amount of time we have spent in each other's company the downs have been minimal.

She's very outgoing and has a love of the outdoors which is reflected in interests like horse riding, swimming and playing tennis and golf, all of which we can do together. We have a lot in common, although unfortunately our stubborness shines through at times. She really is one of my best friends. We love each other and are always there for each other.

Katie certainly was supportive during my playing career, especially when I suffered injuries and general frustration. As I've said, I was like a bear with a sore head, and my mind all over the shop, if I was injured. They say you shouldn't bring work home with you, but football was more than a job to me. People say footballers don't care if they are out because they are paid anyway. That just isn't true.

There's nothing worse than seeing the lads out there training while you are stuck in the treatment room. It affected me so badly I couldn't help but bring it into my private life. It certainly made me miserable and short-tempered, but Katie dealt with it so well, always listening and sympathetic. She always tried to put a positive spin on things.

Katie sacrificed so much for me. After she got her sports business degree at a university in Southampton, she wanted to travel around the world. I had mentioned that was something I wanted to do as well when I stopped playing football. So she put that on hold until I'd quit, without realising how long I would carry on for – about three or four years longer than she had thought.

As my career became more uncertain in the latter years, moving from club to club, she always moved with me without complaint, which, of course, didn't allow her to follow her own career path. But football is like that – you have to be ready to up sticks at a drop of a hat. During this time she trained to be a driving instructor, swimming teacher and Montessori teacher.

It was the Montessori teaching role that was closest to her heart and is now the one she hopes to fill after putting it off for my sake for so long. She is so wonderful with children, and hopefully we'll be able to have our own one day.

Katie's positive outlook on life is reflected in how she lives every day with cystic fibrosis. If you didn't know her you'd never know she had the genetic disorder. She never makes a fuss or complains or feels sorry for herself about having to cope with a problem that is incurable. It makes me feel shitty that she is not feeling on top of the world. It's hard. This is where I try to give her as much support as I can. I'll let Katie explain things. She says:

'Cystic Fibrosis (CF) is a genetic disorder, my Mum and Dad unfortunately both carry the gene and they passed it on to me and my sister, Lizzie. Lizzie sadly died when she was nine years old; she had been on the waiting list for a heart and lung transplant but a donor was not available.

CF mainly affects my chest and pancreas. My pancreas doesn't work, so I have to take pills with every meal to enable my food to be digested and absorbed.

My lungs – and this sounds horrible – constantly produce mucous. To ensure my lungs stay as clear as possible I do a combination of physio and exercise, together with taking a concoction of antibiotics and various nebulisers everyday.

The average life expectancy of someone with CF is around 30–40 years but does vary considerably with each individual. Thanks to ongoing research projects, though, the outlook for CF sufferers is looking better each year.

Darren is extremely supportive and understanding. I don't know how he copes with my continual coughing! He is always encouraging me to do the exercise I need and reminding me to take my pills. We often go jogging or biking together but despite my snails pace Darren will stay with me. He is very patient and thoughtful in that way. Darren really is amazing how he puts up with everything, most men would run a mile!'

Despite a few hospital admissions, at 31 Katie has been fortunate over the years to keep fairly well. She has always been able to live a very normal, active life and really put CF to the back of her mind. Because of this at times she often slips into bad habits and doesn't keep on top of her physio and treatment.

Recently though, Katie had a big wake up call. We were on our way back from America having been to the Super Bowl and been to my friend Joe's Hall of Fame dinner in Philadelphia in 2010. Katie had not been feeling well for a couple of days and on the flight home coughed up a fairly large amount of blood. To say it shocked us is an understatement. I jumped up, grabbed the stewards and explained the situation.

The stewards called for a doctor who assessed her and then told us the decision had been made to turn the plane round and land in St John's, Newfoundland, on the eastern coast of Canada.

Katie was whisked off in an ambulance and taken to the local hospital. Thankfully the bleeding stopped and she was told she just had a very bad chest infection and would be OK. A couple of days later, we flew back home where she spent the next couple of weeks in the Royal Brompton Hospital having a course of intravenous drugs.

The experience has made her realise that, to give herself the best possible of chance of keeping well, she needs to be disciplined and do everything she needs to. Katie has been fantastic since coming out of hospital, doing everything she should; exercising and doing her physio everyday. She is reaping the benefits because she's feeling great at the moment. She is working at keeping well and, touch wood, will keep well.

I recently proposed to Katie in a beautiful hotel in the heart of rural Devon. Fortunately for me, she said 'Yes' after I got down on one knee. It was one of the most nerve-racking things I've ever done. She was in shock as it had taken me so long – 11 years! – to ask. We're now looking to travel and see the world and move back to London and set up a new home.

I'm a very homely person. I love my domestic comforts. Katie is a good cook, but doesn't think she is. I, on the other hand, cooked my first meal when I was 27. After watching Katie prepare her meals, though, I am now able to rustle up my two favourites: steak and chips and spaghetti bolognese.

Also, like a lot of blokes, I think I'm a whiz on the barbecue, although my brothers absolutely batter my barbie skills. I believe I'm quite tidy at home but Katie thinks otherwise, complaining that when I change my clothes they stay where they come off. And when I open doors or cupboard drawers I never close them. That is actually true – and I don't know why I do it.

Now one stage of my professional life is complete, I have to look to do other things to give me a reason to get up in the morning. As a footballer you have your working week, a regime and a boss to report to. Now I'm my own boss it is completely different. You have to use your own brain with the money you have to make it work for you, which is a worry with the way economics have been in the world of late.

I've always had an interest in property, buying and selling. I've even designed my own villa in Spain. We've recently turned a second house in Bournemouth into a nursery, of which Katie and I are part-owners. I've invested in new technology – a mobile charger reliant on solar rather than battery energy – which has been a slow process and opened my eyes to the ways of the business world. It's a bit dog-eat-dog! Some of the people I've met through this aren't particularly honest, which I hate.

I've been doing a few TV appearances like *A Question of Sport* on the BBC and *Goals on Sunday* on Sky TV. I had to give my opinions before, during and after ITV's live coverage of the Tottenham victory over Fulham in an FA Cup replay in March 2010 and – as I said earlier – thoroughly enjoyed it. In fact, I'd love to do some more. And I was delighted to contribute to the Beeb's 2010 World Cup coverage, giving my own reminiscences of 1998 and all that.

Beyond punditry, I have no desire to return to football as either a manager or coach. What I said to Abdul Jaffer at Bournemouth remains true now. It just doesn't appeal, although a small part of me misses playing.

Socially, I've been active. Katie and I have got a wide circle of friends and there's often a wedding, barbecue or dinner to travel to. They will, of course, have to 'come to ours' when Katie and I get married! Neither of us are in a rush to set a date. But it will happen. Watch this space.

My life so far has been an incredible experience. Through my Dad's help, I was able to enjoy an amazing career and now I'm ready to enjoy the rest of my life. My outlook is positive. That's how Dad would want all his kids to be. He wouldn't want us to mope around.

The last couple of years without him have been very tough for me and my brothers and sister. We will always be grateful for the Dad he was to us. He'll never be forgotten.

Postscript

Learning lessons for Brazil 2014 and other thoughts

A positive to come out of England's efforts in the 2010 World Cup Finals is that there should be lower expectations for how well we perform in the next Finals in Brazil in 2014. The so-called 'Golden Generation' obviously did not deliver in South Africa under Fabio Capello, in terms of both performances and results.

Some of that generation will want to stay involved – and I'm sure they will – but there is a need for change, like the one Germany implemented when bringing in youngsters to such good effect in the first World Cup in Africa.

But are our youngsters good enough? There's nothing to suggest they are. A few have been mentioned, like Jack Rodwell, Adam Johnson, Theo Walcott and Jack Wilshere. But generally the success of our Premier League stunts the development of many youngsters.

As long as it remains the richest League in the world, teams are going to pay out £10–£20 million or more on ready-made players rather than bring in and nurture untried youngsters.

I'm glad I came through from a lower division with Portsmouth because I was able to mature so much through playing first-team football early on. If I had begun in Tottenham reserves would I ever have developed into the player I became?

I'm not sure whether the opening of a national centre at Burton would make much difference given the lack of opportunities youngsters get in the Premier League. Maybe the solution might be to limit the number of non-English players in teams so our kids get a chance.

Brazil 2014 is a long way off, but I don't see how our chances of doing well can be high given the way things stand. Whatever we achieve would be a bonus. What will help is learning lessons from our failures in South Africa. Our displays largely showed the 4–4–2 formation to be inflexible, ineffective and outmoded internationally, especially when we were defeated 4–1 by Germany in the first knockout stage, with the likes of Mesut Ozil exploiting the space he had between our two banks of four.

I thought England wouldn't be over-exciting under Fabio Capello but, with his record as a winner and for being a good manager, felt we'd be difficult to beat. After all, Italy won the previous World Cup because they were set up right, rather than being the best team in the world. But Capello got it wrong with his tactics.

Terry Venables said, and I agreed, that the writing was on the wall as far back as the warm-up friendly against Egypt a few months before the Finals. We won it but were overrun in midfield early on playing 4–4–2. There was another warning sign in another friendly against Mexico a few weeks before South Africa where we were outplayed in the first half. In international football you've got to play with the extra man in midfield, otherwise teams will just play through you.

When I played under Glenn Hoddle in the 1998 World Cup, we had five at the back – with wing-backs – which allowed us to play good football and do OK. And with Terry Venables at Euro '96 we had the same and made the semi-finals. At the World Cup in Italy in 1990, England, managed by the late Sir Bobby Robson, were struggling until we changed to five across the back. After we did we should have gone on to win the tournament.

If we had played in the latest Finals either with wing-backs or 4–5–1, we could have got the best out of Steven Gerrard and Frank Lampard. It would have allowed Steven a free role off Wayne Rooney up front, giving our best player the freedom to get involved. Instead, Capello stuck to 4–4–2 and sacrificed Steven in central midfield for Gareth Barry and put him on the wing. The more I think about it the more baffled I am. We had the players suited to five across the pitch. Glen Johnson and Ashley Cole's strengths are going forward and Ledley King, when fit, could have played sweeper.

Capello was unlucky. Rio Ferdinand being injured was a huge blow because Rio had a good understanding with John Terry in central defence, something which is hard to develop at international level. And he was unlucky with Ledley getting injured in our first group game against the United States.

But there were some strange selections. David James should have been in goal from the start of the competition rather than Rob Green, who unfortunately made a mistake in that first game against the States which presented our opponents with their point-saver. David had been there and done it. You need experience in the World Cup. Joe Cole made two belated appearances as a substitute so his talents were pretty much wasted overall. He would have given us something different either on the left side of midfield or playing off Wayne Rooney. And Capello put a lot of emphasis on Gareth Barry beforehand, even though the Aston Villa player wasn't going to be fit until the second game against Algeria. He's a good player, but not a world-beater.

There was no way our players were in top shape either. They'd had a long season in the Premier League and were tired physically and mentally. At some point, we have to have a Christmas break in seasons which run up to major tournaments.

I feel England were in need of someone like the Germany and Bayern Munich doctor, Dr Mueller-Wohlfahrt, who did so much to help me in my career. He's a medical expert who knows what is needed to get the players right in body and mind. His knowledge in that field has certainly helped Germany achieve so much success in major competitions. We always pose the question: 'Why do the Germans always come good at the big events?' It obviously has to be down to their preparation as well as having good players.

There were too many egos among the England players and the team spirit didn't look to be what was hoped for. There were rumours of unrest in the camp, which is the last thing you need when you are trying to win the World Cup. In 1996 and 1998, the team spirit was probably our biggest strength.

In Euro '96, Gazza, who would have been the best player in the world if he'd steered clear of injury, was the perfect example of the team player, not interested in the bullshit of selling 'Gazza the brand'. He was a footballer first and foremost, whereas today's players are heavily involved in marketing and all that stuff around the edge of the game which distracts from what it is all about.

The World Cup in South Africa was a massive disappointment from England's point of view. Although we build up our team too much, we still should have done a lot better. It was a let down for the fans in South Africa and at home.

There was a lot of talk about Frank Lampard's 'goal that wasn't' against Germany – when his shot was clearly went over the line. People spoke of what an injustice it was. And it certainly was. But an even bigger injustice would have been if we had gone in at half-time drawing 2–2 instead of 2–1 down. We could, and probably should, have been four or five goals behind by then. It was embarrassing. There's a way to lose, to go out of a World Cup. And our display against Germany wasn't it.

A lot of managers from the 2010 World Cup Finals have fallen on their swords, while Fabio Capello, contracted until the end of the European Championships in 2012, has been backed by the FA. He has dealt firmly with disciplinary issues like the WAG culture, an unwanted sideshow that didn't help us in the 2006 Finals. But, personally, I would like to see an English manager in charge of the England team. I'm a traditional, patriotic person. Our Premier League has a lot of foreign managers – as well as players – and there's nothing wrong if we have a manager from a different country if he's better than any Englishman we have.

That was the case when Italian Capello replaced Steve McClaren. Glenn Hoddle and Terry Venables, both with their foreign influences at

Monaco (under Arsene Wenger) and Barcelona respectively, were certainly Englishmen up to the task. But Steve probably wasn't.

Harry Redknapp has proved what a top club manager he is by getting Tottenham Hotspur into the Champions League after taking over with the club in the relegation zone. He is a bubbly, personable Londoner who knows how to handle leading players and the media well and understands how the game should be played. Harry reminds me a little of Terry Venables and would be my choice.

There were a few non-England related matches and individual performances which captured the imagination in an otherwise disappointing tournament. Shakira sang and danced the World Cup theme tune, *Waka Waka (This Time For Africa)* at the opening concert, the vuvuzelas trumpeted around the grounds during its matches, Nelson Mandela appeared at its closing ceremony and the South Africans, full of the joy of life, hosted it with a welcoming smile as the global event spread the word about the game. And I watched my old Tottenham teammate Jürgen Klinsmann giving his intelligent analyses of games on the telly.

I recall Diego Maradona's touchline antics and, to be honest, I was far from displeased to see his Argentina, Messi and all, knocked out by Germany in the last eight, especially after what his countrymen did to us in 1998 on and off the pitch.

The long face of Ghana coach Milovan Rajevac made me chuckle. His team, after all, had played with a smile on their faces before becoming the last African team to fall following a missed a penalty in the last minute of extra-time in their quarter-final against Uruguay.

I was stunned Brazil got knocked out in the last eight by Holland. I fancied them to go all the way because of their solid defence and flair upfront, with Robinho looking a totally different player to the one who struggled at Eastlands for Manchester City during the 2009–10 Premier League season.

Spain, highly fancied as European champions, deserved to come through to lift the trophy for the first time with four 1–0 victories in a row, against Portugal, Paraguay, Germany and, in the Final, Holland. The Spanish displayed disciplined defence and a passing game to die for after an opening match defeat against Switzerland. They proved themselves to be the best team, which everybody thought they were going in. The way they try and play the perfect game possibly hindered them, because it meant they were always trying to score the perfect goal. That reminded me of the way Arsene Wenger's Arsenal go about things in our Premier League.

I was delighted to see Spain win in the Final. It was a good result for football with Holland trying to kick them off the park. The Dutch were a disgrace that night.

The German team had impressed me the most with outstanding individual performances from Bastian Schweinsteiger, Metsu Ozil and Thomas Muller and Miroslav Klose – until they were beaten by Spain in the semi-finals. Wesley Schneijder (Holland) played well. Lionel Messi (Argentina) showed a few flashes. But overall Andres Iniesta and Xavi (Spain) were the tournament's two best players. Big names like Cristiano Ronaldo (Portugal) and Fernando Torres (Spain) failed to shine on such a big stage.

The thing I remember most about the 2010 World Cup, apart from the negative feelings I suffered with England and their performances, was those bloody Jabulani official match balls, made by Adidas. They were an absolute scandal; too lively and light. They bounced so high. It was insane. The flight of the ball was so different. Players had to almost mis-hit it to keep it down. It required completely different skills to the norm. It proved farcical. Most teams struggled with it. The Germans had used it in the Bundesliga for part of the 2009–10 season, whereas we didn't. Perhaps that accounted for the contrast in performances. I believe the adoption of the ball was more about a few extra quid in the coffers than trying to improve the spectacle. The World Cup deserved better.

I've probably got more experience than most of the Premier League, having begun my career in the top flight in its first season (1992–93). I spent 13 years in it, and continue to follow its fortunes closely.

It is amazing to see how it has changed from the early days. I watch ESPN Classic games on television which show that the pace was slower at the start. There are more athletes these days, although there is less quality in certain clubs in the lower half. All round it has got better as well as quicker and the increase in money has been fantastic.

The top foreign players and managers have improved the quality no end. Frank Lampard and John Terry have developed 10-fold by playing with the likes of Didier Drogba, Michael Essien and Michael Ballack, and serving Claudio Ranieri, Jose Mourinho, Scolari and Carlo Ancelotti. And, playing in big games every week in the Premiership and Europe. Steven Gerrard has benefited similarly with Fernando Torres and others at Liverpool.

The invaluable experiences picked up under the influence of individuals from abroad seemed to help England players on the international stage – prior to the 2010 World Cup Finals. But there have also been some not-so-clever signings from foreign fields. These are the ones who have stopped good young English players coming through.

There was one at Tottenham I remember, Moussa Saib, the Algerian captain, who helped his country win the Africa Cup of Nations in 1990. He was unplayable in training, but on a Saturday just could not perform. The hustle and bustle of the Premiership makes it different to any other League and he, and others like him, have found it difficult to adjust.

The changes have, mainly, been for the good, apart from the block it puts on the growth of English talent. Hopefully those players can ply their trade in either the Championship or League One and get through to the top that way, while paying their dues.

I certainly think you will see fewer and fewer 17-year-olds bursting into the first team of top clubs, like Nicky Barmby did at Tottenham in my day and Wayne Rooney did at Everton.

I didn't know what to expect the Premier League to turn into in 1992. The way it has gone, I believe, could not have been foreseen. We have many of the best players in the world. Spain's Real Madrid and Barcelona are the only two teams who can compete in status with the top Premier League sides, with Cristiano Ronaldo and Kaka at the Bernebeu and Messi at the Nou Camp.

And all this has been brought about by mainly one thing – money. Lots of it. The Premiership has also provided many teams in the late stages of the Champions League in recent years, with Chelsea, Manchester United, Arsenal and Liverpool all doing well.

My best of the Prem

Teams:
Arsenal
Always totally different to any other. We used to draw against them a lot, and do well without winning. They had the likes of Thierry Henry, Robert Pires, Dennis Bergkamp and Tony Adams. They were all fantastic.

Manchester United
They were especially strong around 1999, of course, when they won the Treble. Roy Keane and Paul Scholes were the two best midfielders in the country, Ryan Giggs was incredible and Becks, arguably, was the fourth-best player out of four in their midfield. The other three were that good!

Dwight Yorke, later to become a Birmingham teammate, and Andy Cole were unstoppable. Teddy was there then but struggled to get a game that season, although he did come off the bench to help them clinch the Champions League.

A few years later, we were beating them 3–0 and ended up losing 5–3. Scholesy, Juan Sebastian Veron, Ruud Van Nistelrooy – what a scorer he was – and Becks tore us to shreds.

Manager
Sir Alex Ferguson
It was dodgy for Fergie when he first went to Manchester United, but he has turned into the best example of sticking by the manager there's ever been. The hunger and desire to keep doing it is incredible. Every year is like his first year. George Graham, when he was my Spurs manager, had that same passion.

Arsenal changed for the better when Arsene Wenger came in and he has proved a great manager. But Fergie has to be the greatest manager the Premier League – if not any League – has ever seen.

Individual opponents
Dennis Bergkamp
A brilliant player and scorer of brilliant goals.

Roy Keane
A winner who got his teams to play.

Paul Scholes
The complete footballer.

Stuart Pearce
Daunting to face.

Teammate
Teddy Sheringham
I've said it all about Teddy.

Many of the players I played against 10 years ago in the Premiership might have had to settle for Championship football with the foreign influx at the top, which, as I said earlier, filters down.

In League One, forwards and midfielders aren't bad, although defenders can be a bit all over the place. But it is more about the team than individuals at the lower levels. If you are difficult to break down, you've got a chance.

The main difference between the top-flight teams and the lower Leagues is pace and power. If Bournemouth played Wigan they'd get steamrollered, although not passed off the park.

Appendix 1

THE DARREN ROBERT ANDERTON FILE

Magnificent Seven (my England goals)

1. Greece 1994 (friendly, Wembley). My second game. Graeme Le Saux crossed a great ball in from the left in between the back of their defence and the 'keeper. Their goalkeeper dived out. No way he was going to catch it. He was just going to push it out. So I read that and basically nipped in front of their centre-back and had a nice easy tap in from six yards. It was lovely. That was the first goal and we went on to win 5–0.

2. Japan 1995 (Umbro Cup, Wembley). The ball came to me out on the right wing. I cut inside the left-back and it opened out for me so I smashed it with my left foot. It caught a slight deflection which wrong-footed the 'keeper and went into the far corner. It put us 1–0 up. They equalised. But we got a penalty late on. David Platt scored from it.

3. Sweden 1995 (Umbro Cup, Leeds). We were 3–1 down with a minute to go. Gazza crossed for David Platt to score to make it 3–2. From the kick-off we got the ball back. Graeme Le Saux smashed it forward. Teddy headed it on to Alan Shearer. I came in off the line and Al headed back to me 25 yards out. I hit it first time. A left-foot half-volley. It went in off both posts. It was my best goal for England. I don't think I've ever hit a ball sweeter. As it was rising, it was very difficult to hit.

4 and 5. Hungary 1996 (friendly, Wembley). Teddy got the ball on the left and crossed. Les Ferdinand dived in but couldn't reach it and I came in at the far post, slid in and tapped it into the corner to make it 1–0. Later David Platt netted and I added the third goal when the 'keeper parried a shot that came back to me and I hit it into the far corner. Two goals. Won 3–0.

6. Columbia 1998 (World Cup Finals, Lens, France). Michael Owen got the ball out wide on the right and as he made a run outside I made my way into the box. He crossed. The defender half-cleared it with his head, but only as far as me on the right side of the box. My touch was good and I smashed it as hard as I could and it flew into the near top corner to put us 1–0 up. We went on to win 2–0 with Becks scoring the second.

7. Czech Republic 1998 (friendly, Wembley). Ian Wright went down the left wing, pulled a cross back to me. From about 16 yards I sidefooted it home with my left foot. With the pace already on the cross, I hit it across my body into the far corner. I thought it was quite a nice finish. It put us 1–0 up. Mers (Paul Merson) also scored. Won 2–0.

My favourites

Football
England teammates: Teddy Sheringham and Gazza.
Tottenham teammate: Teddy Sheringham.
Manager: Terry Venables (again, it's all in the book).
International opponents: Zinedine Zidane (graceful, balanced, strong, the best player of my time), Ronaldo (strong, powerful and pacy) and Roberto Carlos (a dynamo, full of energy, a free-kick specialist, a monster), Michael Laudrup (I admired him at the 1986 World Cup).
Goals: The World Cup strike against Columbia because of the occasion, the one against Sweden, technically my best for England and my long-distance effort for Tottenham against Leeds in the FA Cup.
Ground: Wembley. I grew up watching FA Cup Finals and England internationals. Always wanted to play there. It was a huge thing when it happened.
TV pundit: Andy Gray.
Goal celebrations: Jürgen Klinsmann's dive, Gazza's Dentist's Chair at Euro '96.

Other sports
General sports personality (current): Roger Federer.
All-time greatest sports personality: Basketball legend Michael Jordan. He was so much better than everyone else at his game.
Mobile ring tone: Silent.
Film: *Wedding Crashers.*
Actor: Kevin Costner, Harrison Ford.
Actress: Julia Roberts.
Interests: Playing golf and tennis, watching American football and basketball.
Holiday: Miami, Las Vegas.
Clothes: Jeans and T shirts by designers like Armani, Dolce & Gabbana.
Car: Bentley and Ferrari.
Music: Snow Patrol, Alicia Keys, U2, Madonna, Bon Jovi.

My dream teammates for club and country

Tottenham Hotspur
Goalkeeper
Ian Walker
Defence
Goalkeeper: Ian Walker
Right-back: Stephen Carr
Centre-back: Sol Campbell
Centre-back: Ledley King
Left-back: Mauricio Taricco
Midfield
Gheorghe Popescu
David Ginola
(with me completing it)
Up front
Teddy Sheringham
Jürgen Klinsmann
Les Ferdinand
Substitutes
Gary Mabbutt
Tim Sherwood
Gus Poyet
Steffen Iversen
Robbie Keane
Nicky Barmby

England
Goalkeeper
David Seaman
Defence
Right-back: Gary Neville
Centre-back: Sol Campbell
Centre-back: Tony Adams
Left-back: Stuart Pearce
Midfield
Gazza
Paul Scholes
Paul Ince
(with me)

Up front
Alan Shearer
Teddy Sheringham
Substitutes
David Beckham
Michael Owen
Peter Beardsley
David Platt

Question time

Football
Highs and lows?
Highs: England debut, Euro '96, '98 World Cup (especially my goal), League Cup win, final goal at Bournemouth.
Lows: Start of Tottenham career, Terry Venables departing Spurs, League Cup Final loss to Blackburn, five FA Cup semi-final defeats, injuries, leaving Tottenham, losing against Argentina in the 1998 World Cup and Germany in Euro '96.

What is better about the game?
The medical side has improved, with more fitness coaches and top-class people to look after the club's biggest assets, their footballers. Stadiums, pitches and the depth of quality in squads has also improved.

Diving?
Came into our game with the foreign influence. In internationals it was the most frustrating thing when I saw players diving, and rolling around. It was cheating.

Racism in the game?
There was a bit against the Wallace brothers at Southampton when I was growing up. And I remember when Sol Campbell was a very young kid with Tottenham getting some at West Ham, but it wasn't that bad. As a country I've found we are pretty good with our attitude generally. What was unforgivable is what happened in Spain a few years ago when England played a friendly and their fans displayed out-and-out racism. That was bad.

Television coverage?
It is so huge that players who dive or make bad challenge are monitored. You can't put a foot wrong. Players who get away with diving or any

other misdemeanours can then be punished after the event if his action escapes the officials. Back in the day, tackles were worse but you wouldn't get to hear about them.

Should video technology be introduced?
Yes. It only takes a few seconds to show a replay. Cricket, tennis and rugby have adopted it with success, so why not football? It would have given Frank Lampard a World Cup goal in South Africa!

Match fixing?
Never heard of it happening. A lot of players liked to gamble a few quid on games, but not on ones they are playing in. It's an extra interest.

First FA Cup Final?
1979 when Arsenal beat Manchester United 3–2 with Alan Sunderland getting a last-minute winner. The first one I watched properly was the following year when West Ham beat Arsenal. Paul Allen, who went on to play with me at Tottenham, was in the Hammers side that day, the youngest-ever player to play in the Final.

First World Cup Finals?
1982 when Bryan Robson scored after a few seconds against France. Brazil had a fantastic team, including Zico, Socrates and Falcao, and somehow lost to Italy, who went on to win the whole thing.

Childhood hero?
Kevin Keegan.

Worst trainer?
Steve McManaman, so laid back about it – but in a good way!

Worst away journey?
To Carlisle for the last day of the season with Bournemouth after we'd got relegated. A long eight hours each way! Bondy (manager Kevin Bond) stopped on the way back and let the lads have a couple of beers.

Worst thing that has happened to you on the pitch?
Losing my contact lenses in the World Cup Finals against Argentina. Frustrating and weird. I didn't come off. Physio came round to the other side of the pitch to help me put them back in.

General

Anyone else well known from your school?
The Artful Dodger (A Southampton R 'n B artist).

Are you a romantic?
Katie thinks not!

Does anyone in your family keep a scrapbook of your cuttings?
My Mum.

Last film you saw?
The Blindside about American football. Very good.

Who would you invite to a fantasy dinner party?
Actress Jessica Alba, basketball legend Michael Jordan and comedian Chris Rock.

Politics?
Don't think too much about it. Nor listen to it. It doesn't matter what I think because it will be what it is and you've just got to get on with it.

Religion?
Not religious.

Current affairs?
Interested to a point. Watch the news. Injustice concerns me, like when I see film of starving children.

State of the country?
Pretty average.

What angers you?
Smoking. Rudeness.

What makes you laugh?
Funny people, sarcasm. Seeing people lose their temper in sport makes me laugh quite a lot. I saw my friend Warren Cummings lose it for Bournemouth at Aldershot when a home sub threw the ball from the dug out and it hit him in the face. He was fuming and half-volleyed the ball straight back at their bench. It was hilarious – and he got sent off.

What makes you happy?
Doing nice things for people, I'm lucky to be able to be generous to family and friends.

What would you'd have been if you hadn't been a footballer?
A banker.

Worst travelling experience?
Being stuck on Concorde at New York. It couldn't take off because two of the thrusters weren't working. You didn't expect that with Concorde. I was with my brother Scott. He still tries to claim he flew on Concorde – but he didn't. I tell him the wheels have to get off the ground in order to call it flying.

Appendix 2

DARREN ANDERTON CAREER STATISTICS

Born: Southampton, 3 March 1972.
Career: Portsmouth trainee summer 1988, professional February 1990; Spurs June 1992; Birmingham City August 2004; Wolverhampton Wanderers August 2005; AFC Bournemouth September 2006, retired December 2008.
Senior debut: 9 October 1990 v Cardiff City (FLC).
League debut: 3 November 1990 v Wolverhampton Wanderers.
Spurs debut: 15 August 1992 v Southampton (A).
Honours: England Full 30 caps, B 1 cap, Under-21 12 caps, Under-19 1 cap. Football League Cup-winner 1999.
Position: Forward.

Season	League		FAC		FLC		Others	
	App	Gls	App	Gls	App	Gls	App	Gls
1990–91	20		1		1		1	
1991–92	42	7	7	5	4	1	1	
Portsmouth	**62**	**7**	**8**	**5**	**5**	**1**	**2**	
1992–93	34	6	5	1	2	1		
1993–94	37	6	3	5				
1994–95	37	5	6	1	2	1		
1995–96	8	2	1					
1996–97	16	3	3	2				
1997–98	15							
1998–99	32	3	7	2	7			
1999–2000	22	3						
2000–01	23	2	2	1	1	1		
2001–02	35	3	3	1	6	1		
2002–03	20	1	1					
2003–04	20	1	1	3	2			
Spurs	**299**	**34**	**28**	**6**	**31**	**8**		
2004–05	20	3	2	2				
Birmingham	**20**	**3**	**2**	**2**				
2005–06	24	1	1	1	1			
Wolves	**24**	**1**	**1**	**1**	**1**			

2006–07	28	6	2	1			
2007–08	20	3	1	2			
2008–09	18	3	2	1	3	1	
Bournemouth	66	12	4	2	6	1	
Total	471	57	43	11	41	10	8	1

Others 1990–91–92 Full Members' Cup, 2006–07–08–09 Football League Trophy.

Appearances Match-by-Match (goals scored in brackets)

Portsmouth 1990–91
Football League Division Two
3 November   Wolverhampton Wanderers (h) drew 0–0
24 November   Charlton Athletic (a) lost 1–2
1 December   Oxford United (h) drew 1–1
8 December   West Ham United (h) lost 0–1
15 December   West Bromwich Albion (a) drew 0–0
21 December   Ipswich Town (h) drew 1–1
26 December   Bristol City (a) lost 1–4
29 December   Sheffield Wednesday (a) lost 1–2
9 March   Charlton Athletic (h) lost 0–1
12 March   Millwall (h) drew 0–0
16 March   Plymouth Argyle (a) drew 1–1
19 March   Barnsley (a) lost 0–4
23 March   Newcastle United (h) lost 0–1
30 March   Bristol City (home) won 4–1
2 April   Ipswich Town (a) drew 2–2
6 April   Sheffield Wednesday (h) won 2–0
16 April   Brighton and Hove Albion (h) won 1–0
20 April   Leicester City (a) lost 1–2
4 May   Bristol Rovers (h) won 3–1
11 May   Wolverhampton Wanderers (a) lost 1–3

Football League Rumbelows Cup
Second round, second leg
25 September   Cardiff City (h) won 3–1
     (Portsmouth won 4–2 on agg)

Football League Full Members' (Zenith Data Systems) Cup
Second round
12 December   Oxford United (a) lost 0–1

FA Cup
Fifth round
16 February   Tottenham Hotspur (h) lost 1–2

Portsmouth 1991–92
Football League Division Two
17 August   Blackburn Rovers (a) drew 1–1 (1)
24 August   Port Vale (h) won 1–0
31 August   Middlesbrough (a) lost 0–2
3 September   Sunderland (h) won 1–0
7 September   Brighton and Hove Albion (h) drew 0–0
14 September   Charlton Athletic (a) lost 0–1
17 September   Grimsby Town (a) drew 1–1
28 September   Bristol City (a) won 2–0
5 October   Newcastle United (h) won 3–1
12 October   Barnsley (a) lost 0–2
19 October   Derby County (a) lost 0–2
26 October   Ipswich Town (h) drew 1–1
2 November   Millwall (a) drew 1–1 (1)
5 November   Leicester City (h) won 1–0
9 November   Oxford United (home) won 2–1
16 November   Swindon Town (a) won 3–2 (1)
23 November   Watford (a) lost 1–2
30 November   Wolverhampton Wanderers (h) won 1–0
14 December   Southend United (h) drew 1–1 (1)
21 December   Sunderland (a) lost 0–1
26 December   Bristol Rovers (h) won 2–0
28 December   Middlesbrough (h) won 4–0
1 January   Plymouth Argyle (a) lost 2–3
11 January   Port Vale (a) won 2–0 (1)
18 January   Blackburn Rovers (h) drew 2–2
29 January   Bristol Rovers (a) lost 0–1
1 February   Derby County (h) lost 0–1
4 February   Plymouth Argyle (h) won 4–1
8 February   Ipswich Town (a) lost 2–5 (1)
22 February   Wolverhampton Wanderers (h) drew 0–0
29 February   Tranmere Rovers (h) won 2–0
11 March   Leicester City (a) drew 2–2
14 March   Millwall (h) won 6–1
21 March   Oxford United (a) lost 1–2 (1)

28 March   Swindon Town (h) drew 1–1
31 March   Charlton Athletic (h) lost 1–2
7 April   Tranmere Rovers (a) lost 0–2
11 April   Grimsby Town (h) won 2–0
17 April   Cambridge United (a) drew 2–2
22 April   Watford (h) drew 0–0
25 April   Newcastle United (a) lost 0–1
29 April   Brighton and Hove Albion (a) lost 1–2

Football League Rumbelows Cup
First round, first leg
20 August   Gillingham (h) won 2–1
First round, second leg
27 August   Gillingham (a) won 4–3 (1)
                (Portsmouth won 6–4 on agg)
Second round, first leg
24 September   Oxford United (h) drew 0–0
Third round
30 October   Manchester United (a) lost 1–3

FA Cup
Third round
4 January   Exeter City (a) won 2–1
Fourth round
25 January   Leyton Orient (h) won 2–0 (2)
Fifth round
15 February   Middlesbrough (h) drew 1–1
Fifth round replay
26 February   Middlesbrough (a) won 4–2 (2)
Sixth round
7 March   Nottingham Forest (h) won 1–0
Semi-final
5 April   Liverpool (Highbury) drew 1–1 (1)
Semi-final replay
13 April   Liverpool (Villa Park) drew 0–0
                (aet Liverpool won 3–1 on pens)

Football League Full Members (Zenith Data Systems) Cup
First round
1 October:-   Plymouth Argyle (a) lost 0–1

Tottenham Hotspur 1992–93
Premier League
15 August	Southampton (a) drew 0–0
19 August	Coventry City (h) lost 0–2
22 August	Crystal Palace (h) drew 2–2
25 August	Leeds United (a) lost 0–5
30 August	Ipswich Town (a) drew 1–1
2 September	Sheffield United (h) won 2–0
5 September	Everton (h) won 2–1
14 September	Coventry City (a) lost 0–1
27 September	Sheffield Wednesday (a) lost 0–2
5 December	Chelsea (h) lost 1–2
26 December	Norwich City (a) drew 0–0
28 December	Nottingham Forest (h) won 2–1
9 January	Manchester United (a) lost 1–4
16 January	Sheffield Wednesday (h) lost 0–2
27 January	Ipswich Town (h) lost 0–2
30 January	Crystal Palace (a) won 3–1
7 February	Southampton (h) won 4–2 (1)
10 February	Everton (a) won 2–1
20 February	Leeds United (h) won 4–0
27 February	Queen's Park Rangers (h) won 3–2 (1)
2 March	Sheffield United (a) lost 0–6
10 March	Aston Villa (a) drew 0–0
20 March	Chelsea (a) drew 1–1
24 March	Manchester City (h) won 3–1 (1)
9 April	Norwich City (h) won 5–1
12 April	Nottingham Forest (a) lost 2–1
17 April	Oldham Athletic (h) won 4–1 (1)
20 April	Middlesbrough (a) lost 0–3
1 May	Wimbledon (h) drew 1–1 (1)
5 May	Blackburn Rovers (h) lost 1–2 (1)
8 May	Liverpool (a) lost 2–6
11 May	Arsenal (a) won 3–1

Football League Coca-Cola Cup
Second round, first leg
21 September	Brentford (h) won 3–1

Second round, second leg
7 October	Brentford (a) won 4–2 (1)
	(Tottenham won 7–3 on agg)

FA Cup
Third round

2 January	Marlow Town (a*) won 5–1
	(* switched to White Hart Lane by agreement)

Fourth round

24 January	Norwich City (a) won 2–0

Fifth round

14 February	Wimbledon (h) won 3–2 (1)

Sixth round

7 March	Manchester City (a) won 4–2
4 April	Arsenal (Wembley) lost 0–1

Tottenham Hotspur 1993–94
Premier League

21 August	Manchester City (h) won 1–0
28 August	Aston Villa (a) lost 0–1
1 September	Chelsea (h) drew 1–1
11 September	Sheffield United (a) drew 2–2
18 September	Oldham Athletic (home) won 5–0
26 September	Ipswich Town (a) drew 2–2
3 October	Everton (h) won 3–2 (1)
23 October	Swindon Town (h) drew 1–1
30 October	Blackburn Rovers (a) lost 0–1
6 November	Southampton (a) lost 0–1
20 November	Leeds United (h) drew 1–1 (1)
24 November	Wimbledon (h) drew 1–1
27 November	Queen's Park Rangers (a) drew 1–1 (1)
4 December	Newcastle United (h) lost 1–2
8 December	Arsenal (a) drew 1–1 (1)
11 December	Manchester City (a) won 2–0
18 December	Liverpool (h) drew 3–3
27 December	Norwich City (h) lost 1–3
28 December	West Ham United (a) won 3–1 (1)
1 January	Coventry City (h0 lost 1–2
3 January	Sheffield Wednesday (a) lost 0–1
15 January	Manchester United (h) lost 0–1
22 January	Swindon Town (a) lost 1–2
5 February	Sheffield Wednesday (h) lost 1–2
12 February	Blackburn Rovers (h) lost 0–2
27 February	Chelsea (a) lost 3–4
2 March	Aston Villa (h) drew 1–1
5 March	Sheffield United (h) drew 2–2
19 March	Ipswich Town (h) drew 1–1
26 March	Everton (a) won 1–0
2 April	Norwich City (a) won 2–1
4 April	West Ham United (h) lost 1–4

9 April	Coventry City (a) lost 0–1
17 April	Leeds United (a) lost 0–2
23 April	Southampton (h) won 3–0 (1)
30 April	Wimbledon (a) lost 1–2
7 May	Queen's Park Rangers (h) lost 1–2

Coca-Cola Cup
Second round, first leg
22 September   Burnley (away) drew 0–0
Second round, second leg
6 October   Burnley (home) won 3–1
Third round
27 October   Derby County (away) won 1–0
Fourth round
                Blackburn Rovers (h) won 1–0
Fifth round
12 January   Aston Villa (a) lost 1–2

FA Cup
Third round
8 January   Peterborough United (a) drew 1–1
Replay
19 January   Peterborough United (h) drew 1–1
                (aet. Tottenham won 5–4 on pens)
Fourth round
29 January   Ipswich Town (a) lost 0–3

Tottenham Hotspur 1994–95
Premier League

20 August	Sheffield Wednesday (a) won 4–3 (1)
24 August	Everton (h) won 2–1
27 August	Manchester United (h) lost 0–1
30 August	Ipswich town (a) won 3–1
12 September	Southampton (h) lost 1–2
17 September	Leicester City (a) lost 1–3
24 September	Nottingham Forest (h) lost 1–4
1 October	Wimbledon (a) won 2–1
19 November	Aston Villa (h) lost 3–4
23 November	Chelsea (h) drew 0–0
26 November	Liverpool (a) drew 1–1
3 December	Newcastle United (h) won 4–2
10 December	Sheffield Wednesday (h) won 3–1

17 December	Everton (a) drew 0–0
26 December	Norwich City (h) won 2–0
27 December	Crystal Palace (h) drew 0–0
31 December	Coventry City (a) won 4–0 (1)
2 January	Arsenal (h) won 1–0
14 January	West Ham United (a) won 2–2
25 January	Aston Villa (a) lost 0–1
5 February	Blackburn Rovers (h) won 3–1 (1)
11 February	Chelsea (a) drew 1–1
25 February	Wimbledon (h) lost 1–2
4 March	Nottingham Forest (a) drew 2–2
8 March	Ipswich Town (h) won 3–0
15 March	Manchester United (a) drew 0–0
18 March	Leicester City (h) won 1–0
22 March	Liverpool (a) drew 0–0
2 April	Southampton (a) lost 3–4
11 April	Manchester City (h) won 2–1
14 April	Crystal Palace (a) drew 1–1
17 April	Norwich City (h) won 1–0
29 April	Arsenal (a) drew 1–1
3 May	Newcastle United (away) drew 3–3 (1)
6 May	Queen's Park Rangers (a) lost 1–2
9 May	Coventry City (h) lost 1–3 (1)
14 May	Leeds United (h) drew 1–1

Coca-Cola Cup
Second round, first leg

21 September	Watford (a) won 6–3 (1)

Second round, second leg

4 October	Watford (h) lost 2–3
	(Tottenham won 8–6 on agg)

FA Cup
Third round

7 January	Altrincham Town (h) won 3–0

Fourth round

29 January	Sunderland (a) won 4–1

Fifth round

18 February	Southampton (h) drew 1–1

Replay

1 March	Southampton (a) won 6–2

Sixth round
11 March   Liverpool (a) won 2–1
Semi-final
9 April   Everton (Elland Road) lost 1–4

Tottenham Hotspur 1995–96
Premier League
30 August   West Ham United (a) drew 1–1
9 September   Leeds United (h) won 2–1
16 September   Sheffield Wednesday (a) won 3–1
25 September   Queen's Park Rangers (a) won 3–2
15 April   Arsenal (a) drew 0–0
27 April   Chelsea (h) drew 1–1
2 May   Leeds United (a) won 3–1 (2)
5 May   Newcastle United (a) drew 1–1

Coca-Cola Cup
Second round, first leg
20 September   Chester City (h) won 4–0

Tottenham Hotspur 1996–97
Premier League
17 August   Blackburn Rovers (a) won 2–0
21 August   Derby County (h) drew 1–1
4 September   Wimbledon (a) lost 0–1
7 September   Newcastle United (h) lost 1–2
14 September   Southampton (a) won 1–0
22 September   Leicester City ((h) lost 1–2
16 November   Sunderland (h) won 2–0
24 November   Arsenal (a) lost 1–3
29 January   Blackburn Rovers (h) won 2–1
1 February   Chelsea (h) lost 1–2
15 February   Arsenal (h) drew 0–0
24 February   West Ham United (a) lost 2–3 (1)
4 March   Sunderland (a) won 4–0
15 March   Leeds United (h) won 1–0 (1)
9 April   Sheffield Wednesday (a) lost 1–2
3 May   Liverpool (a) lost 1–2 (1).

Coca-Cola Cup
Second round, first leg
17 September   Preston North End (a) drew 1–1 (1)

Second round, second leg
25 September   Preston North End (h) won 3–0 (1)
                (Tottenham won 4–1 agg)
Fourth round
27 November   Bolton Wanderers (a) lost 1–6

Tottenham Hotspur 1997–98
Premier League
19 October   Sheffield Wednesday (h) won 3–2
25 October   Southampton (a) lost 2–3
1 November   Leeds United (h) lost 0–1
8 November   Liverpool (a) lost 0–4
24 November   Crystal Palace (h) lost 0–1
29 November   Everton (a) won 2–0
6 December   Chelsea (h) lost 1–6
13 December   Coventry City (a) lost 0–4
20 December   Barnsley (h) won 3–0
26 December   Aston Villa (a) lost 1–4
11 April   Chelsea (a) lost 0–2
18 April   Barnsley (a) drew 1–1
25 April   Newcastle United (h) won 2–0
2 May   Wimbledon (a) won 6–2
10 May   Southampton (h) drew 1–1

Tottenham Hotspur 1998–99
Premier League
15 August   Wimbledon (a) lost 1–3
22 August   Sheffield Wednesday (h) lost 0–3
29 August   Everton (a) won 1–0
26 September   Leeds United (h) drew 3–3
3 October   Derby County (a) won 1–0
19 October   Leicester City (a) lost 1–2
24 October   Newcastle United (h) won 2–0
2 November   Charlton Athletic (h) drew 2–2
7 November   Aston Villa (a) lost 2–3 (1 pen)
14 November   Arsenal (a) drew 0–0
21 November   Nottingham Forest (h) won 2–0
28 November   West Ham United (a) lost 1–2
5 December   Liverpool (h) won 2–1
12 December   Manchester United (h) drew 2–2
19 December   Chelsea (a) lost 0–2
26 December   Coventry City (a) drew 1–1

28 December   Everton (h) won 4–1
9 January   Sheffield Wednesday (a) drew 0–0
30 January   Blackburn Rovers (a) drew 1–1
6 February   Coventry City (h) drew 0–0
20 February   Middlesbrough (a) drew 0–0
27 February   Derby County (h) drew 1–1
10 March   Leeds United (a) lost 0–2
13 March   Aston Villa (h) won 1–0
5 April   Newcastle United (a) drew 1–1 (1 pen)
17 April   Nottingham Forest (a) won 1–0
20 April   Charlton Athletic (a) won 4–1
24 April   West Ham United (h) lost 1–2
1 May   Liverpool (a) lost 2–3
5 May   Arsenal (h) lost 1–3
10 May   Chelsea (h) drew 2–2
16 May   Manchester United (a) lost 1–2

Worthington Football League Cup
Second round, second leg
23 September   Brentford (h) won 3–2
(Tottenham won 6–4 on agg)
Third round
28 October   Northampton Town (a) won 3–1
Fourth round
10 November   Liverpool (a) won 3–1
Fifth round
2 December   Manchester United (h) won 3–1
Semi-final, first leg
27 January   Wimbledon (a) drew 0–0
Semi-final second leg
16 February   Wimbledon (h) won 1–0
Final
21 March   Leicester City (Wembley) won 1–0

FA Cup
Third round
2 January   Watford (h) won 5–2 (1 pen)
Fourth round
23 January   Wimbledon (a) drew 1–1
2 February   Wimbledon (h) won 3–0

Fifth round
24 February   Leeds United (a) drew 1–1
               Leeds United (h) won 2–0 (1)
Sixth round
16 March   Barnsley (a) won 1–0
Semi-final
11 April   Newcastle United (Old Trafford) lost 0–2 (aet)

Tottenham Hotspur 1999–2000
FA Carling Premiership
7 August   West Ham United (a) lost 0–1
9 August   Newcastle United (h) won 3–1
14 August   Everton (h) won 3–2
21 August   Sheffield Wednesday (a) won 2–1
12 January   Chelsea (a) lost 0–1
15 January   Everton (a) drew 2–2
22 January   Sheffield Wednesday (h) lost 0–1
5 February   Chelsea (h) lost 0–1
12 February   Leeds United (a) lost 0–1
26 February   Coventry City (a) won 1–0
4 March   Bradford City (h) drew 1–1
11 March   Southampton (h) won 7–2 (1)
19 March   Arsenal (a) lost 1–2
25 March   Watford (a) drew 1–1
3 April   Middlesbrough (h) lost 2–3
9 April   Liverpool (a) lost 0–2
15 April   Aston Villa (h) lost 2–4
19 April   Leicester City (a) won 1–0
22 April   Wimbledon (h) won 2–0 (1)
29 April   Derby County (h) drew 1–1
6 May   Manchester United (a) lost 1–3
14 May   Sunderland (h) won 3–1 (1 pen)

Tottenham Hotspur 2000–01
FA Carling Premiership
19 August   Ipswich town (h) won 3–1 (1 pen)
22 August   Middlesbrough (a) drew 1–1
26 August   Newcastle United (a) lost 0–2
5 September   Everton (h) won 3–2
30 September   Leeds United (a) lost 3–4
14 October   Coventry City (a) lost 1–2
21 October   Derby County (h) won 3–1

28 October   Chelsea (a) lost 0–3
4 November   Sunderland (h) won 2–1
11 November   Aston Villa (a) lost 0–2
19 November   Liverpool (h) won 2–1
25 November   Leicester City (h) won 3–0
2 December   Manchester United (a) lost 0–2
18 December   Arsenal (h) drew 1–1
23 December   Middlesbrough (a) drew 0–0
27 December   Southampton (a) lost 0–2
30 December   Ipswich Town (a) lost 0–3
2 January   Newcastle United (h) won 4–2 (1 pen)
13 January   Everton (a) drew 0–0
20 January   Southampton (h) drew 0–0
31 January   West Ham United (a) drew 0–0
3 February   Charlton Athletic (h) drew 0–0
10 February   Manchester City (h) won 1–0

Football League Worthington Cup
Third round
31 October   Birmingham City (h) lost 1–3 (1 pen)

FA Cup
Third round
6 January   Leyton Orient (a) won 1–0
Fourth round
7 January   Charlton Athletic (a) won 4–2 (1)

Tottenham Hotspur 2001–02
Premier League
18 August   Aston Villa (h) drew 0–0
20 August   Everton (a) drew 1–1 (1)
25 August   Blackburn Rovers (a) lost 1–2
9 September   Southampton (h) won 2–0
16 September   Chelsea (h) lost 2–3
19 September   Sunderland (a) won 2–1
22 September   Liverpool (a) lost 0–1
29 September   Manchester United (h) lost 3–5
15 October   Derby County (h) won 3–1
21 October   Newcastle United (a) won 2–0 (1)
27 October   Middlesbrough (h) won 2–1
4 November   Leeds United (a) lost 1–2
17 November   Arsenal (h) drew 1–1

24 November	West Ham United (a) won 1–0
3 December	Bolton Wanderers (h) won 3–2
8 December	Charlton Athletic (a) lost 1–3
15 December	Fulham (h) won 4–0 (1)
22 December	Ipswich Town (h) lost 1–2
26 December	Southampton (a) lost 0–1
29 December	Aston Villa (a) drew 1–1
1 January	Blackburn Rovers (h) won 1–0
12 January	Ipswich Town (a) lost 1–2
19 January	Everton (h) drew 1–1
30 January	Newcastle United (h) lost 1–3
2 February	Derby County (a) lost 0–1
9 February	Leicester City (h) won 2–1 (1)
18 March	Charlton Athletic (h) lost 0–1
24 March	Fulham (a) won 2–0
30 March	Middlesbrough (a) drew 1–1
6 April	Arsenal (a) lost 1–2
13 April	West Ham United (h) drew 1–1
20 April	Bolton Wanderers (a) drew 1–1
27 April	Liverpool (h) won 1–0
11 May	Leicester City (a) lost 1–2

Football League Worthington Cup
Third round
9 October	Tranmere Rovers (a) won 4–0 (1)

Fourth round
29 November	Fulham (a) won 2–1

Fifth round
12 December	Bolton Wanderers (h) won 6–0

Semi-final, first leg
9 January	Chelsea (a) lost 1–2

Semi-final, second leg
23 January	Chelsea (h) won 5–1
	(Tottenham won 6–3 on agg)

Final
25 February	Blackburn Rovers (Cardiff) lost 1–2

FA Cup
Third round
16 January	Coventry City (a) won 2–0

Fourth round
5 February	Bolton Wanderers (h) won 4–0 (1 pen)

Sixth round
17 February   Chelsea (h) lost 0–4

Tottenham Hotspur 2002–03
Barclaycard Premiership
10 November   Sunderland (a) lost 0–2
16 November   Arsenal (a) lost 0–3
24 November   Leeds United (h) won 2–0
30 November   Birmingham City (a) drew 1–1
8 December   West Bromwich Albion (h) won 3–1
15 December   Arsenal (h) drew 1–1
23 December   Manchester City (a) won 3–2
26 December   Charlton Athletic (h) drew 2–2
29 December   Newcastle United (a) lost 1–2
1 January   Southampton (a) lost 0–1
12 January   Everton (h) won 3–2
18 January   Aston Villa (a) won 1–0
29 January   Newcastle United (h) lost 0–0
1 February   Chelsea (a) drew 1–1
8 February   Sunderland (h) won 4–1
13 February   Fulham (h drew 1–1 (sent off)
1 March   West Ham United (a) lost 0–2
24 March   Bolton Wanderers (a) lost 0–1
5 April   Birmingham City (h) won 2–2
12 April   Leeds United (a) drew 2–2
18 April   Manchester City (h) lost 0–2

Football League Worthington Cup
Third round
6 November   Burnley (a) lost 1–2

FA Cup
Third round
4 January   Southampton (a) lost 0–4

Tottenham Hotspur 2003–04
Barclaycard Premiership
27 August   Liverpool (a) drew 0–0
30 August   Fulham (h) lost 0–3
13 September   Chelsea (a) lost 2–4
20 September   Southampton (h) lost 1–3
28 September   Manchester City (a) drew 0–0

4 October	Everton (h) won 3–0
19 October	Leicester City (a) won 2–1
26 October	Middlesbrough (h) drew 0–0
1 November	Bolton Wanderers (h) lost 0–1
8 November	Arsenal (a) lost 1–2 (1)
22 November	Aston Villa (h) won 2–1
29 November	Blackburn Rovers (a) lost 0–1
6 December	Wolverhampton Wanderers (h) won 5–2
13 December	Newcastle United (a) lost 0–4
21 December	Manchester United (h) lost 1–2
7 January	Birmingham City (h) won 4–1
10 January	Leeds United (a) won 1–0
17 January	Liverpool (h) won 2–1
22 February	Leicester City (h) drew 4–4
9 March	Middlesbrough (a) lost 0–1

FA Cup
Fourth round
25 January   Manchester City (a) drew 1–1
Football League Carling Cup
Second round
24 September   Coventry City (a) won 3–0
Fourth round
3 December   Manchester City (h) won 3–1 (1)
Fifth round
17 December   Middlesbrough (h) drew 1–1 (1)
                (aet Middlesbrough won 5–4 on pens)

Birmingham City 2004–05
Carling Football League Cup
Second round
21 September   Lincoln City (h) won 3–1
Third round
27 October   Fulham (h) lost 0–1

Barclays Premier League
16 October	Manchester United (h) drew 0–0
24 October	Southampton (a) drew 0–0
30 October	Crystal Palace (h) lost 0–1
6 November	Liverpool (a) won 1–0 (1)
13 November	Everton (h) lost 0–1
21 November	Blackburn Rovers (a) drew 3–3 (1)

27 November	Norwich City (h) drew 1–1
4 December	Arsenal (a) lost 0–3
12 December	Aston Villa (a) won 2–1
18 December	West Bromwich Albion (h) won 4–0 (1)
28 December	Fulham (a) won 3–2
1 January	Newcastle United (a) lost 1–2
4 January	Bolton Wanderers (h) lost 1–2
15 January	Charlton Athletic (a) lost 1–3
22 January	Fulham (h) lost 1–2
26 February	Crystal Palace (a) lost 0–2
6 March	West Bromwich Albion (a) lost 0–2
20 April	Manchester City (a) lost 0–3
23 April	Everton (a) drew 1–1
30 April	Blackburn Rovers (h) won 2–1

FA Cup
Third round
| 8 January | Leeds United (h) won 3–0 |

Fourth round
| 30 January | Chelsea (a) lost 0–2 |

Wolverhampton Wanderers 2005–06
Football League Coca-Cola Championship

27 August	Cardiff City (a) drew 2–2
30 August	Queen's Park Rangers (h) won 3–1
10 September	Luton Town (a) drew 1–1
13 September	Millwall (h) lost 1–2
15 October	Sheffield United (a) lost 0–1
18 October	Derby County (h) drew 1–1
22 October	Preson North End (h) drew 1–1
29 October	Watford (a) lost 1–3
1 November	Brighton and Hove Albion (a) drew 1–1
22 November	Sheffield United (h) drew 0–0
26 November	Southampton (h) drew 0–0
3 December	Ipswich Town (a) drew 1–1
10 December	Crystal Palace (a) drew 1–1
17 December	Leeds United (h) won 1–0
26 December	Reading (h) lost 0–2
28 December	Sheffield Wednesday (a) won 2–0 (1)
31 December	Plymouth Argyle (h) drew 1–1
2 January	Coventry City (a) lost 0–2
21 January	Millwall (a) drew 0–0

14 February	Burnley (a) won 1–0
18 February	Ipswich Town (h) won 1–0
25 February	Hull City (a) won 3–2
4 March	Queen's Park Rangers (a) drew 0–0
7 March	Stoke City (h) drew 0–0

Football League Carling Cup
Second round
23 August	Chester City (h) won 5–1 (1)

FA Cup
Fourth round
28 January	Manchester United (h) lost 0–3

AFC Bournemouth 2006–07
Football League One

23 September	Scunthorpe United (h) drew 1–1 (1)
26 September	Bristol City (h) lost 0–1
30 September	Huddersfield Town (a) drew 2–2
6 October	Northampton Town (h) drew 0–0
14 October	Millwall (a) lost 0–2
21 October	Rotherham United (h) lost 1–3
28 October	Tranmere Rovers (a) lost 0–1
3 November	Swansea City (a) lost 2–4
18 November	Carlisle United (h) lost 0–1
9 December	Port Vale (h) lost 0–4
16 December	Gillingham (a) drew 1–1
23 December	Blackpool (h) lost 1–3
30 December	Scunthorpe United (a) lost 2–3
1 January	Brighton and Hove Albion (h) won 1–0
6 January	Brentford (h) won 1–0 (1)
13 January	Crewe Alexandra (a) lost 0–2
20 January	Huddersfield Town (h) lost 1–2
3 February	Chesterfield (a) won 1–0
10 February	Leyton Orient (h) won 5–0 (3)
20 February	Yeovil Town (h) lost 0–2
17 March	Millwall (h) won 1–0 (1)
24 March	Tranmere Rovers (h) won 2–0
31 March	Rotherham Unied (a) won 2–0
7 April	Bradford City (h) drew 1–1
9 April	Carlisle United (a) lost 1–3
14 April	Swansea City (h) drew 2–2

28 April	Gillingham (h) drew 1–1
5 May	Port Vale (a) lost 1–2

Football League Trophy
31 October	Millwall (a) lost 0–2

FA Cup
First round
11 November	Boston United (h) won 4–0

Second round
12 December	Bristol Rovers (h) lost 0–1

AFC Bournemouth 2007–08
Coca-Cola Football League One
11 August	Nottingham Forest (a) drew 0–0
18 August	Huddersfield Town (h) lost 0–1
25 August	Doncaster Rovers (a) won 2–1
1 September	Port Vale (h) lost 0–1
8 September	Leyton Orient (a) lost 0–1
15 September	Northampton Town (h) drew 1–1 (1)
22 September	Swindon Town (a) lost 1–4
29 September	Carlisle United (h) lost 1–3
2 October	Brighton and Hove Albion (h) lost 0–2
6 October	Crewe Alexandra (a) won 4–1 (1)
14 October	Swansea City (h) lost 1–4
20 October	Millwall (a) lost 1–2
27 October	Walsall (h) drew 1–1
3 November	Bristol Rovers (a) won 2–0
6 November	Leeds United (h) lost 1–3
5 April	Swansea City (a) won 2–1
12 April	Bristol Rovers (h) won 2–1 (1)
19 April	Walsall (a) won 3–1
26 April	Crewe Alexandra (h) won 1–0
3 May	Carlisle United drew 1–1

Football League Carling Cup
First round
14 August	West Bromwich Albion (a) lost 0–1

Football League Trophy
4 September	Walsall (h) won 2–0
9 October	Bristol Rovers (a) won 1–0

AFC Bournemouth 2008–09
Coca-Cola Football League Two
9 August   Gillingham (h) drew 1–1 (1)
16 August   Aldershot (a) drew 1–1
23 August   Exeter City (h) lost 0–1
30 August   Port Vale (a) lost 1–3
6 September   Notts County (a) drew 1–1
13 September   Macclesfield Town (h) lost 0–1
20 September   Bradford City (a) won 3–1
27 September   Darlington (h) won 3–1
4 October   Wycombe Wanderers (a) lost 1–3
11 October   Rotherham United (h) drew 0–0
18 October   Shrewsbury Town (a) lost 1–4
21 October   Dagenham and Redbridge (h) won 2–1
25 October   Lincoln City (h) lost 0–1
1 November   Chesterfield (h) drew 1–1
15 November   Accrington Stanley (a) lost 0–3
21 November   Grimsby Town (a) drew 3–3 (1)
25 November   Morecambe (h) drew 0–0
6 December   Chester City (h) won 1–0 (1)

Football League Carling Cup
First round
12 August   Cardiff City (a) lost 1–2

Football League Trophy
2 September   Bristol Rovers (h) won 3–0
7 October   Milton Keynes Dons (a) won 1–0 (1)
4 November   Colchester United (h) lost 0–1

FA Cup
First round
8 November   Bristol Rovers (h) won 1–0
Second round
29 November   Blyth Spartans (h) drew 0–0

Club Career Goals (League unless stated)

For Portsmouth:
17 August 1991 Blackburn Rovers (a) D 1–1
27 August 1991 Gillingham (a) W 4–3 FLC1 2L

2 November 1991 Millwall (a) D 1–1
16 November 1991 Swindon Town (a) W 3–2
14 December 1991 Southend United (h) D 1–1
11 January 1992 Port Vale (a) W 2–0
25 January 1992 Leyton Orient (h) W 2–0 (2)
8 February 1992 Ipswich Town (a) L 2–5
26 February 1992 Middlesbrough (a) W 4–2 (2) FAC5R
21 March 1992 Oxford United L 1–2
5 April 1992 Liverpool at Highbury D 1–1 aet FACSF

For Tottenham Hotspur:
7 October 1992 Brentford (a) FLC2 2L
7 February 1993 Southampton (h) W 4–2
14 February 1993 Wimbledon (h) W 3–2 FAC5
27 February 1993 Queen's Park Rangers (h) W 3–2
24 March 1993 Manchester City (h) W 3–1
17 April 1993 Oldham Athletic (h) W 4–1
1 May 1993 Wimbledon (h) D 1–1
5 May 1993 Blackburn Rovers (h) L 1–2
3 October 1993 Everton (h) W 3–2
20 November 1993 Leeds United (h) D 1–1
27 November 1993 Queen's Park Rangers (a) D 1–1
6 December 1993 Arsenal (a) D 1–1
28 December 1993 West Ham United (a) W 3–1
23 April 1994 Southampton (h) W 3–0
20 August 1994 Sheffield Wednesday (a) W 4–3
21 September 1994 Watford (a) W 6–3 FLC2 1L
31 December 1994 Coventry City (a) W 4–0
5 February 1995 Blackburn Rovers (h) W 3–1
1 March 1995 Southampton (a) W 6–2 aet FAC5 R
3 May 1995 Newcastle United (a) D 3–3
9 May 1995 Coventry City (h) L 1–3
2 May 1996 Leeds United (a) W 3–1 (2)
17 September 1996 Preston North End (a) D 1–1 FLC2 1L
25 September 1996 Preston North End (h) W 3–0 FLC2 2L
24 February 1997 West Ham United (a) L 3–4
15 March 1997 Leeds United (h) W 1–0
3 May 1997 Liverpool (a) L 1–2
7 November 1998 Aston Villa (a) L 2–3 (pen)
2 January 1999 Watford (h) W 5–2 (pen) FAC3

24 February 1999 Leeds United (h) W 2–0 FAC5R
5 April 1999 Newcastle United (a) D 1–1 (pen)
5 May 1999 Arsenal (h) L 1–3
11 March 2000 Southampton (h) W 7–2
22 April 2000 Wimbledon (h) W 2–0
14 May 2000 Sunderland (h) W 3–1 (pen)
19 August 2000 Ipswich Town (h) W 3–1 (pen)
31 October 2000 Birmingham City (h) L 1–3 (pen) FLC3
2 January 2001 Newcastle United (h) W 4–2 (pen)
7 February 2001 Charlton Athletic (a) W 4–2 FAC4
20 August 2001 Everton (a) D 1–1
9 October 2001 Tranmere Rovers (a) W 4–0 FLC3
15 December 2001 Fulham (h) W 4–0
5 February 2002 Bolton Wanderers (h) W 4–0 (pen) FAC4
9 February 2002 Leicester City (h) W 2–1
8 November 2003 Arsenal (a) L 1–2
3 December 2003 Manchester City (h) W 3–1 FLC4
17 December 2003 Middlesbrough (h) D 1–1 lost 4–5 on pens FLC5

For Birmingham City:
6 November 2004 Liverpool (a) W 1–0
21 November 2004 Blackburn Rovers (a) D 3–3
18 December 2004 West Bromwich Albion (h) W 4–0

For Wolverhampton Wanderers:
23 August 2005 Chester City FLC1
28 December 2005 Sheffield Wednesday (a) W 2–0

For AFC Bournemouth:
23 September 1906 Scunthorpe United (h) D 1–1
6 January 2007 Brentford (h) W 1–0
10 February 2007 Leyton Orient (h) W 5–0 (3)
17 March 2007 Millwall (h) W 1–0
15 September 1907 Northampton Town (h) D 1–1
6 October 2007 Crewe Alexandra (a) W 4–1
12 April 2008 Bristol Rovers (h) W 2–1
9 August 2008 Gillingham (h) D 1–1
7 October 2008 Milton Keynes Dons (a) W 1–0 FLT
21 November 2008 Grimsby Town (a) D 3–3
6 December 2008 Chester City (h) W 1–0

Did You Know?

Tottenham Hotspur
● Darren was among the rapid-fire goalscorers when Spurs turned a 0–1 deficit into a 4–1 lead against Southampton on 7 February 1993. He scored the third goal, timed at 57 minutes 51 seconds, little more than three minutes after Teddy Sheringham had equalised for Spurs. In between, Nick Barmby had put Spurs 2–1 ahead. Sheringham added Spurs' fourth less than two minutes later to give four goals in four minutes 48 seconds. Iain Dowie had given Southampton a 22nd-minute lead and Richard Hall netted their second goal in the 67th minute.

● One of Darren's goals for Tottenham was chalked off by the Premiership dubious goals panel. He was originally credited with the first goal in a 2–0 win at Newcastle on 21 October 2001, but this was subsequently deemed to be a Gary Speed own-goal.

● Darren first wore the Spurs captain's armband in unusual circumstances. That was in a 0–1 defeat at West Ham United on 7 August 1999 when regular skipper Sol Campbell went off injured after 27 minutes. Justin Edinburgh took over the armband until he too was forced off by injury on 70 minutes and Darren led the side for the remainder of the game.

● Darren scored from eight of the 11 penalties which he took for Spurs during normal play. His first two were unsuccessful, at Queen's Park Rangers on 27 November 1993 and at home to Aston Villa on 2 March 1994. Both games ended 1–1. He scored from his next seven spot-kicks from November 1998 until 2 January 2001. Having converted his first penalty of the evening three minutes earlier to put Spurs 2–1 ahead, he saw his second spot-kick saved by Newcastle's Steve Harper during the 33rd minute.

Birmingham City
● Darren scored the goal which gave Birmingham their first victory over Liverpool at Anfield in 26 years in November 2004. Up to the end of the 2009–10, they haven't triumphed in front of the Kop since.

Wolverhampton Wanderers
● Darren scored what has been put down as Wolverhampton Wanderers' 7,000th League goal with the second goal in a 2–0 win

over Sheffield Wednesday at Hillsborough on 28 December 2005, although the club's press office claim the achievement has recently been disputed by one or two Stattos.

AFC Bournemouth

- Darren scored on his League debut for AFC Bournemouth in a 1–1 draw at home to Scunthorpe on 23 September 2006.

- Darren scored the first (and only) hat-trick of his professional career for AFC Bournemouth against Leyton Orient on 10 February 2007 at Dean Court. A crowd of 5,985 witnessed his three goals in a 5–0 Cherries victory. The other scorers were Marc Wilson and James Hayter.

- Darren came on as a late substitute in the home match against League Two relegation rivals Chester City on 6 December 2008, having already announced this would be the last match of his professional career. He scored the winning goal with a late long-range strike.

England

- When netting against Colombia at France '98, Darren became the fifth Spurs player to score a goal for England at the World Cup Finals. He followed Jimmy Greaves (1962), Martin Peters and Alan Mullery (1970) with one apiece and Gary Lineker (1990) with four. Jermain Defoe joined the list at the 2010 tournament.

England International Career

Under-19

25 May 1991   – Spain at Wembley drew 1–1 Friendly

Under-21 (12 appearances, five goals)

8 September 1992 – Spain at Burgos won 1–0 Friendly
                          – scored one goal
16 February 1993 – San Marino at Luton won 6–0 UEFA U21 qualifier
                          – scored one goal
27 April 1993   – Netherlands at Portsmouth won 3–0 UEFA U21 qualifier
                          – scored one goal
28 May 1993   – Poland at Jastrzebie Zdroj won 4–1 UEFA U21 qualifier
                          – scored one goal

1 June 1993	– Norway at Stavanger drew 1–1 UEFA U21 qualifier
7 June 1993	– Portugal at Miramas won 2–0 Toulon Tournament
9 June 1993	– Czechoslovakia at Toulon drew 1–1 Toulon Tournament
11 June 1993	– Brazil at Draguignan drew 0–0 Toulon Tournament
13 June 1993	– Scotland at La Ciotat won 1–0 Toulon Tournament Semi-final
15 June 1993	– France at Toulon won 1–0 Toulon Tournament Final
7 September 1993	– Poland at Millwall lost 1–2 UEFA U21 qualifier – replaced by Mike Sheron
17 November 1993	– San Marino at San Marino won 4–0 UEFA U21 qualifier – scored one goal

B

| 21 April 1998 | – Russia B at QPR won 4–1 Friendly – replaced |

Full (30 appearances, seven goals)

9 March 1994	– Denmark at Wembley won 1–0 Friendly
17 May 1994	– Greece at Wembley won 5–0 Friendly – scored first goal 23 mins, replaced by Matt Le Tissier
22 May 1994	– Norway at Wembley drew 0–0 Friendly – replaced by Ian Wright
7 September 1994	– USA at Wembley won 2–0 Friendly
15 February 1995	– Republic of Ireland at Dublin Friendly – abandoned after 27 minutes
29 March 1995	– Uruguay at Wembley drew 0–0 Friendly
3 June 1995	– Japan at Wembley won 2–1 Umbro Cup – scored first goal 48 mins
8 June 1995	– Sweden at Leeds drew 3–3 Umbro Cup – scored third goal in injury time
11 June 1995	– Brazil at Wembley lost 1–3 Umbro Cup
18 May 1996	– Hungary at Wembley won 3–0 Friendly – scored first goal 39 mins and third goal 62 mins
23 May 1996	– China at Beijing won 3–0 Friendly
8 June 1996	– Switzerland at Wembley drew 1–1 European Championship Finals
15 June 1996	– Scotland at Wembley won 2–0 European Championship Finals

18 June 1996	– Netherlands at Wembley won 4–1 European Championship Finals
22 June 1996	– Spain at Wembley drew 0–0 won 4–2 on penalties European Championship Finals quarter-final – replaced by Robbie Fowler
26 June 1996	– Germany at Wembley drew 1–1 lost 5–6 on penalties European Championship Finals semi-final
23 May 1998	– Saudi Arabia at Wembley drew 0–0 Friendly
27 May 1998	– Morocco at Casablanca won 1–0 Friendly
15 June 1998	– Tunisia at Marseille won 2–0 World Cup Finals
22 June 1998	– Romania at Toulouse lost 1–2 World Cup Finals
26 June 1998	– Colombia at Lens won 2–0 World Cup Finals second round – scored first goal 20 mins, replaced by Rob Lee
30 June 1998	– Argentina at St Etienne drew 2–2 lost 3–4 on penalties World Cup Finals quarter-final, replaced by David Batty
5 September 1998	– Sweden at Stockholm lost 1–2 European Championship qualifier – replaced by Rob Lee
10 October 1998	– Bulgaria at Wembley drew 0–0 European Championship qualifier – replaced by David Batty
14 October 1998	– Luxembourg at Luxembourg won 3–0 European Championship qualifier – replaced Rob Lee
18 November 1998	– Czech Republic at Wembley won 2–0 Friendly – scored first goal
10 February 1999	– France at Wembley lost 0–2 Friendly
2 September 2000	– France at Paris drew 1–1 Friendly – replaced by Keiron Dyer
15 November 2000	– Italy at Turin lost 0–1 Friendly – sub for Ray Parlour
10 November 2001	– Sweden at Old Trafford drew 1–1 Friendly – sub for Trevor Sinclair

● Statistics compiled by Bill Pierce, Andy Porter (Tottenham Hotspur FC historian) and David Barber (the FA historian).